SEARCHING
FOR A DEMON

SEARCHING FOR A DEMON

THE MEDIA CONSTRUCTION OF THE MILITIA MOVEMENT

Steven M. Chermak

NORTHEASTERN UNIVERSITY PRESS   BOSTON

Northeastern University Press

Library of Congress Cataloging-in-Publication Data
Chermak, Steven M.
Searching for a demon : the media construction of the militia movement
/ Steven M. Chermak.
p. cm.
Includes bibliographical references and index.
ISBN 1–55553–542–9 (cloth : alk. paper)—
ISBN 1–55553–541–0 (pbk. : alk. paper)
1. Militia movements in mass media.   2. Mass media—United States.
I. Title.
P96.M542   U543   2002
322.4'2—dc21   2002004920

Designed by Lou Robinson
Composed in Palatino by Coghill Composition in Richmond, Virginia.
Printed and bound by Thomson-Shore, Inc., in Dexter, Michigan.
The paper is Writers Offset, an acid-free sheet.

MANUFACTURED IN THE UNITED STATES OF AMERICA

06   05   04   03   02   5   4   3   2   1

CONTENTS

TABLES AND CHARTS

PREFACE

September 11, 2001. Few events are as memorable and as tragic as what happened in New York City and Washington, D.C., on that day. The images of the airplanes en route to their tragic destination, the video of the towers collapsing, and the voices of Flight 93 provided an incredibly powerful need to revisit concerns about terrorism. We are still trying to grasp the enormity of the destruction, but society reacted immediately to the attacks on the World Trade Center and the Pentagon in several different ways. The public was fearful, angry, and resentful. People feared opening their mail, flying on airplanes, and entering tall buildings. These concerns led to increases in the sale of goods with which to better prepare in case of another attack, increases in visitation to counselors and therapists, and decreases in airline travel. People visited Ground Zero to pay tribute to the victims, and ad hoc memorials appeared everywhere. Department stores could not keep American flags on their shelves. Some people contacted old friends after the event, and others used it to reevaluate their lives. Citizens gave blood, held vigils, and worshiped, and the discussion of a memorial for the victims began almost immediately. Some people's hatred intensified as the number of crimes committed against Arabs increased dramatically. Policymakers responded to the public's demand for justice. These events started a war, have influenced foreign and domestic policy decisions, and have changed the role of federal law enforcement at home and abroad. Terrorism has been defined as the most significant social problem facing the nation.

It may seem like ancient history, but it was only seven years ago when another mass-casuality act of terrorism impacted the public culture in similar ways. This book began April 19, 1995—the day Timothy McVeigh revenged the deaths of David Koresh and the Branch Davidians. Media coverage of the Oklahoma City bombing was interesting, but more intriguing to me was the media's construction of the militia movement. I was puzzled that a group that was presented in such an alarming way had been completely ignored prior to the bombing. This book is my attempt to make sense of the panic regarding the militia movement in the 1990s. I look closely at the presentation of militias in news and popular culture, but I also wanted to understand these groups and their ideology. So I went out to talk to them—on the telephone, at local diners, at gun events, and at preparedness expositions. Between 1996 and 2000, I conducted one hundred interviews with active militia members. Extracts from these interviews are scattered throughout the text. I discuss the motivations of people involved in the militia movement, how the media presented these motivations, and why militia groups were presented in certain ways. By exploring media coverage of this movement, I hope this book helps people better understand the role of the media in the construction of social problems.

ACKNOWLEDGMENTS

I would like to thank Bill DeLeon-Granados and the reviewers for their substantive critiques. Kelly Damphousse, Hal Pepinsky, and Josh Freilich provided valuable insights, information, and useful criticisms along the way. Angela Maitland collected and inputted data; searched for relevant films, television shows, and editorial cartoons; and conducted extensive research on the Senate hearings and the Roy Lampley case. Jeff Gruenewald and Greg Prophet helped with data collection. Alex Gonzalez and Amy Kearns provided valuable reference assistance for discovering editorial cartoons. Judy Kelley and Kathy Baker transcribed the interviews. My sincere thanks to David Lasocki for his fine editing work. I would also like to thank Margery Kingsley, Robert Bausch, and the staff and students of the Oklahoma Scholar Leadership Enrichment Program. I presented some of this work at Cameron University as part of that program, and the feedback was very helpful. Thanks to Helen DeBolt for taking time to show me the Oklahoma City Memorial. I would also like to thank Northeastern University Press. Bill Frohlich kept encouraging me to get him a manuscript. Sarah Rowley was very helpful in preparing the manuscript and extraordinarily patient in responding to my long lists of questions. Emily McKeigue and the editorial staff did an outstanding job.

My greatest debt is to the subjects of this study. My understanding of the militia panic would not have been complete without their cooperation. Hal Pepinsky, Tracy Smith, and "Renee Bullard" provided key contacts. My wife, Alisha Chermak, provided encouragement and criticism. My colleagues at Indiana University provided a supportive environment. My family has always supported me in any way they can, and this book is dedicated to the memory of Dan and Evelyn Whitney, Doris Brookover, and Diana Chermak.

SEARCHING
FOR A DEMON

Constructing Community Boundaries

On April 19, 1995, Timothy McVeigh parked a truck loaded with ammonium nitrate fertilizer outside the Alfred P. Murrah Federal Building in Oklahoma City. This truck "bomb" detonated at 9:02 A.M., killing 168 people and injuring nearly 600. Images of the destruction caused by the bomb are now familiar fixtures in American public culture. It is easy for the public to imagine the bloody landscape and the removal of the victims in body bags. An amateur photographer's Pulitzer Prize–winning snapshot of a baby girl in the arms of a rescue worker after being recovered from the debris has been reproduced in newspapers, magazines, and books around the world. This photograph "became a worldwide symbol of the tragedy."[1] Media coverage included the pained faces of spokespersons and rescue workers providing a daily list of casualties. Video images of the destroyed building were stunning: the façade of the building was reduced to rubble, and what was left standing looked more like the ancient ruins of a lost civilization than a modern government center.

The nation was shocked and disturbed by the bombing, and many felt violated and intensely afraid. Oklahoma City was an apparently random target, so people living in every other city in the United States now felt vulnerable to such an attack. This randomness shook the public's sense of security and forced citizens to revisit what they had taken for granted about living in a democratic society. The bombing also reshaped the priorities of society's social control apparatus. Terrorism, which had been a social problem of concern but of low priority, jumped to the front of the policy line. As generally occurs in response to an event of national importance, the U.S. Senate initiated hearings almost immediately to search for appropriate policy initiatives. The Senate Subcommittee on Terrorism, for example, held hearings on the militia movement within sixty days of the bombing. The purpose of these hearings was "examining the scope of militia organizations . . . the nature of their activities, their reason for existence, and the extent to which they pose a threat to American citizens." President Bill Clinton recommended the creation of a counterterrorism center, amended the ban on involving the military in domestic law enforcement, and broadened the power of federal agents to investigate extremist groups. The new visibility of terrorism and the momentum for policy change has since carried a high public price tag: spending on antiterrorism initiatives has increased by 5 billion dollars since 1995.[2]

Another of the immediate reactions to the bombing was to search for someone or something to blame. Shifting the focus to a scapegoat is vital for stability and security. Public trust, faith in one's fellow citizens, and perceptions of safety are profoundly disturbed by such crisis. Attribution of responsibility to a source provides the opportunity to direct the fear and anger conjured up by the incident, and the attribution of blame brings balance back to daily social interaction, instilling or renewing faith in the existing structures of society and reaffirming the legitimacy of social control institutions.

The first scapegoat was a well-known and frequently used bogeyman—the Middle Eastern terrorist. On the one hand, this target was a logical choice. Osama bin Laden's terrorist network was well established, and it had demonstrated that it was capable of committing such acts. Moreover, the links between bin Laden, Arab terrorists, and the World Trade Center attacks of 1993 were still fresh in the public's mind. On the other hand, it was equally plausible that a domestic terrorist group was responsible for the bombing. April 19 carries special meaning for such groups, including that it marked the tragic end of a fifty-one-day standoff between the Branch Davidian religious group and federal law-enforcement officers in Waco, Texas. Although some reporters appreciated the significance of April 19 and argued that the bombing might be the work of a domestic terrorist group, most decided that the Oklahoma City bombing had to be the work of foreign terrorists.

It was immediately pointed out that the modus operandi of this attack—a truck bomb placed strategically near a heavily populated meeting place—was similar to terrorist methods in Israel and Europe. Sue Anne Pressley, writing for the *Washington Post* on the day of the bombing, remarked that "the explosion quickly turned the placid, tree-shaded downtown into a scene more reminiscent of the aftermath of the bombings in Beirut or Tel Aviv."[3] Reporters compared the Oklahoma City tragedy to the 1993 World Trade Center bombing, reminding readers that Middle Eastern terrorists were ultimately arrested for that bombing. Some initial stories also cited "unconfirmed reports" that law-enforcement agencies were looking for three men, two of whom were described as Middle Easterners with dark hair and beards. Officials speculated that the bombing could have been the work of Islamic fundamentalists or Arab terrorists.

The Middle Eastern terrorist became the favorite explanation for the bombing because he has been a recurrent threat. The media play a significant role in the demonization of potential threats such as terrorism, and they gave substantial coverage to terrorism in the 1980s and early 1990s. Well-known terrorist events were scrutinized intensely in the press, providing opportunities for interested parties and political power brokers to define the country's vulnerability to terrorism and suggest an appropriate course of action. The Middle Eastern terrorist has also become a staple bad guy in crime-related popular culture. Blockbuster films, novels, crime fiction, and a wide variety of television shows have exploited the international terrorist threat by presenting him as a foe worthy of the forces of good in society. Thus, when rumors circulated that Middle Eastern terrorists were responsible for the Oklahoma City bombing, the public accepted them without scrutiny because such a conclusion was consistent with expectations.

The nation therefore was confused when Timothy McVeigh was arrested and linked to the bombing. McVeigh was not a Middle Eastern terrorist but a U.S. citizen who had had enough commitment to the country to serve in its armed forces, fight in the Gulf War, and receive the Army's Bronze Star for meritorious duty. At first, it was difficult to explain McVeigh's actions. He was not a mentally crazed sociopath like the Unabomber, who committed his acts because he was unable to distinguish between right and wrong. Although there was some evidence of drug use by McVeigh, the extent of the destruction from this bombing was not consistent with preestablished frames for drug offenders. Rather, McVeigh was motivated by his anger at the government, and since he did not fit squarely into any existing stereotypes, it was necessary to shift society's social control boundaries and create new ones that provided an adequate explanation. The new demon was the militia.[4]

Public concern about militia groups, and their understanding of such groups, changed dramatically once the mass media emphasized a link to McVeigh. It is irrelevant that McVeigh was not a member of a militia group. Although it is true that he embraced a philosophy consistent with some militia ideology, was angry with the actions of the government at Ruby Ridge and Waco, and thought about forming a group, he was not a leader of the militia movement and never followed up on his plans to form a group. It is also now clear that McVeigh was frequently interacting with various extremist groups and radicals prior to the bombing, and it would have been as correct to label him a neo-Nazi or highlight his ties to the Ku Klux Klan or the Aryan Republican Army. However, the mass media used the militia to reshape public consciousness in a way similar to how it has influenced the public's shared understanding of international terrorist threats.

One of the objectives of this book is to examine the contributions of news and popular entertainment media to the creation of the public's understanding of militias. Newspapers, "infotainment," reality-based television programming, magazines, and editorial cartoons have become important arenas for the transmission of accepted behavior in society. Despite increases in the number and types of media outlets available, and easier access to a variety of different mediated voices via the World Wide Web, the mass news media remain a central power in the dissemination and control of information in society. Public consumption of news-mediated images remains high, and other sources of institutional power continue to further their agendas by manipulating the presentation of public issues in a way that supports specific positions. Popular culture also plays a vital role in reaffirming the extremes of acceptable and unacceptable behavior in society. Many of the ideas, storylines, plot twists, and significant characters in popular culture resemble the truths and half-truths told in reality-based sources. For example, public understanding of serial murder has been influenced by news analysis of murderers like Jeffrey Dahmer, John Wayne Gacy, and Ted Bundy, as well as by popular fictional accounts of Hannibal "The Cannibal" Lecter, and the various retellings of the murders committed by Jack the Ripper.[5]

In this book, media coverage of the militia movement is examined using both quantitative and qualitative content analysis. Newspaper articles between 1994—the first year in which an article about the militia movement appeared in one of the newspapers sampled—and 1998 were collected and analyzed. The concluding chapter presents additional analysis of media coverage of militias until and through McVeigh's execution in 2001, and it examines the similarities between media coverage of militias and bin Laden's terrorist network following the September 11 attacks. The focus of the news analysis is on newspapers because of the format advantages of this medium. The 1990s militia movement was undefined until the Oklahoma City bombing. Newspapers provided the space for reporters to investigate the characteristics of this newly discovered threat and fully cover the significant events, like political hearings and criminal trials, that helped define the nature of this new threat. I also examine how militia groups became a convenient source of evil on television and in film after the news media targeted militias.

The images of militias presented in the news are influenced by the key processual elements that structure how forces of good and evil in a society are created, disseminated, and understood. Thus it is important to examine *why* certain social issues become moral crusades and how these issues are presented to the public. I argue that mechanical processes (e.g., how information is selected, processed, and disseminated in society), ceremonial processes (e.g., how decision making is given legitimacy), and feedback processes (e.g., the interplay between news and entertainment media) shape the way problems are defined in society. These processes provide the structure through which problems are socially constructed, help illuminate the moral contours of society, and define which individuals and groups achieve deviant status.

My insights into these processual elements have been influenced by interviews with militia members, extremist watchdogs, law-enforcement officers, and media representatives. From 1996 to 2000, I interviewed one hundred active militia members. Some of these informants were high-profile figures in the movement, but most were leaders or members of local militia groups. I used three different strategies to find potential informants. First, I used militia Web sites as contact points, sending e-mail inquiries to a sample of groups publicizing their activities on the Web. Second, I attended public events that attract a large number of militia members, including preparedness expositions, gun shows, and gun shoots. Third, I attempted to contact people cited in news stories about the subject. I used any contact made through one of these strategies as an opportunity to identify additional interviewees. I used similar techniques to contact extremist watchdogs, law-enforcement officers, and journalists and thereby broaden my understanding of the key players in the social construction of militias.[6]

These qualitative data provide an opportunity to describe the philosophies, activities, and strategies of the members and leaders of militia groups. There are few scholarly accounts that describe militia thinking and militia life, and nobody has yet to describe the militia perspective. This research, therefore, fills a significant hole in research to date by describing the activities of militia groups from their own perspectives. These firsthand accounts are also used as contrasting data to the images of militias constructed by the mass media.

Defining Community Boundaries

Of Emile Durkheim's many contributions to sociology, his thoughts on crime are some of the most intriguing. In *The Division of Labor in Society*, for example, Durkheim struggles with the issue of social solidarity, and discusses how the evolution of societies can be understood by examining how they move from a mechanical to an organic division of labor. Crime is an important concern affecting the solidarity of a group. He argues that "crime may actually perform a needed service to society by drawing people together in a common posture of anger and indignation." Just as gossip and rhetoric currently swell around a celebrated case, Durkheim discusses how moral scandal affects a small town: "Crime brings together upright consciences and concentrates them. . . . [The people] stop each other on the street, they visit each other, they seek to come together to talk of the event and to wax indignant in common. From all the similar impressions which are exchanged, for all the temper that gets itself expressed, there emerges a unique temper . . . which is everybody's without being anybody's in particular. That is the public temper."[7]

An individual's interpretation of reality is influenced by contacts with the social world. Friends, family, strangers, political and social institutions, and images received from the mass media shape these interpretations of reality. Yet Durkheim demonstrates that ideas do not exist solely in an individual's mind, but rather are influenced by what he refers to as a "collective conscience." He discusses how "the totality of beliefs and sentiments common to average citizens of the same society forms a determinate system which has its own life." James Duke elaborates on how the collective conscious becomes a key influence on individual interpretations of reality:

The collective conscience represents those subjective or ideational factors that are shared by many or most people in the society. It contains those values, norms, and orienting assumptions that are common to the group and which define the nature of the social world to the individual group member. . . . [It] has a separate existence apart from individual consciences. It is external to the individual. In addition, the collective conscience constrains the individual to bring his own thought processes in line with it. Individuals by taking thought can have little if any influence upon the collective conscience. Conversely, the collective conscience exerts great influence upon individual consciences.[8]

Durkheim presents his thoughts on crime in detail in *The Rules of Sociological Method*, concluding that crime is found in "all societies of all types." He notes that the behaviors considered criminal may change over time, but "everywhere and always, there have been men who have behaved in such a way as to draw upon themselves penal repression." Durkheim concludes that crime is a normal aspect of social life and that society could not exist without it. He also argues that societies may even evolve because of the existence of crime: "Where crime exists, collective sentiments are sufficiently flexible to take on a new form, and crime sometimes helps to determine the form they will take."[9]

Kai Erikson's classic study of seventeenth-century Puritan life elaborates on Durkheim's thesis by illustrating the capabilities of communities to construct and maintain boundaries. He remarks that "human behavior can vary over an enormous range, but each community draws a symbolic set of parentheses around a certain segment of that range and limits its own activities within that narrower zone. These parentheses, so to speak, are the community's boundaries." Erikson demonstrates that the persecution of deviants helped to redefine the boundaries of the Puritan community. He discovered that the Puritans experienced three crime waves in the 1600s: The Antinomian Controversy of 1636, the Quaker persecutions of the 1650s, and the witchcraft hysteria of 1692. A crime wave "dramatizes the issues at stake when a given boundary becomes blurred in the drift of passing events, and the encounters which follow between the new deviants and the older agents of control provide a forum, as it were, in which the issue can be articulated more clearly, a stage on which it can be portrayed in sharper relief." Erikson argues that the Puritans' crime waves helped their society clarify their position in the world and resulted in the development of new community boundaries.[10]

These boundaries reflect the expectations, shared understandings, and identities common, or believed to be common, to the mass unit, but they are constantly shifting and evolving. The boundaries of a seventeenth-century Puritan community were relatively easy to delineate, but boundaries in modern society are much more elusive. Economic expansion, social mobility, population growth and migration, technological innovation, competition, and cultural diversity have accelerated the rate at which societies change. Community visions are incredibly unstable and are being constantly manipulated. This manipulation occurs on many different levels, but the representatives of powerful institutions try to create a community vision that is consistent with their goals, and they use their access to the media and their control of various legitimacy ceremonies to manufacture support for their preferences.

The social construction of groups or individuals as demons plays an important role in defining and justifying the boundaries of a community, illuminating a community's contours, and stabilizing a constructed view of community. Extremists can be used accordingly as a tool that may ultimately contribute to stability in society. They are beneficial because they provide a pivotal contrast between individuals living within the contours of accepted behavior in a community and individuals who remain at the periphery. Extremists challenge authority, question the legitimacy of existing social institutions, and offer alternative viewpoints on key social issues. Nicholas Kittrie highlights the importance of studying extremists: "Being a mover and shaker, whether in furthering societal cohesion or in tearing society apart at its seams, the rebel's central role in the struggle for legitimacy must not be ignored or misunderstood."[11] Social-control officials define extremists and rebels as threatening and as living outside society's majority, but that definition has the value of neutralizing extremist efforts and reaffirming and stabilizing the core beliefs and values of a society. The study of the social construction of one of these extremist groups allows us to understand not only the processes that produce an issue of concern but also how people with power maintain their position in society by manufacturing boundaries that are consistent with their preferences. Such boundaries are awesome mechanisms of social control.

THE MEDIA'S ROLE IN SHAPING PUBLIC CONSCIOUSNESS

Emile Durkheim was primarily interested in the link between punishment and community solidarity. In *The Division of Labor in Society*, Durkheim states that "we can thus say without paradox that punishment is above all designed to act upon upright people, for, since it serves to heal the wounds made upon collective sentiments, it can fill this role only where these collective sentiments exist and commensurately with the vivacity."[12] Approaches to punishment, however, have evolved considerably over time. In some eras, for example, punishment was primarily a public affair, and prisons were simply holding cells for deviants until they could be brought before the community to endure some method of torture or execution. Public hangings were popular, and corporal punishments frequent. Such a public display of punishment provides a clear statement of appropriate and inappropriate behavior to the rest of society.

The gallows, the rack, and the ducking stool have long ago disappeared as public expiating tools. In modern society, the public is provided only minor glimpses into the actual workings of the criminal justice system. Police officers are the most accessible agency of social control, but key police procedures such as interrogations, bookings, and investigatory decision making are completely hidden from public view. The criminal trial is supposed to provide the public with a role in processing a deviant, but most cases are resolved—without such input— through plea bargaining. More importantly, once the accused is sentenced, public interest in a case disappears. The serious offender is no longer paraded in the streets as an important reminder of the consequences of deviating from community standards, but instead is sent to a prison facility in a remote location.

Although Erikson focuses on a period when the town center often provided a stage on which core Puritan society could flex its punishment muscles, he acknowledges that in more advanced societies, community boundaries must be maintained through other means. He furnishes the important insight that public punishment began to disappear at about the time when society developed the means to mass-produce news, suggesting that media attention to deviance has the same boundary-defining power as punishment. He remarks that "perhaps this is no more than an accident of history, but it is nonetheless true that newspapers (and now radio and television) offer much the same kind of entertainment as public hangings or a Sunday visit to the local gaol."[13]

Gus Schattenberg significantly advances Erikson's hypothesis in exploring how the modern mass-entertainment media affect the construction of shared moral sentiments. He argues that the mass media serve to diffuse information about moral boundaries and that it "appears to have taken over the same types of social-control functions that Durkheim ascribed to actual punishment. Violent entertainment may represent a persistent form of the elemental control mechanisms characteristic of the segmental relationships of mechanical solidarity." Schattenberg also confirms two of the most enduring themes of research on media content. First, he concludes that the media do not provide an accurate representation of crime in society but rather overemphasize violent crime. Second, he notes that the media emphasize that crime does not pay. He concludes that the fictional representations of punishment presented in television dramas "can spread information about the location of moral boundaries as effectively as real ones. Not only are they cheaper and more frequent, but their contrived nature forces them to be more explicit about the lesson that is to be learned. The processes of typification and moral entrepreneurship raise explicit issues that are resolved by symbolic punishments in unambiguous terms." The public does not have access to the inner workings of criminal justice, and most people have never been inside a prison, but the public can fantasize about these realities because of fictional accounts provided in popular culture.[14]

Since Schattenberg published his important application of Durkheim's and Erikson's work, the mass media and the criminal justice system have changed dramatically, exacerbating the media's role. Although most decision-making processes remain invisible, there has been significant growth in all areas of the criminal justice system, with the largest expansion being in prison populations. Prisons are completely inaccessible, and the public does not appear to be concerned with their growth, instead accepting that the rational goal for building prisons—that they will reduce crime—is a legitimate truth.

Despite crime data indicating that the United States is experiencing a downward trend in violent and property crime, the media's emphasis on violence remains unchanged. Images of violent crime and concerns about safety and the effectiveness of criminal justice remain staple themes of media coverage. News organizations continue to make crime a priority topic and, although the various criminal justice decision-making points remain relatively removed from direct public view, the media's surrogate role has expanded. Television shows like COPS and other "reality" programs clearly delineate the roles of pursuer and pursued, and they provide the public with access to police decision-making processes for investigations and arrests. Most states permit camera access to the formal stages of the court process, and broadcast news organizations use this access to show the public the system's ability to effectively process deviants by stressing plea and sentencing decisions. Court TV does provide more than mere sound-bite coverage of the court process, but it is important to note that the cases emphasized are typically high profile and sensational. Media access to corrections remains extraordinarily limited. News and entertainment media virtually ignore life in prison as appropriate subject matter. Media publicity is intense when an offender is charged with a death-eligible offense, and such cases provide interested claims-makers with many opportunities to etch new boundaries for society, but efforts to televise executions have been met with legal and ethical objections.

It follows that the mass media are among society's most important institutions of social control because of their role in establishing and maintaining community boundaries. Part of their importance is due to the simple fact that, through their ubiquity, they have become the primary filter for information sharing and policy debate. The public's limited access to a full range of information on issues, coupled with people's limits on the amount of time available to investigate issues beyond their own immediate primary life concerns, has created a reliance on vicarious sources of information. The public consumes information but often does not critically analyze or ponder the issues highlighted, and it generally ignores whatever is not presented about the issues. The mass media can also control the scope of public debate in a democratic society by determining what facts are relevant, who the authoritative voices on issues are, and when a minority or alternative viewpoint is worthy of consideration. In this way the media prevent the public from viewing a problem from a different perspective. The public will simply accept the media's priorities and their interpretation of events as fact without questioning the legitimacy of their claims or searching for another viewpoint.

The significance of the media is also seen in their role in determining society's hierarchy through promoting individuals to positions of authority and relegating others to outsider status. Other social-control institutions rely on the media as a public outlet for self-promotion. The media's control of information, and their ability to shape the accepted realities of a social problem, can determine what organizations and institutions will be provided financial, material, personnel, and legitimacy rewards. These organizations know that the media provide a key battleground on which to determine the priorities that become the public's priorities. Representatives of social-control institutions learn that they need to exploit media access in order to distance themselves from threats in their environment. An effective mechanism for enhancing this distancing is the creation of exemplars of unaccepted and deviant behavior. Descriptive categories, such as "serial killer," "drug lord," or "sexual predator," become convenient caricatures of behavior. Such outsiders are demonized in order to provide a clear contrast to the rest of society and illuminate who should be the target of responses to social problems. For example, it is demonstrated in Chapter 3 that President Clinton was able to gain control of a very threatening environment because of his role in the creation of the militia demon.

The media's status as an important social-control agency can also be observed through a number of different realities of media coverage. One of these realities is the standards and procedures used to present daily events. The ordinary coverage of events can grind away at public consciousness through repetition. Although each individual event presented in the news is different in its facts and in the involvement of individuals and institutions, the presentation of events to the public is eerily similar. The news selection process, the way a news story is produced, the reliance on institutionally affiliated sources, and expectations about how news should be presented to the public all represent the established working routines of news personnel. Thus individual events simply slip in and out of public consciousness, and all events meld together over time.

The media's coverage of crime provides a good example of how unique events are framed in a similar fashion. The research on media coverage of crime is large, and has examined various media, historic periods, locations, and media-market areas. Yet the findings from these studies are not significantly different: certain types of crime, usually violent crime, are preferred; the individuals involved in an incident may elevate the salience of a story; the representatives of criminal justice organizations provide most of the information included in stories; and the causes of crime are simply ignored. Although the "who," "what," and "where" change in each crime story, the end product resembles all prior and future crime stories because it is produced using the established working routines of crime production.

Commonplace and everyday events can grind away at the public's thought processes, and the standard frames and procedures used by the media provide consistent reminders of society's preferred behaviors. However, moral panic and celebrated cases offer more dramatic lessons that often set new community standards. Often the most unusual and unrepresentative events can dominate media coverage for a long period of time, providing an opportunity to reshape public thinking about an issue. From the earliest days of mass production of news, editors, news owners, and others have recognized the value of sensational events. Much of the public's reliance on the news media and the profit potential of newsmaking are linked to the media's ability to satisfy the public craving for information. Sensational cases startle the public into accepting a new understanding by evoking the public's fears and frustrations. The media define these events, relying primarily on representatives from institutions typically used in the construction of news. These cases also ignite other processes that are crucial to the manipulation of the "collective conscious."

Sensational events emerge in an existing public culture that determines how they are presented and how they impact the collective conscience. A new event thus gets presented in old ways. Public thinking is first stirred by an event, and then it is directed and transformed by existing societal structures, processes, and ceremonies. Moreover, in order for events to remain current and worthwhile over a period of time, newsmakers must find ways to maintain their relevance. A celebrated event may have a short "shelf life" because, although its facts are consistent with news values, it does not ignite these other processes. Another celebrated event, however, has staying power because it evolves into an issue worthy of public, policy, and bureaucratic attention. Single events grow into larger atrocities, and are used as exemplars to evoke traditional social-control responses and stimulate a media-led hunt for similar tragedies. Linking an event to an issue thus provides an opportunity for a moral crusade.

Celebrated Cases and Moral Panics

In July 1994, Jesse Timmendequas coaxed a seven-year-old neighbor named Megan Kanka into his house to pet a puppy. He did not have a puppy, but rather used this lie to abduct, rape, and murder the girl. After he dumped her body in a nearby park, he joined groups of volunteers searching for her. He later confessed to the crimes. Megan's parents and the community were stunned and outraged when they discovered that Timmendequas's prior criminal history included two convictions for sex offenses involving young girls. The parents felt that if they had been made aware of his history and told that his two roommates also had prior sexual offense convictions, they would have taken the necessary precautions to protect their daughter.

Many crimes against children generate an enormous amount of media publicity, and the Kanka case received prolonged local and national news attention. The intense media coverage of the event generated fear, outrage, and disappointment over the failure to protect a child. Such scrutiny and concern ensures that society will respond in some manner to the event. For example, in response to Megan's death, New Jersey policymakers created new legislation about sex-offender notification. This law requires that all persons convicted of certain sex offenses register with local law-enforcement officials. Those officials then use registration information to determine who should be notified in the community about the presence of a sex offender. Since the New Jersey legislation was passed, all states have enacted laws requiring sex offenders to register with local authorities, and most states allow for some type of public notification.[15]

The Kanka/Timmendequas case is one of a long list of celebrated cases presented in the media during the last ten years. Some other high profile defendants of the 1990s included Jeffrey Dahmer, O. J. Simpson, Colin Ferguson, Louise Woodward, Susan Smith, Dylan Klebold and Eric Harris, and Benjamin Smith. Although the facts and policy interests generated by each case were different, such cases share two general characteristics. First, none of the cases were consistent with our statistical expectations of criminal activity in society. Guns are, of course, frequently used in crime, but offenders usually do not go on a shooting spree motivated by racial hatred. Domestic violence and domestic homicide are common—but we do not expect them of a Hall of Fame athlete and high-profile celebrity. Fights among teenagers are common and often motivated by the tensions between competing groups, but an attack on an entire school with high-powered weapons and homemade bombs is rare.

The second thread binding many celebrated cases is their power to influence the public's psyche. These events become part of the public culture, transforming or confirming how people should think about specific issues. Many social problems exist, of course, but most are publicly invisible. Our society is structured in a way that has produced a public primarily concerned with its own personal success and aspirations. Most individuals feel disenfranchised and unwilling to sacrifice their own goals for a common negotiated good. The low present-day participation in community life—such as voting for political representatives, engaging in public discussions of social issues, attending neighborhood association meetings, or volunteering their leisure time to help others—provides some indication of a general public apathy toward participation in a shared community vision. Celebrated cases, however, are powerful resources that often result in bringing more people than usual into public conversation about an issue, and increasing "the amount of 'surplus compassion' [the public] can muster for causes beyond their usual immediate concerns."[16] These news events are not mundane, and once covered intensely they pick up a momentum that pushes the event into other aspects of public life. If individuals ignore a celebrated event, they risk feeling alienated from the rest of society. These events are often retold or reworked within other types of public discourse, including individual and group conversations, and can often initiate social decision-making processes. The intense media coverage of these extraordinary events—and the waves of communication and social process generated from that coverage—then contribute to the creation of a new, visible, and shared public understanding of a social problem.

Celebrated events do, however, impact the public and other social processes to varying degrees. Some of these events catch the public's fancy but do not move beyond media drama. At first such events are highly newsworthy, but they soon disappear from public view. After Susan Smith drowned her two children, she tried to divert attention from herself by tapping into racial prejudice and public fears concerning an existing carjacking panic. Her story proved to be a hoax, and she was ultimately held responsible for her actions. This case was a national news story scrutinized in the press, broadcast news, and other media outlets such as radio and television talk shows. Yet no fury of legislative initiatives was introduced, no criminal justice agencies adjusted their crime-fighting priorities, and no child-protection groups used the facts of her case as an example of abusive parenting. The incident angered the public, but it did not ignite other social processes.

Some celebrated cases, however, not only impact public consciousness directly but also force social-control agencies to respond by altering their response to an issue. The expectation of a response to a sensational event forces local, state, and national political representatives to give priority to a specific issue. Criminal justice organizations cast a wide, but not all-inclusive, net in their response to crime. The celebrated case can add extra weight to the criminal justice system's social-control net or highlight a need to redistribute the limited resources of that system. Citizen watchdog groups, advocacy centers, think tanks, and other social-movement organizations may be created or may refocus and re-frame their concerns in response to a celebrated case. The synthesis of such varied entities creates a powerful message that enhances its potential to create new community boundaries.

Celebrated cases that evolve into moral panics provide the best example of how the media impact the public perception of social problems and the social processing of deviants. Research on moral panics documents how they tend not to represent the realities of a social problem accurately and how solutions implemented in response to the exaggerated problem often fail. What is important to the argument presented here is that moral panics have become a central tool used in reshaping community boundaries and forming new social orders. When a celebrated event is linked to an issue, and that issue ignites a societal response, claims-makers hurry to capitalize on the heightened attention to the issue. Consequently, these panics provide important moral lessons that guide public thinking and activity.[17]

Gun violence, for example, is a recurring moral dilemma. In the last thirty years, few criminal justice issues have received more policy attention than guns. Thousands of statutes, hundreds of programs, and numerous intervention strategies have been created and implemented in an effort to respond to gun violence. Policy issues and public concern for this topic have developed through a steady trickle of change. That trickle changes to a stream of activity and change when a high-profile gun event captures the public's imagination. The list is long but includes the assassinations of John F. Kennedy, Martin Luther King Jr., and Bobby Kennedy; the attempted assassinations of Gerald Ford and Ronald Reagan; and the shooting sprees of Patrick Purdy and the Columbine High School students. Yet the shape, form, and nature of the panic that follows such events are always shaped by the structure of public debate in society and the contentious claims-makers who have access to the arenas where that debate occurs. High-profile gun crimes are responded to in the following manner: politicians hold legislative hearings to implement a legislative response; law-enforcement officials, lobbyists, and researchers testify about the legislation; and eventually a substantially watered-down version of the original law is passed.[18]

Stanley Cohen's analysis of the panic surrounding youth disturbances is the seminal scholarly piece on moral panics. He describes such panics in the following way:

> Societies appear to be subject, every now and then, to periods of moral panics. A condition, episode, person or group of persons emerges to be-

come defined as a threat to societal values and interests; its nature is presented in a stylized and stereotypical fashion by the mass media; the moral barricades are manned by editors, bishops, politicians and other right-thinking people; socially accredited experts pronounce their diagnosis and solutions; ways of coping are evolved or (more often) resorted to; the condition then disappears, submerges or deteriorates and becomes less visible. Sometimes the subject of the panic is quite novel and at other times it is something which has been in existence long enough, but suddenly appears in the limelight. Sometimes the panic passes over and is forgotten, except in folklore and collective memory; at other times it has more serious and long-lasting repercussions and might produce such changes as those in legal and social policy or even in the way society conceives itself.[19]

Cohen's description and other moral panic research have collectively identified seven common characteristics of such panics. First, the term "moral panic" refers to a collective type of behavior that occurs in response to concern or fear about a threat. Second, public concern is often fueled by unsubstantiated claims about the extent of the problem. Third, the concern about a specific type of behavior appears suddenly and often disappears just as quickly. Fourth, the majority of the public believes that this threat is real and becomes intensively hostile toward the group targeted in the panic. Fifth, panics often coincide with social crises, and the targets are threatening because they challenge the core interests of society; responding to them provides opportunities to establish social order. Sixth, the panic often ignites political, legal, and social-control processes. Seventh, over time, as a realistic appraisal of the behavior emerges, it is discovered that the actual threat was far less than the perceived threat.[20]

Although society has always been faced with moral panics about crime and deviance, it appears that the rate of the rise and fall of issues as panics has increased dramatically in the past ten years. It is no mere coincidence that this increased rate corresponds to the end of the cold war and the instability of new world boundaries. Thompson illustrates how there is now a rapid succession of moral panics; as one ends another often begins immediately, with no clearly defined boundaries.[21] A panic about a particular issue can feed off the energy generated by an earlier panic. Moreover, the molding of issues into panics has become a familiar established process. The structure of such panics, the language used to describe them, and the claims-makers involved in their solutions all borrow from an existing culture of moral panic construction.

THE CREATION OF CRIME NEWS, CELEBRATED EVENTS, AND MORAL PANICS

The public's understanding of militias was transformed after these groups were catapulted into public view by the Oklahoma City bombing. The work that has gone into this study is an effort to understand the presentation of militias in the news and other mass-mediated sources, and then to link this presentation to the larger processes that determine it, as well as to the panic surrounding these extremist groups. The results provide understanding of how the mass media help to shape community boundaries—invisible boundaries that are powerful sources of social control and decision making. This study also examines how stereotypes are manufactured in society, how social-control organizations set justice priorities, how social problems are framed for public consumption, and how entertainment media feed off the images created in the news media to reinforce the directions of public concern about social problems.

Chapter 2 provides background information on the militia movement. It describes the primary concerns of militia members and how those concerns contributed to the emergence of the militia movement prior to the Oklahoma City bombing. Two high-profile cases, the Ruby Ridge and Waco incidents, are discussed because they have elicited the anger and concern of the people involved in the movement.

The mechanical processes that shape how social problems are presented in the news are discussed in Chapters 3, 4, and 5. Chapter 3 investigates how celebrated cases can open a gateway to the "social-problems marketplace." Bureaucratic organizations are susceptible to triage decision making. Since it is impossible to respond to all of society's social problems, priorities have to be set, maintained, and readjusted because of the limitations of time and resources. Social problems are often thrust onto policymakers' agendas by celebrated cases, upsetting the standard operating procedures and forcing social-control institutions to respond. Militias, for example, became an issue of concern only because of media coverage of the militia movement after the Oklahoma City bombing.

Chapter 4 focuses on what sources were used by the news media to define and describe the militia movement. Although a vast number of sources are used by news organizations and many more are available, this chapter highlights the dichotomizing tendencies of news construction. On the one hand, most sources are used to represent the core interests of society: government and criminal justice officials, advocates and experts, and victims and citizens. On the other hand, the media also rely on deviant voices for a contrasting viewpoint. Heightened attention to militias meant that celebrity figures associated with the movement and other active militia members had access to the public through the media.

Chapter 5 presents the dominant frames used to describe militias in the news media. Such frames are well known, easily understandable, and represent shorthand references that people use to make sense of events and issues. These frames also are efficient because they increase the production capacity of news organizations. Chapter 5 also argues that these frames are reflections of the bias of media structure and the limitations of the routines of news construction. Moreover, these frames are meaningful because they tap into broader themes that dominate the public culture.

Chapter 6 focuses on the ceremonial processes through which institutions often respond to crises in order to satisfy broad concerns about their legitimacy. Public organizations are especially concerned about protecting their autonomy. One way to do so—and an equally important objective in the processing of information through such organizations—is the development and adoption of strategies that allow for the maintenance of public legitimacy in society. The decisions, rules, and priorities of these organizations have to be accepted in order for them to continue to function autonomously as arms of social control. If these organizations are able to placate the public, they are isolated from attacks on their legitimacy. News organizations also have a high stake in legitimacy and must capitalize on the "watchdog mystique" whenever possible so that the public continues to accept the news product as a fair summary of daily events. The rituals invoked in response to celebrated cases proceed in a sequential and self-confirming fashion. The media confirm the seriousness of a social problem by its priority coverage, and then other rituals—such as political hearings, criminal trials, and memorial dedications—confirm the legitimacy of newly established community boundaries.

Chapter 7 focuses on the interplay between popular culture and the news media. Images presented in the news feed off the energy that exists in the culture and also influence the creativity represented in other media outlets. Media coverage of militias thus tapped into familiar cultural images that helped create a moral panic. Other media, such as editorial cartoons, television, and films, used militia groups as threats worthy of society's greatest fears, thereby solidifying public opinion about militias.

In conclusion, Chapter 8 explores how the media's demonization of militias helped to legitimize one of society's new threats. In addition, it discusses how the media, when describing the terrorist acts of September 11, recycled some of the key imagery created during the militia panic.

Ruby Ridge and Waco Revisited

There are many historical examples of extremist groups being used as powerful catalysts of social unification. Groups from the extreme Right and Left, such as the Order, Sheriff Posse Comitatus, the Weathermen, and the World Church of the Creator—have slipped into public consciousness, exerted a brief but strong solidifying presence, and then disappeared. Many extremist groups develop during periods of rapid social and economic change, but the development itself occurs slowly, unevenly, and almost invisibly. Pockets of disenfranchised individuals come together, but their activities and philosophy are generally outside the peripheries of public concern. The size of the threat, and public perceptions of it, is not large enough to be competitive in the social-problems marketplace.[1] Unable to gain momentum, most groups have a short and undistinguished history, and rarely do independent groups coalesce into a national movement. Some groups, however, burst onto the public's radar screen. Public perceptions of an extremist group's threat can escalate rapidly for a period of time, usually following a convincing event. For example, militias are a relatively new addition to the very diverse extremist landscape. They had a relatively anonymous beginning, rose rapidly to the pinnacle of public concern, and then receded to the remote regions of public consciousness. Yet their brief achievement of celebrity has left a lasting impression about the realities of militia life and thinking.

When reading militia literature or interacting with militia personnel, one may observe a range of far-right ideological and strategic influences, including the religious philosophy of Christian Identity adherents, the racial hatred of skinheads, the conspiracy thinking of the John Birch Society, and the paper-terrorism strategies of common-law devotees. The lack of unanimity and the decentralized structure of the militia movement allow these independent groups flexibility in developing their ideological positions, so it is difficult to make broad generalizations when describing militia philosophy and activities. Probably the best way to characterize the extremist thinking of the individuals involved in the militia movement is to position individuals on a continuum, ranging from those just outside mainstream thinking to those violently opposed to such ideology who are looking for ways to act out their anger. Several of the individuals interviewed supported this characterization. For example, one militia activist stated:

> The most moderate elements of the militia movement are the right-wing libertarian element that tends to concentrate on Libertarianism with an evil twist. Slightly more extreme than that are people who are also extreme gun fanatics. They are single-mindedly concentrated on guns to the exclusion of everything else—much more than the average NRA member. The level above that is the person that starts accepting some of the conspiracy theories, like the stickers on the back of street signs, UN troops in the national parks, the New World Order, and black helicopters. Some may get into conspiracies just a little bit and some a tremendous amount. [Conspiracy beliefs are] a big part of the spectrum. Beyond that are people fully into conspiracy theory stuff, but who also tend to be in Christian Identity or something like that. That is sort of the ultimate radical.

There are three reasons for the diversity in the militia movement and the overlap between militias and other extremist groups.

First, the militia movement has no national structure. Militia groups are generally independent, decentralized, and fragmented. Although some groups are connected by independent newspaper publications, fax chains, Web pages, and shortwave radios, and some regional and statewide organizational efforts have occurred, efforts to nationalize the movement and bring groups under a common umbrella, organizational structure, and identity have been unsuccessful. One explanation for this fragmentation is the lack of a unifying presence in the militia movement. Although several high-profile figures have been designated as mouthpieces for the modern militia movement, no one individual has possessed the power and the charisma to unite the diverse militia community under one umbrella. Another source of disunity are the many conflicting personalities and differences in opinion on what should be the underlying ideological tenets of the militia movement. In addition, having a national structure conflicts with the basic organization of these groups. Many militia groups have embraced the paramilitary structure recommended by leaders of the far Right who believe that individuals should by organized independently into small, fragmented cells. This organizational structure, called "leaderless resistance," makes it difficult to monitor such groups, reduces the risk of infiltration by law-enforcement officers, and promotes group independence. A final explanation for there being no national militia presence is that joining under a broad umbrella would erode feelings of solidarity in the small groups. Individuals involved in the movement embrace social and ideological isolation from mainstream society. Coming together as a larger movement would fail to satisfy the yearning to belong to a tight-knit group.

A second reason for the wide range of ideas found among militias is the movement of individuals between groups. Militia groups are not isolated from other extremist groups, but rather are influenced by the network of individuals involved in other extremist groups. Many of the individuals currently active in the militia movement have dabbled in other types of extremist activity, been involved as members of other groups, or attended rallies and public meetings that often attract a range of extremists. There are many extremist chameleons or cross-pollinating opportunists who flow in and out of different groups. These types may travel across states to give speeches or show people how to organize a local militia group. Over time, individuals who join the militia movement are often exposed to a range of extremist ideas through informal contacts and interactions with members of different groups at various assemblies or events. One of the reporters interviewed described the intermingling of groups, "[Christian] Identity people will show up at the same things as the militias, and they'll accept each other. They do, some of them, end up attending the same events together."

Third, militia diversity can also be linked to the influence of a widely available extremist literature, designed to have broad appeal. Writers, publishers, and distributors of these materials are interested in making a profit as much as they are in disseminating an extremist perspective. The influence of the diverse literature can be observed when listening to militia rhetoric in public speeches, when reading the literature, pamphlets, and newsletters produced and disseminated by extremist groups, and when viewing militia materials posted on the World Wide Web. Clearly, militias and other extremist groups actually share, copy, and plagiarize materials from many of the same published sources.

Extremist leaders and key militia promoters have distributed organizational and informational packets widely. The popularity and growth of the Internet has accelerated the distribution rate of these materials and also has delivered them to a larger and more diverse audience. Technological advances have made it easier for individuals and groups to share ideas and concerns. Evidently, these materials influenced the individuals who first got involved in the militia movement in the early 1990s. A public information specialist for one militia group described how his involvement started when he and two friends decided to start a community-help organization. This organization had about ten members when they received a pamphlet called *Operation Vampire Killer*, distributed by Police Against the New World Order, an organization founded and run by Jack McLamb, a retired Phoenix, Arizona, police officer. McLamb is well known by extremists for *Operation Vampire Killer*, his *Aid and Abet* newsletters, and his numerous appearances on radio shows, including his own. *Operation Vampire Killer*, about seventy pages long, warns of a conspiracy between the United States and the United Nations to establish a New World Order.[2] It argues that law-enforcement officers will play a critical role in enforcing laws against citizens in support of the New World Order, and it discusses how economic, political, media, educational, and religious institutions are all part of a larger conspiracy that would allow the United Nations to rule the world, including the United States. Quotations gleaned from a variety of publications and public speeches are used as evidence supporting the existence and threat of this New World Order. The public information specialist described the profound impact that receiving *Operation Vampire Killer* had on him and his community organization:

> We received that, and we all went through it, and over it and we read it about thirty times apiece, and we started checking into it. We're all investigative by nature. And we checked into it and found out that a lot of what is in *Vampire Killer* was exactly what was happening. And that's when we decided that we needed to change our community-help organization, which had done help functions for homeless children and Christmas drives and stuff like that, into what we considered a militia group.

Preparedness expositions also provided easy access to extremist literature for newly organizing militias. These events were enormously popular in the mid- to late 1990s due to the approaching new millennium and the resulting apocalyptic fervor that captivated the public. These expositions were attractive gathering places for militias because "being prepared" is a central concern, and their popularity provided an opportunity for individuals, groups, and organizations to sell and promote various products and publications.

I attended one of these preparedness expositions in October 1997. The three-day event featured products, services, and information to educate and prepare people "for the future possibilities that lie ahead." The types of products sold included "the latest in Emergency & Disaster Supplies, Food & Water Storage, Alternative Energy, Self-reliant Living, Homeopathic Remedies, Alternative Health Products, Home Security & Self-Protection, Emergency Shelter, Survival Gear, [and] Wilderness and Camping Supplies."[3] Magazine, book, and newspaper publishers were also represented at the exposition. For example, there was CPA Book Publisher, described in its publication material as "an arm of the CHRISTIAN PATRIOT ASSOCIATION (CPA), which is a Christian Political Educational Association, secured by the Holy Bible as the word of YAHWEH (God Almighty) and its Laws to all men." The publisher's catalog was seventy pages long and had over 1,000 extremist publications for sale. Among the other newsletters and magazines distributed were *Taking Aim* by the Militia of Montana, *The Spotlight* by the Liberty Lobby, *The Patriot Report* by the Present Truth Ministry, and McLamb's *Aid & Abet*.

Militia groups used this exposition to recruit individuals, educate the public, and spread their ideological rhetoric. The booths manned by militia groups or militia supporters had vast libraries of materials on display. The Militia of Montana (M.O.M), for example, had a broad array of materials available, including books, videos, and newsletters. M.O.M.'s 1997 *Preparedness Catalog* was over thirty pages long and included materials on preparedness and survival, self-defense, the military, medicines and herbs, and documentation and education. The section on documentation and education included publications with titles such as "Black Helicopters Over America," "The Mark of the New World Order," "US Government Mind Control Experiments on Children," "Weather Control," the "Militia and Networking Handbook," and the "Militia Packet."

These materials sold well during the exposition. The individuals who worked the booths were skilled at identifying people's interests and concerns and then offering materials that might meet their needs. Most of the items were extremist publications, but one militia group had a very large display of preparedness materials. I talked with a member of this group about a range of topics, including the purpose and objectives of militias, his group's history, how and why he got involved, gun control, preparedness, and the media's representation of militias. He was animated when discussing this last issue, and he gave me a short essay by Robert Homan called "Newspaper Control in America," and an article by the research staff of *National Vanguard Magazine* called "Who Rules America?: The Alien Grip on our News and Entertainment Media Must be Broken." These articles supported his argument that media organizations are controlled by a Jewish conspiracy and play an important supporting role in furthering the goals of the New World Order.

This exposition provided numerous opportunities to interact with the members of the public in attendance. A large percentage were primarily interested in the preparedness products, but many groups and individuals picked up extremist materials and information. I spoke with one man who had traveled about 500 miles to spend two full days at the exposition, attending the supporting seminars and roundtable discussions. Titles of the lectures included, "The Federal Government's Cover-up of the Oklahoma City Bombing," "Mark of the New World Order," "Lucid 2000: The International Identification and Monetary System for the New World Order," and "Your Right to Bear Arms—Why It Is Being Revoked." This man said that he attended the exposition because it provided an opportunity for him to meet and interact with people he admired, and to gather ideas from other individuals and groups in attendance. He said he spent all the money he had brought for the weekend on the materials and information on display.

A Paramilitary Tradition

The militia movement that was discovered and defined in the 1990s was only the latest manifestation of several extremist traditions. For example, Mark Pitcavage argues that "it is out of the dual traditions of the right-wing paramilitary and the Posse ideology that the militia movement emerged."[4] One of the most acknowledged features of the militia movement is its paramilitary orientation, but plenty of other extremist groups, including the Ku Klux Klan, the Aryan Nations, the Minutemen, the Order, and the Covenant, Sword, and the Arm of the Lord, were organized similarly.[5] Many of these groups, and particularly the groups involved in the militia movement in the 1990s, also borrowed extensively from a broader culture that has been influenced by paramilitary images, structures, and tactics.[6]

Some writers have also argued that the militia movement was significantly influenced by several 1980s extremist groups, including the Posse Comitatus, the Order, and the Committee of the States.[7] The Posse was started in California by William Potter Gale and in Oregon by Henry Beach in the early 1970s, and by the early 1980s its activities had been documented in nearly twenty states. Much of its growth was tied to its leaders' exploitation of the farm crisis.[8] One of my interviewees discussed the influence of the Posse on the militia movement:

> Well, the militia movement is different from the Posse, but it comes from the Posse. The Posse as an organization died out in the mid-1980s, but the ideology stuck around. In the mid-1990s you have seen a resurgence of that ideology in two different ways. The Posse had this paper terrorism and paramilitary activity. In the 1990s, you see the paper terrorism in the common law courts and sovereign citizens, and the paramilitary activity is seen in the militia movement. It is kind of a strange thing. The common law courts and the sovereign citizens are more of a direct descendant of the Posse, and the militia movement is an offshoot of the Posse, but there are some connections there.

There are several direct connections to Posse Comitatus that clearly influenced the militia movement of the 1990s. Posse adherents believed that the only "true form of government was a near anarchic, highly localized form of government centered on the county sheriff." The sheriff, they argued, was the law of land, because the Constitution provided law-enforcement powers only to him. The Posse believed that the federal government was part of a great conspiracy to deprive individuals of their rights and that the country needed to return to the basic text of the Constitution. The Posse movement also was influenced by survivalist practices. Survivalists prepare for society's collapse by storing weapons, food, water, and other supplies, and practicing field maneuvers in order to defend their lives and property.[9]

Members and leaders of Posse Comitatus had fairly regular conflicts with state and federal law-enforcement officials over issues such as gun ownership, and some of these conflicts ended in violence. Gordon

Kahl's confrontation with law enforcement in 1983 was a defining event.[10] Kahl refused to pay taxes, was a follower of Christian Identity, and recruited for Posse Comitatus. He, like many members of Posse, used the farm crisis as a recruiting tool, blaming a conspiracy orchestrated by Jews. Warrants were issued for Kahl's arrest after he failed to appear at several court hearings. When federal and local law-enforcement officials attempted to arrest him after a Posse meeting in North Dakota, a gun battle ensued. Two federal marshals were killed, and three other officers were wounded in the battle. Kahl escaped and was a fugitive for over four months. The FBI tracked him down to a farmhouse in Arkansas, but Kahl refused to surrender peacefully. In the standoff, a local sheriff was killed, as was Kahl after the FBI set on fire the farmhouse were he was staying.

His death produced one of many martyrs of the far Right. David Neiwert calls the process whereby martyrs are created from the ranks of extremists on the Right a "storied tradition."[11] Most of these martyrs of the Right defied authority by refusing to surrender to law-enforcement officials and dying for their cause. Kahl became a martyr when he died for his beliefs, and he became "a catalyst for the revolution espoused by the Order, CSA [Covenant, Sword, and Arm of the Lord], and the White Patriot Party."[12] Other martyrs, such as Robert Matthews of the Order, died in a similar fashion. When the leaders of various groups cited these cases as evidence that the government was indeed a threat, other extremists moved into action. The availability of a martyr can contribute to significant growth in radicalism. The militia movement had two: Randy Weaver and David Koresh.

MILITIA MEMBERSHIP

Most of the people active in the militia movement are white, male, and politically and socially conservative. Some writers argue that militia members are also economically disadvantaged. Joel Dyer's *Harvest of Rage: Why Oklahoma City is Only the Beginning* provides a description of why rural residents and workers are enraged at the federal government. He writes that "Rural America as a whole is collapsing under the weight of a rapidly changing world. Industries such as mining, oil, and timber have been hit hard in recent decades. Increasing government regulation and dwindling resources at home have made it more profitable for today's multinational corporations to mow down the forests and rip the minerals from the earth in distant Third World countries." He discusses how politicians knew but did not care that such changes and regulations would adversely impact rural people because they are not a significant voting block. He also explains that these citizens reacted in two ways: they turned their anger inward, causing large increases in suicide, depression, and other mental health problems; or they directed their anger toward the government. This latter group, he explains, accounts for the growth in various antigovernment extremist movements.[13]

Dyer's book contributes an explanation for why rural and economically disenfranchised individuals may have joined extremist groups, but the movement was certainly not isolated to rural areas. There is a militia presence in suburban and urban areas, and many of the people I interviewed had good jobs. Some operated their own businesses and were modestly successful, and some were making a good living working for others. Furthermore, other research does not support the conclusion that individuals joined militias in response only to economic conditions. Joshua Freilich, for example, examines the variables that differentiated states with high and low militia presence in 1994 and 1995. His state-level analysis generates little support for economic influences, as rural, farm-depressed, and economically depressed states were found not to have the strongest militia presence. It is noteworthy that the states with the strongest paramilitary culture, measured by an index including the number of ardent gun owners, police officers, active military personnel, and veterans of the Vietnam and Persian Gulf Wars, had the strongest militia presence.[14]

MILITIA CONCERNS

People involved in the militia movement prefer to be isolated geographically, politically, economically, socially, and ideologically. Many militia members, prior to their involvement in the movement, would have been considered strong conservatives, and they spent the 1980s and early 1990s fuming about social and economic shifts in the country. It is important to remember that they may have actively participated in traditional and mainstream democratic processes, or they may not have felt the need to be engaged at all because their vision for what it means to live in America was not being threatened. Gradually, they felt increasingly threatened by outside forces, frustrated, resentful of the democratic process, and concerned about how society was changing. These concerns and fears were then directed toward what they believed was a growing, overreaching, out-of-control, and intrusive federal government—a government, they believed, that infringed on individual rights, thereby violating the basic premises of the Constitution. A government involved in a global conspiracy to eliminate the American identity would be replaced by a one-world order.

Several high-profile political issues were particularly salient. Many of these issues, such as the North American Free Trade Agreement (NAFTA) and the attempts to move to a national healthcare policy, were pushed forward by a Democratic president despised by the Right. The anger generated by such broad policy efforts was aggravated as the early leaders of the militia movement provided the following evidence to support the conclusion that the federal government was willing to do anything to accomplish the goals of a global conspiracy.

Gun-control legislation is among the greatest concerns of the militia, and it is one of the best recruiting devices used by militia leaders. The historically contentious gun-control debate again consumed a significant portion of federal policymakers' time in the 1980s as they debated two issues: short waiting periods to allow for background checks, and banning the manufacture and sale of semiautomatic assault weapons. An attempt to assassinate Ronald Reagan in 1981 brought the waiting-period initiative into play, and a school-yard massacre in 1987 motivated federal policymakers to move against semiautomatic weapons. Both issues received significant political and media attention, and two pieces of federal gun-control legislation were passed in 1993 and 1994. Watered down as the versions of this legislation signed into law were, politically conservative gun owners were enraged and threatened by these intrusions: "I've never seen a firearm harm anyone," stated one militia member. "It's always people that use them. I've never seen a car hurt anyone. It's always the person at the controls. I mean, if they're going to ban guns, they ought to ban cars long before guns. A car is a hundred times more dangerous than guns." Another militia member said, "Constitutional rights are being taken away by a one-world government, and there's gun confiscating happening all over the world, including this country." Policymakers revisit gun issues and introduce new gun legislation frequently, which provides militia members with sustaining evidence of the government's threat.

Regulations imposed on private citizens in the interest of protecting land, the environment, and endangered species also alienate militia groups. For example, because of the passage of the Endangered Species

Act, the federal government plays a central role in devising strategies to prevent the extinction and help the restoration of specific threatened species. Protecting many of these species affects businesses, property owners, local governments, and citizens, and impacts a range of issues including access to federal lands, grazing fees, mining and timber restrictions, building, wetlands protection, ranching, and hunting. Citizens affected by these restrictions are angry because they felt that the resulting "land grabs," and a decision-making process far removed from citizen and local input, were threatening their way of life and ability to earn a living. Two members of a militia group discussed with me how they believed that a governmental commission was protecting a million acres of land they claim had been designated a biosphere reserve that would be ceded to the United Nations. One remarked that

> people are really restricted by this commission; by the laws, regulations, or constitutional law on how to build, or where to place a septic tank, or you can't build this, or you can't build that. The people are just getting fed up because they are handcuffed all the time. The building permits are restricted heavily by an unelected body of people. This commission has incredible powers, and it answers to no one!

These two individuals learned about the existence of such biospheres by reading literature distributed by a militia that actively promotes organizing and distributes low-cost materials and educational videos. The leader of a group that circulates information nationally described his concerns about biospheres:

> Why haven't they told the public about the biosphere grabs of America? The biospheres, the parks? The buffer zones, which are tens of thousands of square miles of private and public property. The corridors that connect them all, which take away more land than the interstate system ever took, and the only part of America beyond those three is called "zone of cooperation." How does it feel to be living in a zone of cooperation if they allow you to cooperate? We can't find a definition to that. They won't tell me. We've attended a lot of different meetings, sponsored by the Forest Service, the Department of Agriculture, to find out answers to our questions, and we just can't get them. They're just like, it's just like they're hiding behind a cloud of mysticism of some sort and here in Montana and Idaho, Washington State, there's a giant cry for answers. People's property is being usurped to these biosphere grabs, these giant UN bio-

spheres, and we're not getting answers, we're getting lies. . . . It's boiling. And I can understand why.

Militia members were also concerned about the changing international world order. Once the Berlin Wall fell and the cold war ended in 1989, there was great instability as international boundaries and power were reconfigured. The United States had a large stake in these new boundaries, and government officials aggressively intervened to influence their definition. The United States was the central force driving a new international world agenda, assisted efforts by the United Nations to stabilize the world, and was a key figure in peacekeeping efforts in countries such as Somalia, Rwanda, and Bosnia. President George Bush, in a speech to a joint session of Congress in September 1990, said: "A new partnership of nations has begun, and we stand today at a unique and extraordinary moment. The crisis in the Persian Gulf, as grave as it is, also offers a rare opportunity to move toward an historic period of cooperation. Out of these troubled times, our fifth objective—*a New World Order*—can emerge: A new era—freer from the threat of terror, stronger in the pursuit of justice, and more secure in the quest for peace" (emphasis added).[15] Bush never described what he meant by the "New World Order," but other conservatives like Pat Robertson and Pat Buchanan defined the term for him as evidence of a looming threat to national sovereignty. They argued that Americans should put the interests and needs of America first—a philosophy that resonated with conservatives. The great threat was no longer communism but globalism, and militia leaders capitalized on this discussion of a New World Order by demonizing the United Nations as a threat to sovereignty. The United Nations was the centerpiece of a conspiracy, involving bankers, politicians, corporations, and other leaders, to undermine everything that was America. One militia member described his fear:

> I am convinced that there is a big socialist plot to give away, incrementally, our sovereignty to the United Nations. You're going to start with the East Sea, the European Commonwealth, we're going to dissolve all the borders there, and they're going to be like one big happy family. And then you've got the United States, Canada, and Mexico through NAFTA, and you've got one big happy country. Oh, it's going to be wonderful, with nothing left to fight over and no more wars. When I say that and you look at this thing about melting away of borders and melting away of religious distinctions between people because there will be nothing left to

fight over, you've got to realize these peace-type people really think that way. I think you will probably see eventually the sovereignty of the United States will be dissolved and that we will be just chattel for the UN, and our country will be just milked to prop them up, them and all their little Third World countries out there, until we're reduced to the same level that they are.

These domestic and international threats helped fuel the general belief voiced by one militia leader that "our rights, duties, and responsibilities are being watered down and taken away from us piecemeal." He went on to describe how the federal government is seeping into all aspects of private lives:

[People] are starting to question more and more what the government is doing with NAFTA and GATT [General Agreement on Tariffs and Trade] and the United Nations and the New World Order and several different things like that. This is more than just one issue. It's hitting us from every angle. The educational angle, the judicial, the judiciary, our legislators, the executive branch, the money, all our foreign trade with NAFTA and GATT, like I said. These are all issues that have to be explained to people in detail to make them understand what's happening to this country and to raise their consciousness and awareness to what our government is doing. We have been sold out—literally sold out to the New World Order.

Similarly, other militia members talked about the federal government's encroachment on rights, citing IRS abuses, civil forfeiture actions, dynamic entries, and undercover police operations as evidence of a power-hungry federal government.

It is possible that these isolated conservatives would not have taken the next steps towards extremism if not for the standoffs at Ruby Ridge and Waco. Such speculation can only be supported by what we know, which is that these two events are the demonstrative evidence used by militia personnel to prove that the government is a major threat to its citizenry. In the following statement, a militia leader emphasizes the significance of these two events:

The people were bitter about the government with all their regulations and telling you that you must do this and you can't do that and it was getting worse all the time. The rage was building, but what really pushed people over the edge was the debacle in Waco—a terrible, terrible mistake. Also up in Northern Idaho, when they shot that woman and blew her head off—unarmed and holding her baby in her arms. These two things happened pretty close to each other, and then militias started springing up all over the country.

These "last-straw" events moved many people into the militia movement. Ruby Ridge and Waco have become convenient shorthands that carry intrinsic meaning and motivation for the people involved in the militia movement. "I stood and watched Waco on television," said a militia member, "and I watched our government take tanks and go in there and knock down that building, whether it was set by them or the Branch Davidians, when I saw that happening, I was enraged. And I realized that it could very well be me that they were doing this to. And up until that time, I didn't even own a gun." I spoke with another militia member as he was preparing for a confrontation with local law-enforcement officials. He had been stopped for driving without a license plate and arrested for not having a driver's license. After he was released on bail, he refused to appear at court, and a warrant was issued for his arrest. He discussed Ruby Ridge and Waco:

I'm fifty-one, and I can see a marked difference in the nation from the time when I was a child into a young man growing up to what we have today. I don't know if you've been around long enough to see it or if you've ever been looking, even. But the freedoms that we've had in this country at one time are being eroded. I mean, my God, my friend, think of Ruby Ridge. What did they do there? Eight hundred men around one man and his family and murdered his wife. Shot her through the face! What did they do at Waco? They burned to death those people plus shot them to death. Do you remember? There were seventeen children under the age of five that burned in that building. Seventeen—and that's just the ones under the age of five. Now, if that doesn't alarm you, you've got your head up your butt. Because I'll tell you what, that happens in America! This is America, my friend. I've got photographs of those "men" after the compound or building or church or whatever you want to call it was burned to the ground, slapping each other on the ass and laughing. They had a great time in there murdering those people. These are Americans against Americans. Isn't something wrong here?

The events at Ruby Ridge and Waco in 1992 and 1993, the fact that federal agents were enforcing gun laws, the mistakes that occurred when attempting to resolve these situations, and, perhaps most importantly, the attempts to cover up the wrongdoings were sinister enough to breed suspicion and anger necessary to strengthen and solidify an individual's resolve to respond in protest. It is important to present a synopsis of what occurred because these two events are significant to active members of the militia movement. Similar antigovernment sentiments have certainly existed for a long time, and many militia strategies, especially the paramilitary tactics and structure, are borrowed from earlier extremist activities, but Ruby Ridge and Waco became symbolic rallying points for the militia movement of the 1990s. Ruby Ridge was a solidifying event that was recognized by far-right extremists as a promotional opportunity. Waco was even more significant because it both reaffirmed existing concerns and provided the necessary momentum and growth to create and sustain a movement. People searched for an outlet for their anger; many found the militia movement.

Ruby Ridge: "A Martyr is Made"

Randy Weaver embraced a life outside the boundaries of mainstream society. The Weaver family moved in 1983 from Iowa to Idaho because it was a state with a reputation for being sympathetic to people with unorthodox viewpoints. Weaver preferred to live life as independently as possible. He and his wife lived in a small primitive cabin, they home-schooled their children, and they lived from what the land could provide. Such activities are not extraordinary, but more intriguing were his unorthodox political and religious views. Weaver's ideology was Christian Identity, and he believed that the United States government—he called it "ZOG" (Zionist-Occupied Government)—was controlled by a conspiracy of Jews.[16]

The Aryan Nations, founded by Richard Butler, is probably the best-known extremist group residing in Idaho. Two of the key foundational principles of the Aryan Nations' belief system are racism and religion. Aryans are white supremacists who adhere to Christian Identity beliefs. Christian Identity devotees believe that white Christians are God's chosen people, that the Old Testament provides a history of the white race, that Adam is the father of only the white race, and that Jews and blacks are subhuman species who are "children of darkness" or "children of Satan." Randy Weaver attended at least three events at the Aryan Nations' compound near Hayden Lake, Idaho. At one of these events, he met a biker who was also an informant for the Bureau of Alcohol, Tobacco, and Firearms (BATF). This biker, using the pseudonym Gus Magisono, offered Weaver cash if he could produce sawed-off shotguns. Weaver, who was in desperate need of money, delivered two shotguns with the barrels sawed off at thirteen inches. Weaver was subsequently arrested on weapon charges. The BATF did not target Weaver because he was a high-volume illegal arms dealer, but rather because federal authorities had hoped to enlist his assistance as an informant in its investigation of the Aryan Nations. Weaver refused to cooperate, and he was indicted for illegal weapon sales.

The government's first mistake in *United States vs. Randy Weaver* occurred after his arraignment in January 1991. He was told that his trial would occur by February 19—a date later changed to February 20. However, a letter was delivered to Weaver telling him that his trial was delayed until March 20. In February, when he did not appear for a trial date he did not know existed, he was indicted for failure to appear, and a warrant was issued for his arrest.

The government's second mistake in this case was that the U.S. attorney demanded that efforts to negotiate a peaceful surrender through intermediaries be terminated. Weaver had committed a crime that was defined as a relatively serious offense, but it was apparent that he was not an immediate threat to public safety. Yet there was also evidence that he would not go peacefully if directly confronted by federal law-enforcement officials. With the possibility of a violent confrontation, it made sense to work through intermediaries toward a peaceful solution. Unfortunately, the U.S. attorney did not recognize the value of such a strategy and the risks inherent in a more aggressive approach.

The U.S. Marshals Service considered a variety of different options for apprehending Weaver after this decision, and it pursued its choices carefully for eighteen months, from February 1991 through August 1992. The Marshals Service decided that the best choice, because it was the one that posed the least risk both to the Weaver family and to law enforcement, was to use an undercover operation whereby the marshals would buy nearby property and lure Weaver into a situation where he could be arrested without resistance.

During surveillance of Weaver's property for the undercover operation by six agents on August 21, Weaver's dog detected the surveillance team. It is not clear who shot first, but the U.S. marshals killed the dog. Sam Weaver, Randy's son, fired at whomever killed his dog and was subsequently killed by the marshals; and Kevin Harris, a close family friend of the Weavers, killed U.S. marshal William Degan. Randy Weaver and Harris took Sam's body and retreated to the Weavers' cabin, and the Marshals Service retreated from Rudy Ridge and turned the case over to the FBI.

The government's third mistake, by far its most critical, was its deployment of the FBI's Hostage Rescue Team (HRT) to respond to the incident at Ruby Ridge. The deployment of the HRT was not an error per se, but the FBI did not have sufficient intelligence for adequate decision making. More importantly, the HRT crisis team was sent into the field with specifically formulated "rules of engagement," instructing the team that they could shoot any armed man appearing outside the cabin even if he did not pose an immediate threat. These newly contrived rules "departed from the FBI's standard deadly force policy" and also "contravened the Constitution of the United States."[17]

On August 22, Special Agent Lon Horiuchi, operating under these new rules of engagement, fired one shot that wounded Randy Weaver when he left the cabin to check on Sam's body in an adjoining shed. Kevin Harris was with Randy and was retreating back into the cabin when Horiuchi fired again, seriously injuring Harris and killing Randy Weaver's wife, who was behind the cabin door.

Over the next eight days, as radicals, concerned neighbors, and curious citizens gathered and protested, the FBI attempted to negotiate an end to the siege. Without success, they turned to an intermediary. The intermediary was Bo Gritz—a highly decorated Vietnam veteran and a well-known antigovernment radical. Fortunately, Gritz was able to negotiate Weaver's surrender, putting an end to the siege at Ruby Ridge.

However, numerous mistakes took place in the aftermath of the siege. First, the U.S. attorney decided to pursue the death penalty, even though "the applicable federal appellate court had held that the offense charged could not constitutionally support the imposition of a death sentence."[18] Second, the FBI was delinquent in producing documents and evidence to the U.S. attorney, and the U.S. attorney was delinquent in reproducing materials for the defense. Third, during the trial, at which Randy Weaver was acquitted, the FBI admitted to tampering with evidence.

Randy Weaver served a short sentence for the original gun charge. He and his family were awarded over 3 million dollars from his civil suit against the government for its handling of the siege. In the aftermath, Weaver has become a metaphor for government abuse of power—a perfect martyr and antihero. In the handling of the case, the government lied, conspired, fabricated, and attempted to hide significant wrongdoing. Individuals wanting to incite a movement had a useful and noteworthy example to offer as evidence to support their fear of government abuse, and the Weaver tale was peddled energetically throughout the far Right.

Individuals already fully engaged in some extremist activity immediately recognized the value of the Ruby Ridge incident. Not since the deaths of Posse Comitatus leader Gordon Kahl and the Order's Robert Matthews had extremist leaders had such a useful martyr. Pete Peters, a leader in the Christian Identity movement, organized a three-day strategy session about two months after the Ruby Ridge incident in Estes Park, Colorado.[19] Over 160 people from at least fourteen different states attended the Estes Park gathering. Among those in attendance were Larry Pratt, founder of Gun Owners of America; Richard Butler, founder and head of the Aryan Nations; Kirk Lyons, best known as an attorney for the far Right; John Trochmann, leader of the Militia of Montana and friend of Randy Weaver; ex-Klansman Louis Beam; and tax protestor Red Beckman. This diverse group of extremist leaders was able to agree that the federal government was everybody's enemy. Many of these groups continue to use aspects of the Ruby Ridge incident to meet their goals and objectives. Although many of the individuals who have become involved in the militia movement have brought other concerns and issues with them, the militia movement generally has thrived because of its focus on fears of an overzealous federal government. The Randy Weaver case supported those fears.

Ruby Ridge might have been written off as an aberration, and the militia movement might have slowed considerably or come to a halt, had it not been for the stunningly similar debacle that occurred at Waco, Texas, in 1993. Just over thirty days after the fifty-one-day Waco siege ended on April 19 in a fiery blaze, the federal government indicted Randy Weaver.[20] Because of the similarities and timing of these events, they have melded together in the minds of militia members as the requisite evidence validating their concern about the federal government's encroachment on fundamental rights and liberties.

WACO: "THE MESSIAH IS ATTACKED"

David Koresh was the unique leader of a religious community living in Waco, Texas.[21] In *The Ashes of Waco*, Dick Reavis discusses how Koresh, who dressed casually, often wearing old dirty T-shirts and khakis, came into power. Koresh maintained a connection with his followers, the Branch Davidians, through his engaging religious interpretations, often delivered in celebratory song, and it is clear that he truly believed that he was an anointed prophet or messiah. James Tabor, a religious studies professor who offered assistance to federal authorities during the siege, states that Koresh believed "he was the chosen one who was to open the seven seals of the Book of Revelation and bring on the downfall of 'Babylon.'"[22] Koresh also thought that federal agents would be central figures in bringing about the apocalypse.

Koresh was extremely practical, recognizing that his influence on his followers was tied in part to the community's self-sufficiency. His business savvy helped the community live with limited outside interference, but it also brought him to the attention of federal law-enforcement officials. Koresh developed a good understanding of the profits that could be made from dealing in guns, and over time he purchased a large number of guns for investment purposes. In the early 1990s, Koresh knew that the federal law banning semiautomatic weapons would eventually pass. In order to profit from increasing demand, he bought a large number of semiautomatic weapons, and entered into a partnership with a gun dealer to buy parts to assemble other weapons for later sale. When the law passed, Koresh expected to realize a huge profit.

The BATF did not define Koresh and the Branch Davidians as gun dealers but as criminal threats. They used the following information to secure a search warrant for the compound.[23]

• David Koresh and the Branch Davidians came under scrutiny after the local sheriff's department alerted the BATF that a UPS driver delivered dummy hand grenades to the compound.
• The BATF also discovered that ninety pounds of powdered aluminum, used to make grenades, were delivered to the compound.
• The residents had spent about $40,000 on guns, including a large number of semiautomatic weapons.
• The BATF suspected that someone at the compound was converting semiautomatic weapons to fully automatic weapons. Nobody living at the compound had the proper permits to own fully automatic weapons.

On February 28, 1993, when about one hundred law-enforcement agents attempted to execute a search warrant that was issued based on admittedly weak evidence,[24] a gun battle between federal authorities and members of the community occurred. Four agents were killed and fifteen wounded in the ninety-minute battle. Media footage was breathtaking. Bullets blasted in and out of the complex, and cameras captured agents scurrying for their lives. News cameras were able to get close to the compound because the federal authorities had planned to use the arrest of the Branch Davidians as promotional publicity. This strategy backfired in three important ways. First, the Branch Davidians knew the federal agents were coming because of a chance meeting between one of their members and media personnel. Second, since the news media were in a position to provide video coverage of the "dynamic entry," federal officials felt pressured to go through with the raid even after they knew a surprise attack was compromised. Third, the whole world, including people critical of the U.S. government, had a front row seat to the standoff. When the result was tragic, both sides had deep emotional wounds that limited the options for a peaceful resolution of the situation.

As at Ruby Ridge, the FBI and its Hostage Rescue Team took over at Waco after the execution of the warrant failed miserably. Over the next fifty days, operating under a set of engagement rules that prohibited agents from firing unless they were in imminent danger, officials attempted to negotiate a peaceful surrender. When their psychological tactics failed, the FBI stopped negotiating, and federal authorities launched an assault on the compound on April 19. The video footage of the end to the siege was even more powerful than that shown to the public fifty-one days earlier. In the early morning hours, tanks punched holes into the complex and injected CS gas (a type of tear gas) into the building. As high winds swept through the area, flames engulfed the wood structure, killing David Koresh and seventy-five Branch Davidians.

There have been numerous books, congressional hearings, media stories, court trials, and journalistic exposés taking positions on what occurred at Waco. But there are many conflicting reports and missing data, making it impossible to know what actually happened. What is important for this analysis, however, is an understanding of how the militia movement has constructed their own truth about Waco and used it to justify a commitment to their ideology. They cite numerous governmental errors in the initiation, handling, and aftermath of the siege, many of which were similar to mistakes made at Ruby Ridge.

First, militias have problems with the purpose of the Ruby Ridge and Branch Davidian investigations and the methods used in them. The arrest and prosecution of Randy Weaver and David Koresh were not the primary objectives for carrying out these law-enforcement strategic actions. Weaver was targeted in hopes he would become an undercover informant. The Branch Davidian raid was going to be used by BATF officials in order to justify budgetary increases for the federal agency. With budget hearings approaching, the BATF attempted to time the raid to maximize publicity. Thus, federal authorities went ahead with the raid even when BATF officials knew that the secrecy of the mission had been breached. Undercover agents, one a paid informant and the other a federal agent, were key figures in both investigations. Militias view such undercover activities as highly corrupt, providing the government opportunities to choose targets, entrap them, and then create cases against nonthreatening, law-abiding citizens.

It is also significant that both Weaver and Koresh were targeted by law-enforcement officials for gun offenses. Members of militias believe that the actions of the officers in these two cases demonstrate a significant violation of the Second Amendment and represent a broader plan to prevent citizens from fully exercising this right. These fears were confirmed in late 1993 and early 1994 when Congress enacted legislation requiring waiting periods and banning semiautomatic assault weapons.

The second government error that has been enormously useful to militia leaders is the overzealous law-enforcement response. Law-enforcement officials easily could have arrested Koresh outside the compound without incident, as he did leave it occasionally.[25] He was willing to answer questions from authorities about his gun dealings. Other examples of aggressive law enforcement that were part of this case and are also consistently cited by militia leaders as being problematic are the use of no-knock search warrants by law-enforcement officials, the use of military personnel in domestic law-enforcement activities, the use of military equipment by law-enforcement agencies, and weak evidence to define legal gun activities as criminal.

Militias cite the tactics used in carrying out the assault as a third error. Altering the rules of engagement led to the death of Vicky Weaver. At Waco, federal officials conducted an air and ground assault. Helicopters were used in the raid, but they were supposed to follow the ground team's execution of the warrant. However, the helicopters arrived simultaneously, and there is evidence that law-enforcement snipers were the first to fire on the compound.[26] Moreover, once the opposing side had retreated and there was an attempt to negotiate a peaceful solution, federal authorities were inept. They made promises that were not kept in exchange for concessions by the Davidians; they used psychological tactics, such as playing loud music, Tibetan chant, sirens, and sounds of rabbits being slaughtered over loudspeakers; and they refused to exercise patience and diplomacy, bowing to public and governmental pressure. It is highly likely that the Davidians would eventually have surrendered peacefully because they had limited food, water, and other supplies. Militias cite these issues as evidence that federal law-enforcement officers never had any intention of resolving this standoff in a peaceful manner.

The militias also cite concerns about the hiding and fabrication of evidence. Federal agents and the U.S. attorney were not completely forthcoming with evidence in the Weaver case. Similarly, federal agents refused to cooperate with Texas rangers conducting the initial inquiry into the siege. And for some reason, BATF surveillance cameras did not work the day of the Waco raid. When agents first approached the compound to execute the warrant, Koresh and a couple of followers met them at a double front door. The left door, at which Koresh met the agents and from behind which the Davidians fired their guns, survived the blaze intact. The right door was pummeled with incoming rather than outgoing rounds. BATF officers insist that the first shots came from inside the compound. This claim is controversial because "agents deny firing any shots through the front doors; their standing orders, they say, are to fire only at clearly identifiable targets."[27] Survivors of the fire, and Koresh in media interviews during the siege, claimed that the BATF agents fired first. After the fire burned the compound to the ground, the right door was missing. This coincidence is troublesome for an objective observer; for individuals attempting to excite a movement, it is recruiting propaganda. Later, after the numerous investigations and reports about the incident, the FBI finally admitted to using pyrotechnic devices in the final days of the standoff. This information was known by several law-enforcement officials in 1993, but it was hidden from investigators and the public for six years and may never have come to light had it not been for a whistleblower. Such disclosures only serve to strengthen the claims made by militia leaders that other damning evidence was, and remains, hidden.

THE DIFFERENT TRUTHS OF RUBY RIDGE AND WACO

In order to survive and thrive in a competitive bureaucratic world, organizations must be able to provide measurements of their output. It is not important that the output data be a good predictor of how effectively the organization is functioning; it solely provides justification for the organization's continued existence. This output data can be distracting because in most cases it protects organizations from outside influence. For example, police organizations cite arrest and clearance figures, and prosecutors cite conviction rates and length of sentence information. These outputs do not really capture the informal processes that are characteristic of criminal justice decision making; however, the news media publicize the former and ignore the latter. The media's emphasis on the output data of criminal justice organizations may be illustrated in several ways. First, the presentation of crime in the news media exactly parallels the textbook account of the stages of criminal justice: the media emphasize arrests, arraignments, trials, and sentencing stages, ignoring the decision-making processes that occur between decision points. Second, the media portray criminal justice as a rational bureaucratic system. The key representatives of the state social-control apparatus, police and prosecutors, are shown working together closely to accomplish the single goal of reducing crime. Arrests and convictions are given top priority because they provide the best evidence that the system is effectively accomplishing its goals. Third, media coverage is incident-specific: media personnel present the "who," "what," and "where" of individual events and never consider how the events might be linked. These descriptive elements are easily gleaned from police and court documents, then reformatted to create a news story.

It is important to consider what is ignored by the emphasis on criminal justice outputs. The final decisions made by criminal justice actors, presented to the public as outputs, are not necessarily representative of the decision-making processes of the system. For example, the police often decide to resolve a case with no further criminal justice involvement. Police officers filter cases out of a system that is too overburdened to accept all instances of crimes. Court personnel are equally likely to influence the outcome of a court case by participating in informal bargaining sessions that lead to the establishment of shared understandings of how a case should be processed. Thus, the news media's focus on outputs furthers the goals of criminal justice organizations and helps them maintain legitimacy, but it is also demonstrates and publicizes a limited understanding of criminal justice in action.

High-profile cases like Ruby Ridge and Waco not only highlight some of the important outputs of the system but also open investigations into the invisible decision-making processes. Celebrated cases are high-stakes affairs. It is not enough now that somebody was arrested, shot, or convicted of a crime. Questions arise about why an outcome occurred, whether it could have been prevented, who is at fault, and whether the errors made represent common or even systematic defects of everyday decision making. The errors, the many attempts to hide them, and the unanswered questions that remained in these two cases were substantial, and it was essential to follow them up with fact-finding inquiries. Journalists, scholars, politicians, attorneys, and law-enforcement personnel have all attempted to discover the truths of what went wrong at Ruby Ridge and Waco.

Due to two key obstacles, however, such inquiries are inherently limited in their ability to uncover valid truths. First, many such inquiries are directed at organizations that have the ability to limit access to information by controlling the amount and type released. Second, the structures that limit access to data also isolate the organizations from blame, instead focusing on individual scapegoats and ignoring systematic defects. Ruby Ridge and Waco were not coupled together as examples of bureaucratic corruption and overzealousness, but rather were seen as isolated events that could be explained away as the result of bad procedures and the wrong people making decisions. The government has certainly investigated these events, conducting numerous hearings and investigations, but the scope of their inquiries has been very narrow.

The government's use at Waco of three pyrotechnic tear-gas rounds, provides a good illustration of how these two obstacles work in practice. Law-enforcement investigators and prosecutors knew that pyrotechnic gas—of a type that could have sparked the fire that ended the siege—was used in 1993, but they did not publicly disclose this information. Evidence of the pyrotechnic gas being used then went missing or was intentionally destroyed.[28] Also, the individuals who knew of the use of this gas hid it from investigators until 1999. It only came to light when Bill Johnston, one of the federal prosecutors at Waco, admitted that he and others had covered up the knowledge of the pyrotechnic gas. This revelation spurred yet another investigation into the Waco incident, this time headed by Senator John Danforth. Johnston and two other U.S. attorneys were punished for their role in the cover-up, but the investigation did not go beyond criticizing a few individuals nor did it identify who destroyed the evidence.

Although the investigation of the events at Waco received intense coverage and there was some criticism directed at how agents handled the siege, militias and others in the far Right simply were not satisfied with the nature and conclusions of the inquiries. It seemed doubtful to them that the government and U.S. attorney general Janet Reno—the organization and individual whom militias have concluded should be held responsible—would seriously investigate themselves. Moreover, the lack of access to the inner workings of the organizations involved adds significant fodder to a suspicious belief system, allowing conspiracy thinking to thrive.

To militia leaders, the conclusions of the federal probes and numerous congressional hearings on Waco are biased and without merit. Instead, the militias have created their own accounts of these events, and they rely on their own sources of information—three videotapes—as supporting documentation. These videos—useful as conspiracy fodder— were created using a mixture of truths, half-truths, and a narrow view of the truth to construct powerful imagery that exemplifies government corruption. Linda Thompson, an Indianapolis attorney and active militia member, manufactured two of the videotapes, *Waco: The Big Lie* and its sequel *Big Lie II*. These videotapes cut and splice footage from a variety of sources, ultimately concluding that government officials intentionally killed the Branch Davidians. Among the claims made in the videos are that three of the federal agents killed were murdered by another federal agent to cover up a CIA plot, that the tanks shot flames into the compounds to end the siege, and that the federal government purposely blocked building exits with gunfire to maximize the number of deaths.[29] The third video, *Waco: The Rules of Engagement*, is a more credible account of what occurred at Waco and was nominated for an Academy Award. It argues that the BATF agents attempted to use Koresh's arrest as a publicity stunt and that the FBI purposely started the fire, and it clearly documents the attempts to obstruct justice in the case. As I discussed Waco with various militia members, almost all of them encouraged me to view this videotape, and several even offered to send it to me. One militia member described *Rules* in the following way:

It will make you sick to your stomach. You'll cry. It shows government— this is all government photography taken from the U.S. government helicopters and light planes that overflew Waco twenty-four hours a day. It shows them shooting the Branch Davidians as the place is burning and they're trying to get out. It shows them shooting them. They killed everyone intentionally.

Similarly, another militia member said:

At the time there were and subsequently for the last few years there have been people who have speculated that the government set the fire and that the government massacred at least some of the Davidians. When you see this film, I think you'll come to the conclusion that that is exactly what happened. When the militia concluded after Waco that the government had set the fire and massacred the Davidians, we were called paranoid wackos and all sorts of other things. But it now turns out that what we feared about Waco was true: doesn't that make us not paranoid but prophets? . . . We're here to make a noise and to alert people that your constitutional rights are going down the toilet. And when you see the movie, I think you'll understand what I'm saying.

It is clear that Ruby Ridge and Waco were significant events that set two processes in motion—processes that would be brought together soon after the bombing of the Murrah building in Oklahoma City. First, these incidents helped solidify antigovernment rhetoric and activities into what is now called the militia movement. Ruby Ridge was an important event, especially because Weaver survived the confrontation. However, Ruby Ridge did not generate nearly the publicity given to Waco. The media access and coverage opportunities provided to reporters at Waco to generate publicity for additional federal funds backfired miserably. Second, Waco had a profound impact on Timothy McVeigh. He was at Waco during the siege, he watched the end of it on television, and he visited the site on several occasions after its tragic conclusion. Waco was the central motivating force that led McVeigh to commit the devastation in Oklahoma City.[30]

The Rise and Fall of Militias

Militias used the wrongdoings and unanswered questions from the Ruby Ridge and Waco incidents to solidify the militia movement and recruit new members. Early leaders of the movement recruited using various strategies, including disseminating pamphlets, mailings, newsletters, and other descriptive literature at public meetings, get-togethers, gun shows, and on the World Wide Web. Many other groups, especially after the Oklahoma City bombing, had open public meetings to disseminate militia materials and describe their concerns and activities. Other militia groups discussed how public-service activities are worthwhile because they benefit the community, combat their image in the news media, and bring interested people to their meetings. "We have an adopt-a-highway program," noted one militia member, "we do toy drives for kids, we do Halloween drives with candy." Gun shows and gun shops have also been important recruitment locations for militias. Militia groups will post notices of upcoming meetings at gun stores and Army-Navy surplus stores to attract "like-minded" people. One member of a multicounty militia owned a gun shop, where materials describing the philosophy and goals of the militia were scattered throughout. When customers inquired about the posted materials, he had a captive audience.

Many of these broad-based recruitment strategies, including disseminating newsletters and promotional materials at key events (e.g., gun shows) and key locations (e.g., gun shops), were used by larger militias with the financial resources and personnel to produce and disseminate promotional materials. These large groups (75–500 members) tend to cover a state, a portion of a state, or even a region. Their typical structure includes an umbrella group with elected or appointed leadership positions that is the decision-making and communication hub for all groups within its jurisdiction. The local groups included under the umbrella also have locally elected or appointed officers. For example, the commanding officer of a regional militia with nineteen countywide regiments described its structure. He described himself as being an active member of the militia movement since 1992, and at that time he was the elected leader of a county group. After his group visited with other county militias in the region, they decided to form a group that was "larger and had a wider variety of people with different backgrounds." "What we had was a lot of different independent county militias, and it's much easier to respond if you do have some natural disaster or something happens and you need the manpower if you have got all of these under an umbrella group: where you know who the commanders are, you can coordinate everything." He was elected the commander of the regional group when it formed, and then his wife was elected to take his vacated position in the county group.

The majority of militias, however, make only minimal effort to have a public face and attract new members. The number of public recruitment efforts has also declined significantly over time. Consistent with their underlying philosophy and the driving reason for participating, most militias rely on individuals seeking a group after they realize that the government is a threat. One militia member described such a passive approach to recruitment:

> We don't have to do anything to recruit members—the government does it all for us. Every single day of the year somebody somewhere feels like his or her rights have been violated and feels powerless against the government. You know, they feel like the government is supposed to derive its power from the people, but many people feel powerless against the government. Every single day somebody feels like their rights have been violated and they feel like they need an "out." They need to tell someone about it who is going to sympathize with them and understand, and then help them prevent it from happening again. Every time that happens, once the word gets out that there is a militia in the area and the name of the contact, you get calls. You get calls continuously. Whether they join the militia or not, if you can get them information to help them so they can then help themselves, that goes a long way.

Probably the most effective strategy used, especially in the period between the Ruby Ridge standoff and the Oklahoma City bombing, was informal networking among family, friends, and acquaintances. Most militias have few members (six to ten), are geographically specific, and bring their members together through various informal social ties. This structure is consistent with the "leaderless resistance" cell structure, although many of these smaller groups are not concerned about maintaining secrecy about their activities. Efforts to recruit others generally involve talking to people they know: friends, neighbors, hunting buddies, brothers-in-law, and co-workers. For example, one interviewee discussed how wearing a T-shirt with the name of his militia to work became a topic of conversation. Several co-workers purchased the shirts, a few started to attend meetings, and a couple actually joined the militia.

Although Ruby Ridge and Waco stimulated growth, and many of the people who became interested in militias after these two incidents became active, the activities, philosophies, and recruitment efforts of the militia movement remained outside the peripheries of the public's consciousness. The public was unaware of and unconcerned about the existence of militias because the media, policymakers, and law-enforcement officials were not interested in their activities and did not see a need to educate the public about them. The Oklahoma City bombing dramatically ended this indifference: militias immediately became a priority issue. The panic lasted for a couple of years, but since then militias have been drifting away as an issue of concern.

The rest of this chapter focuses on how and why militias entered and exited the public's consciousness in the 1990s. It begins with a discussion of the inherent limitations of the social-problem marketplace. It then describes three distinct eras of the existence of militias in the public's mind—the period prior to the Oklahoma City bombing, the two years following it, and the subsequent period when public interest waned. Explanations for why militias underwent this transition are explored, and the issues highlighted provide insights into the processes that shape public understanding of social problems.

THE LIMITATIONS OF THE INFORMATION MARKETPLACE

A community's formal system of social control is limited in its capacity to respond to social problems. All public bureaucracies suffer because they have created the expectation that they can provide a diversity of services but do not have the time, resources, or personnel to tend to all legitimate concerns. Prioritizing by the highest-ranking need is a natural by-product of these capacity limitations. The highest-ranking problems can reflect what may be of greatest risk or concern to the populace, but generally the ranking is more likely to reflect other pressures, such as the concerns of politicians and activists. Research on agenda setting discusses how the number of discretionary agenda items considered by politicians is inherently limited because a large part of the agenda is consumed by annually occurring items and events such as budgetary sessions, committee work, and ceremonial commitments.[1] Similarly, the criminal justice system cannot respond to an indefinite number of crimes. Various constraints, including personnel, resources, space, and desire, create the need for criminal justice personnel to exercise a great deal of discretion in deciding what cases are formally processed through the system. Activist groups also set priorities or simply address a small array of issues. The main objective of most political claims-makers, however, is to influence public perception of the issues about which they are concerned while also maintaining isolation from external pressures.

Since the capacity for all bureaucratic organizations to respond to social problems is inherently limited, it should not be surprising that many social problems lie dormant. These problems exist, and there may even be efforts by grassroots entrepreneurs to raise public awareness about them, but the environment is resistant to giving serious consideration to them in the public arena. Joel Best, in his discussion of social construction theory in his book on threats to children, discusses how various claims-makers have to compete for attention in the social problems marketplace, because the number of claims far exceeds its "carrying capacity."[2] Some social problems are viewed as commodities in this environment and consume a disproportionate amount of the limited resources of a community's social-control apparatus. Once politicians, bureaucrats, media personnel, and moral entrepreneurs view a problem as an opportunity to generate capital, then these claims-makers compete for control or ponder ways in which they can benefit from the attention the problem may generate. These chances are fleeting. A problem is identified, there are opportunities to shape how the criminal justice system responds to it, and then it disappears. Some of society's more contentious issues may be frequent visitors to the social-problems marketplace because there is a balance of power among the decision makers attempting to capitalize on an opportunity. But when the response to the social problem is not affected by divergent viewpoints or else the groups with the dissenting view are powerless or considered deviant, significant changes in policies, organizations, and public understanding occur. Concomitantly, the response to an issue by those in power increases the status of deviant groups, solidifying the latter's commitment to their ideology and attracting new members.

Competition is the most important variable influencing how social problems become the temporary rulers of this marketplace, and there are several important characteristics of this competition. First, competition to achieve priority status is fierce. This imbalance has produced a very unstable marketplace—a "revolving-door" structure in which the attention paid by the media and politicians to many problems rapidly comes and goes with the political current. One of the unfortunate aspects of this instability is that the processes that made a problem significant leave a permanent impression on the fears and concerns of the community. The instability also influences the way these problems are defined and the appropriate responses to them.[3]

Second, the competition exists both across and within categories of social problems. Attention to crime as a serious social problem has to compete with concerns about the environment, the economy, poverty, energy consumption, political scandal, health issues, education, and automobile safety. Social problems that occur outside the geographic boundaries of the United States are almost always overshadowed by key domestic social problems. These problems are also affected, however, by competing social problems within a category. Crime is a broad area, and thus problems such as drugs, guns, and prostitution have to compete against drunk driving, serial murder, and domestic violence for heightened public attention. In order to fully understand why certain social problems occupy a prominent place in the social-problems marketplace, one must examine the predominant competing concerns.

Third, the limits of this marketplace and the stiff competition for attention produce crisis-management decision making. Most crime and criminal justice policy that has been implemented reflects this crisis mentality. Crime is very competitive in the social-problem marketplace and has consistently entered and dominated it. Celebrated cases often provide the needed entryway to this competitive marketplace, and frequently become of broader social concern. Issues like crime are important because of the inherent moral messages that can be woven into the discussion of them. Crime can also be discussed in a manner that is consistent with existing cultural frameworks. Consider the popularity of crime-control strategies. Stuart Scheingold discusses how crime is a "valence issue" and "the only challenge with respect to valence issues is to present them in ways that work for you and against your opponents." Law-and-order policies are emphasized, and politicians claim "that they are serious about reducing street crime, but they insistently emphasize punishment and marginalize the social and economic programs that criminologists and criminal justice professionals alike see as essential components of crime prevention." Social problems that are consistent with the dominant law-and-order framework are more likely to enter the marketplace and be defined as worthy of a policy response.[4]

Fourth, not all social problems are even eligible to be considered serious. The construction of a social problem in this marketplace must coexist with the objective reality of the problem. Because of this coexistence, problems that do not pose a significant threat to the community may receive attention, while other problems that are threatening may be ignored. Similarly, some problems may indeed be a threat to the community but are constructed in a way that produces a response out of proportion to the actual threat, thereby wasting or exhausting resources. It is difficult to predict which cases will produce a disproportionate response, but several issues appear to be significant. The first is the extent to which the case is able to generate fear. The second is whether the policy concern linked to the case is "ideal." If it can be solved in ways that are familiar and consistent with the preferences of policymakers, it has a greater chance of succeeding in the marketplace. The third issue, intertwined with the previous two, is the existence of a "good demon." The target that is identified as causing the social problem must be an effective threat and can usually be responded to using strategies preferred by political claims-makers.

It is important to note that there is a core group of players that have some role in all matters that become defined as significant social problems. Individuals and groups do not have equal access to the public arena. Some experts, for example, are only occasional visitors and have an inconsistent impact on the definitional processes that occur in the social-problems marketplace. There are, however, political and bureaucratic institutions that play a role in responding to social problems, and although the nature of the problem varies, these institutions define and implement responses to all social problems in a similar way. Officials representing these institutions are involved in all stages of social-problem construction, the result being the framing of problems in a way that supports their interests. This is quite significant because the initial framing of a problem influences the public's understanding of it by structuring how claims-makers discuss it and eliminating the consideration of a range of alternative frameworks. Ideal policy issues thus will be constructed in similar ways, but it is important to note that the opposing frameworks preferred by various policymakers may limit their construction. For contentious political issues, in which both policymakers and interested parties have a stake in problem definition, the amount of change following celebrated cases is limited. But when the nature of the problem involves an ideal defendant, and there is limited resistance across this core group of key players, then the amount of attention to a problem and the changes implemented are significant.

The rise and fall of militias is an excellent example of how the strict size of the marketplace forces panicked responses to social problems. Media coverage of militias from 1990 to 1998 helps to illustrate how the social-problems marketplace evolves, how celebrated events are key defining moments, and how certain individuals and institutions shape the definition of social problems.

MEDIA COVERAGE OF MILITIAS, 1990–1998

Table 3.1 presents data on the number of articles in which militias and militia activity were featured in newspapers from two databases: NewsBank and LexisNexis.[5] NewsBank produces a sample of media articles from local market areas by indexing a large number of newspapers representing different-sized market areas and different regional areas. Newspapers as diverse as the *Los Angeles Times*, the *Washington Post*, the *Dallas Morning News*, the *Atlanta Journal and Constitution*, the *Wichita Eagle*, the *Sacramento Bee*, and the *Greensboro News* are included. The range and regional representation of newspapers in this database provide a good estimate of how militias seeped into both national and local conversations.

Table 3.1 Number of Militia Articles Presented Over Time

Year	NewsBank	%	New York Times	%
1990	0	0.0	0	0.0
1991	0	0.0	0	0.0
1992	0	0.0	0	0.0
1993	0	0.0	0	0.0
1994	5	1.4	3	1.5
1995	209	58.9	104	53.3
1996	84	23.7	52	26.7
1997	42	11.8	30	15.4
1998	15	4.2	6	3.1
Total	355	100.0	195	100.0

The second database examined for this analysis was LexisNexis, searching for articles about militias published in the *New York Times*. This newspaper was selected for two reasons. First, it is a good example of the national media's attention to policy agenda items. Second, it provides an opportunity to examine variations in the intensity of coverage of militias over time in one large media source.

These two data distributions support three important findings. First, media attention to militias suddenly increased after the Oklahoma City bombing and then steadily declined. Only five articles were included in NewsBank and only three *New York Times* articles were published prior to 1995. In 1995 and 1996, nearly 300 articles were published in the newspapers indexed by NewsBank and 156 articles appeared in the *New York Times*. Since 1995, however, the intensity of media coverage has steadily declined. In 1997, forty-two articles about militias were published in the NewsBank newspapers, and there were thirty articles in the *New York Times*. The number of militia-related articles published in 1998 declined significantly. It is interesting that the patterns of coverage locally and nationally are almost identical.[6]

Second, the link between militias and Timothy McVeigh allowed militias to become competitive in the social-problems marketplace. Over half of the entire sample of militia-related newspaper articles was published in the same year as the bombing. In 1995, prior to April 19, there were only ten newspaper articles about militias in NewsBank and none in the *New York Times*. After the bombing, 190 articles were printed in newspapers indexed by NewsBank and 104 in the *New York Times*, with a heavy concentration within sixty days of the bombing. This concentrated coverage is presented in Chart 3.1. The chart indicates that there were just

Chart 3.1 Number of Articles in NewsBank in 1995 by Month

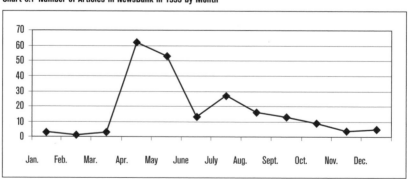

over sixty articles published in April in the newspapers indexed by NewsBank. Only three of these articles were published prior to April 19. There were fifty-three articles published in May 1995, but nearly 70 percent were published before the middle of the month. Thus, between April 19 and May 15, nearly one hundred articles were published. It is important to note that these numbers underestimate the attention to militias because articles discussing the Oklahoma City bombing but not specifically mentioning militias were excluded from the counts. The public had come to associate McVeigh with militias, however, and thus the coverage of the bombing indirectly contributed to concern about these groups.

Third, these data support the conclusion that there have been three distinct eras of media coverage of militias. Prior to the Oklahoma City bombing, the social-problems marketplace resisted identifying militias as a serious social problem. Despite considerable growth during this time period, the primary institutions that set the tone for this marketplace ignored militias. After the Oklahoma City bombing, militias were heavily scrutinized. The characteristics and size of militias did not change immediately following the bombing, but the public perceived them as a significant social problem needing to be addressed. More recent coverage of militias shows them as receding from public concern. Interest in militias virtually disappeared once McVeigh and Nichols were convicted.

MARKETPLACE RESISTANCE (1990–APRIL 19, 1995)

One militia member interviewed described how he grew up in the mountains and was always around guns. He and his friends were firm believers in the Constitution, the Bill of Rights, and family values. He was proud to look like somebody in the military: "I have a shaved head. I've got a Marine Corps high and tight that I've had on my head since I was thirteen years old." Although interested in the military, he never joined. He did, however, organize a militia soon after the Ruby Ridge and Waco incidents.

The militia group he organized started as just "two of us—two friends got together . . . two people turned to three, three turned to five, five turned to ten, and it grew and grew and grew." Later, he found out about another unit operating in a nearby county and arranged a meeting with them. "We got to talking and we got together, and they knew another group which is about another sixty miles from them, and that put one actual group in each end of the state and one in the center. And we went from there and sat down, and we got together and we bickered over things and came up with a policy and decided that we could do a statewide program." He described this militia group as a closed-cell organization.

> We do not advertise a chain of command. We do not post our entire plans for everything on the Internet. We operate in a closed-cell structure, just like the militia was intended to operate. Communication occurs in person by courier. We don't transmit information over the Internet, we don't talk on the telephone, we do not use faxes, and we don't even send anything through the mail. We deliver everything in person.

He talked about how units did military training, stocked weapons, food, and supplies, and were ready to respond. This group had active units operating in two-thirds of the counties in the state.

This development of a statewide militia group occurred when the public was not paying attention. It is difficult to know how representative this growth was because reliable data on the movement's size do not exist. Such information is difficult to collect because of the secrecy of closed-cell militias and the range of structures and strategies employed by militia groups. The interview data, however, support the conclusion that there was substantial growth in militia membership after the Waco incident, but the development of a statewide presence in such a short time was not common. The majority of people interviewed claimed long-term involvement in the movement and were active prior to the Oklahoma City bombing. One member said he had communicated with units in over forty states simply to gather information and share ideas when his group first started organizing in 1993. Other interviewees consistently discussed the growth that occurred between Waco and Oklahoma City. "About five years ago a couple of gentlemen started a county unit. I was just a member of that unit. I was very active and very interested in it, and it started to grow really fast. We ended up having to split our regiment up into companies."

Since militias were new to the extremist landscape, organizations that monitor such activity had difficulty reliably approximating the size of the movement. Early estimates of the size of the movement ranged from finding a militia presence in ten to thirteen states, to at least twenty states, to over thirty states. Although the estimates varied considerably, watchdog groups were concerned enough to monitor and gather data about militias prior to Oklahoma City. For example, Kroninger reported that "the Southern Poverty Law Center, the Center for Democratic Renewal, Political Research Associates, Planned Parenthood, Greenpeace, the Sierra Club, and the Anti-Defamation League of B'Nai B'rith had been ringing the alarm bells, as had many local antiracism groups, but hardly anyone seemed to be listening."[7] One longtime employee of an activist group that was interviewed said

> We actually noticed the militia movement before Oklahoma City. That was something we noticed for a couple of years. It was something that we found in a bunch of states—we actually reached a point where we had found militia activity in about thirteen states. These groups were incredible, very opposed to the gun control movement and very upset by Waco and Ruby Ridge.

Yet political activists, although they made an effort to inform the public about their concerns about militias through the media, still had little success in generating publicity.

A few reports published prior to Oklahoma City did highlight the dangers, growth, and racism of the militia movement. One militia activist was very critical of these early reports for containing inaccurate information and exaggerating the links between militias and white supremacist groups.

> Those reports were the first detailed look that anyone had given the militia movement up to that point, and it had a tremendous weight on the media, who would refer for quite some time to those early pamphlets. The problem is that the reports concentrated on one element of the so-called patriot movement—the white supremacists. The way they discovered the militia movement is by tracking white supremacists. They discovered that some white supremacists end up in the militia movement. They reasoned from that, or concentrated on that, that the militia movement was saturated with, led by, and controlled by white supremacists. . . . Every militiaman was a Klansman in "camo." The militia movement and its relation to race are really complex. There are a lot of militia people out there where race is not why there are in the militia movement, not why they were angry—it was not even remotely an issue. And they were certainly more mainstream than say a Phineas priest or something like that.[8]

The reporters interviewed echoed the notion that interest in militias prior to Oklahoma City was very limited. Several reporters had noticed the growing militia movement after Ruby Ridge and Waco and had established contact with it. But their attention to militia activities was poorly received by news editors, and although they were able to generate some stories, they were discouraged from following up. One of the reporters said:

> [I] had proposed doing a story to my editors on the rise of citizen militias. It would have been a good story, and I was watching them grow. I was told that there's no interest in that, and I think the exact quote was "Our readers have no appetite for that kind of story." At the time, there was an attitude that we [the media] shouldn't do too much of this stuff. It was okay to write an occasional story when there's something good, but we don't want to just write about what this militia is doing or there's a new militia here or whatever. I had a lot of trouble getting some stories in the paper. In fact a story I did on Christian Identity took two to three weeks to get in the paper. It ran on the front page but it took a long time to get it through just because . . . I don't know, there was still some of that "We don't want to be covering wackos" type of thing, and "Don't even tell us about it." It was very frustrating.

There was scant news coverage of the militia movement prior to the Oklahoma City bombing. Some stories did focus on the general activities of the militia groups and the growth of the movement. The more alarming stories highlighted several issues, including the size of the movement, but they were simply isolated investigative reports that did not generate any momentum or additional media coverage. For example, Sam Walker, a staff writer for the *Christian Science Monitor*, described the growth of militias in late 1994. "Armed with assault rifles and full of contempt for many federal laws, particularly recent gun-control measures, groups calling themselves 'militias' have held training exercises across the nation and claim to have recruited as many as 10,000 foot soldiers." The majority of the article describes militia concerns about gun-control legislation and reactions to federal policymaking activity on guns. He concludes: "People stereotype these guys as a bunch of redneck weekend warriors; but they're not. I see a dark day ahead with these folks running around with assault rifles. It's scary." Similarly, Keith Schneider published an article in the *New York Times* estimating that there was a militia presence in at least twenty states. He discussed the ideology and paramilitary structure of militias generally, and examined the Michigan Militia as representative of the movement. Law-enforcement officials and extremist watchdogs were quoted, emphasizing the dangers of the militia movement. Ironically, though early media interest in militias and the discovery of the Michigan Militia did not generate a public panic, a vague reference to McVeigh attending one meeting of a militia group in Michigan ignited a media and policymaking frenzy after the bombing.[9]

Other media stories published prior to the Oklahoma City bombing discussed militias as an issue secondary to some other concern. Many stories focused on antiabortion activity and the various intimidation tactics being used by extremist groups, including militias, to harass workers at abortion clinics. Abortion issues almost always generate significant news interest, and in the early 1990s abortion-clinic intimidation and terrorist tactics received publicity after several high-profile incidents, including the murders of doctors in Boston, Massachusetts, and Pensacola, Florida. Several antiabortion activists even advocated organizing militias as a way of accomplishing their goal of shutting down abortion clinics.

THE INSIGNIFICANCE OF THE PRE–OKLAHOMA CITY MILITIA MOVEMENT

The growth of the militia movement prior to the Oklahoma City bombing was already significant enough to raise concern among groups who monitor the far Right. These groups attempted to use what access they had to the media to publicize these concerns and raise public and law-enforcement awareness of militias. Moreover, individual reporters were curious about militia activities and worked diligently to understand the ideology of newly forming militia groups. Yet these concerns and activities were still not powerful enough to create a marketplace-worthy social problem. Militias were unknown commodities. Media coverage was sporadic, infrequent, and scarcely noticed. Prior to the Oklahoma City bombing, the social-problems marketplace was resistant to the coverage of militias because they were defined as insignificant "wackos" and not yet considered a real threat.

Militias were ignored in part because there were other issues or specific cases that concerned media organizations. For example, as we have seen, Ruby Ridge and Waco produced both celebrated media coverage and congressional investigations. The processing of these two cases through the criminal and civil-justice systems provided many opportunities to revisit them in the early 1990s. The cases could have been framed into larger systematic concerns about law-enforcement corruption, aggressive police practices, or government cover-up, especially since both cases followed the Rodney King case and its aftermath, and a coalition of strong claims-makers, including the ACLU and the NRA, was calling for the investigation of such abuses. Yet the focus of the Ruby Ridge and Waco investigations was not on these broader policy issues, but rather on determining the facts and assigning blame for what happened in these two cases. Although the scope of the investigations did not include a broader systematic review, it is significant that both the FBI and BATF were heavily criticized for their handling of the cases. These cases also opened political opportunities. The early congressional investigations were important opportunities to discredit and attack President Clinton and his leading law-enforcement official. Janet Reno was, of course, not attorney general when the Ruby Ridge event occurred in 1992, but she was the one who ordered the raid on Waco. Republicans attempted to emphasize her role at Waco in an effort to have her removed from office. As with the Whitewater and Vincent Foster suicide investigations, attacking Reno provided another opportunity to highlight problems with Clinton's presidency.

Other crime-related issues occupied a considerable amount of time for policymakers and the media during the early 1990s. The gun-control debate on waiting periods and semiautomatic assault weapons was winding down, and legislation on those issues was passed in late 1993 and early 1994. Research examining the media's coverage of these two issues indicates that the vast majority of coverage supported the implementation of these policy changes, creating an environment resistant to the concerns of gun enthusiasts.[10] Policymakers also found an ideal target for new crime policies in the sexual offender against children. There was considerable discussion of community notification statutes and sexual predator laws in the early 1990s, as well as about international terrorism incidents and international groups posing threats to targets at home and abroad. Finally, O. J. Simpson's arrest for a double homicide consumed almost all the time and space given to extraordinary cases in 1994.

Militias were growing in 1992 and 1993, but it is understandable why they did not break into the social-problems marketplace during this period. Media reporters did not have the necessary context or the existing framework they could use to illustrate that militias were threatening. At first, as one militia leader said, the media thought of them as "a bunch of buck-toothed, inbred, pickup driving, beer-drinking hillbillies that couldn't find our way out of a paper bag with a map." Key watchdog groups were only just learning about these groups, and little data was available yet. Even in 1994, when the media provided some coverage to militias and watchdog groups released information pointing to significant growth in militias, the marketplace continued to resist defining militias as a serious social problem. Although the articles discussed earlier cited growth statistics and specific crime incidents, the militias were not yet considered threatening enough to be a valuable news commodity. If the media had looked, they could have found other incidents in which such groups intimidated, threatened, or injured government officials. Militias were not yet a threat, however, because they did not have a celebrated face. This changed dramatically on April 19, 1995.

THE OKLAHOMA CITY EXPLOSION

A reporter who worked for a newspaper in a large Midwestern city had taken early notice of the militia movement, but she was assigned to the political beat, responsible for developing legislative stories. She had her hands full, as most reporters do, fulfilling the routine requirements of this beat. But, in her spare time, she kept tabs on the militias. And while covering the abortion issue, she made some militia contacts. "The reason I got interested in the militia movement was because some of the more radical pro-lifers that I was covering were starting to get involved in it, and that's what introduced me to them. I guess it made sense for pro-lifers to be antigovernment, because they think the government is sanctioning baby killing." When she moved to another newspaper in early 1994, she continued to follow militias, had a good list of sources in the movement, and talked to them on a fairly regular basis about their activities and strategies. She was working at the legislature on the day of the bombing, so other reporters from her newspaper were sent to Oklahoma City. "I was kind of depressed, because I had to sit and watch CNN from the state capitol." Once the media linked Timothy McVeigh to the militia movement, however, she immediately got a call from an editor who asked: "'Can you do this stuff?' . . . I ran home and got out all of my files and starting going over everything. . . . I think after the bombing they just started listening more closely when I would bring up something that was militia-related." When I asked her to estimate how many stories she has done on militias since the bombing, she responded: "Probably a couple hundred. I would have to go back and look, but I've done a lot."

When an event of the magnitude of the Oklahoma City bombing occurs, no other news matters that day. All other news is just filler for the limited amount of excess space available. There is no other front-page headline, no other story can push it out of the top slot in a television broadcast, and an even more breathtaking event would have to occur to prevent it from adorning the covers of weekly news magazines. The timing of the event is less significant in an era of around-the-clock news coverage. Reports, video images, photographs, and World Wide Web coverage made dissemination of the known facts immediate. Moreover, rumors travel fast in our technologically linked society, and the public was starved for information. The media unleashed whatever personnel were available, sending hundreds of reporters to Oklahoma City, assigning others to search for local ties, and asking others to make sense of all the incoming data. Don Brown, who was the city manager of Oklahoma City on April 19, estimated that over 300 different news agencies had visited the bomb site by the time the search and rescue operation had closed down.[11] Because of the conglomeration of the media environment, the existence of wire services, and the ability to transmit video by satellite and computer, almost every media organization in the world had some presence in Oklahoma City.

It is obvious why the Oklahoma City bombing was such a celebrated media event. The media did not know the number of people killed or wounded during the immediate aftermath, but it was clear that the harm was substantial. The building was heavily populated, and the images of its physical destruction implied that a long list of casualties would be forthcoming. The public's feelings of safety and security were profoundly disturbed. One leader of a militia group who talked at length about the news coverage of the Oklahoma City bombing said that "nobody cares about what happens anywhere until it happens to them." The random selection of this target made it seem as if it could have happened to anyone. The attack took place in Oklahoma City, but it was defined as an attack on the United States. This sentiment was captured poignantly in Jack Ohman's editorial cartoon published immediately after the bombing. (See Figure 1.)

Some media scholars have described the news production process as "routinizing the unexpected nature of news."[12] The resulting routines add predictability and stability to the process of collecting and dissemi-

1. *Jack Ohman, How Many Hurt?* © *Tribune Media Services, Inc. Reprinted with permission. All Rights Reserved.*

nating the news, and they increase the efficiency of the news production process. But they also bias what news is covered as well as how it is covered. Although events like the Oklahoma City bombing disrupt these routine processes, news media can handle them with relative ease because the media environment has advanced technologically and organizationally. Media competition is almost nonexistent because a limited number of organizations own media outlets, and they pool their resources in response to such celebrated events. Although there may be an initial struggle to get to the center of a celebrated story when it first occurs, the panic subsides as media workers recognize familiar boundaries that give shape and meaning to the story. These boundaries that define the nature of events reflect existing cultural frameworks and the ethos of the profession. They allow the media to manage a crisis in an efficient and effective manner because the stories are familiar, but they also guarantee that certain preferred meanings rather than alternative frameworks will be used in the interpretation of the events.

Initial coverage of a celebrated crime focuses primarily on describing the incident and its impact. Reporters also attempt to explain who committed the act and why. The Oklahoma City bombing was immediately framed as a terrorist attack. Although no group had taken responsibility for the bombing, news personnel were familiar with the destruction and the method used in the attack because media coverage of the World Trade Center bombing had lasted through 1994. They therefore jumped to the conclusion that it was terrorism, and the logical demon for the media to accuse was the figure most closely associated with the framework: the Middle Eastern terrorist. In the critical period immediately following the bombing, some reporters entertained the possibility that the terrorists were domestic rather than foreign because they recognized the historical significance of the date of the bombing—the day the Waco siege ended. Several of the reporters interviewed admitted that they thought that the link to the Middle East was bogus, but the bulk of media coverage focused on Arab terrorists. This conclusion was not based on any factual information; however, it was consistent with media and public expectations. Moreover, since the supposed link to Middle Eastern terrorists was public knowledge, other organizations perpetuated this idea because news reporters borrow heavily from other media when constructing stories, assuming that printed or broadcast assertions are truths.

Two days after the bombing, media organizations reported that an arrest had been made, but they did not report the suspect's name. For example, Ron Martz reported on April 21 in the *Atlanta Journal and Constitution* that a suspect was being held.

> One man was reported arrested today in the terror bombing that smashed a huge chunk in a federal office building and killed at least 57 people. The man was seized in the town of Perry, less than 100 miles north of Oklahoma City, television networks reported. . . . In Michigan at mid-afternoon, an FBI official said federal agents were also making a raid on a farmhouse in Decker, Mich., in connection with the bombing. . . . ABC News reported that two people were arrested there. The raid had been in the works for some time, the network said. *It said authorities said both of the men on the run were said to be members of Michigan Militia, an "extreme-right-wing" organization connected to other organizations around the country. . . . ABC reported that the Michigan Militia had links to the Branch Davidians* [emphasis added].[13]

At this point, the news value of this story increased dramatically for two reasons. First, the media could now dissect the lives of the suspects.

Second, as the story evolved, media personnel could go beyond describing the event to explaining why it happened. They could talk to family members, acquaintances, teachers, co-workers, and friends to get life histories, and perhaps identify the events that triggered the suspects' actions. The media also tried to keep pace with law-enforcement agents as they pieced together the evidence against the suspects. As suspects were discovered and the investigation continued, the body count grew. People who survived the blast, and family members of those who were lost, worked through grief and trauma with no privacy.

Society had a problem to cure and an ideal policy issue that needed fixing. An interviewee said that all militias "were guilty by association" and needed to be responded to as domestic terrorists. Moreover, militias were only one of many existing terrorist groups. Domestic terrorism became the latest in a long list of moral panics, and its status as an important social problem dominated the marketplace for nearly a year. We had a problem that needed to be analyzed and understood, we had a target that needed to be eradicated, and we had a legitimate threat to be feared. Policymakers and government bureaucrats needed to formulate a response. These officials had a cultural framework within which to work because the terrorist was well accepted as a respectable fear, and they also had the freedom to call for significant changes because there would be no legitimate opposition to the demonization of far-right extremists plotting terrorist acts.

The obvious response for politicians was to increase the social-control capacity of the political and criminal justice system, a strategy consistent with the law-and-order frame that has dominated policy making since the early 1980s. Groups who tried to make the public aware of the threat well before Oklahoma City now had a public face for their antihate agenda. The bombing had lifted the veil of secrecy over homegrown terrorist groups. Media analysis of any far-right extremist group now became competitive in the social-problems marketplace. It was, however, the media's prior coverage of militias, and the early conclusion that Timothy McVeigh was a member of the Michigan Militia, that focused interest on the previously invisible militia movement.

As soon as the Michigan Militia were wrongly implicated in the bombing, reporters flocked to get interviews and public comment. Several of the people interviewed in Michigan were active members of the movement well before Oklahoma City. They described being overwhelmed by national and international media. One leader of a large regional group estimated that he probably did close to 300 media interviews in the week after the bombing. Another militia member did about a hundred interviews within a few days after the bombing.

The Michigan Militia, however, was not the only story. In fact, as news media realized that the link between McVeigh and the Michigan Militia was spurious, attention shifted to discovering whether other threats existed. News personnel across the country were instructed to go out and find the local militia threat. "Mainstream news organizations discovered militias and antigovernment groups for the first time after Oklahoma City," said one reporter. Reporters could now put a face on existing statistical estimates of the problem, and it was important to see whether other groups like the groups in Michigan were widespread. Everybody wanted to do a story, and, as illustrated by the NewsBank and *New York Times* data discussed earlier, reporters were very successful.

THE IMPACT OF MEDIA COVERAGE

The Oklahoma City bombing elevated militias to priority status, and public understanding of militias was significantly changed by how they were presented in the news in the following months. This celebrated event had a significant impact on the size of the militia movement. On the one hand, the publicity of the bombing pushed many people toward militias. Researchers have documented how membership in deviant subcultures expands dramatically following media publicity, calling this growth the "paradox of social control."[14] Two types of believers joined the movement after the bombing. Some of the people were true believers, who shared the concerns of the militias and felt the same anger voiced by people receiving publicity. The publicity increased their awareness and motivated them to search for local groups. According to one militia leader, "We had no idea of the amount of people doing the same thing that we were doing. We thought we were by ourselves until the Oklahoma City bombing." Yet many of the people who formed or joined militias after the bombing were simply opportunists. Their motivations varied from seeking celebrity status to the hope of achieving monetary rewards. Such opportunists have since moved away from the movement. For example, a public information specialist of one militia group described how the publicity of the Oklahoma City bombing impacted membership: "We had a little run on membership. We may have lost three or four members who, they 'just couldn't,' you know—it scared them. But we probably picked up a hundred. But again, of those people who came around after the bombing, we probably only see six or eight of them anymore. Now, you know, of course, our group is probably very typical of other groups too."

On the other hand, the bombing pushed many people away from the militia movement. First, the publicity threatened the isolation of many of its members, and people started to feel pressure from friends, relatives, and members of the public who were critical of militias because of the stereotypes being created in the media. Those who left the movement were the "weekend warriors," who viewed their involvement as more social than political. One militia leader, who had been the commander of a county militia since 1993, discussed how Oklahoma City had this dual effect on the movement's size. After the bombing, "we lost some members in our unit. We lost eight people, though I don't really look at it as losing them. I look at it as eight people I didn't have to begin with. Anybody who is going to get scared and quit over something they didn't have anything to do with—I don't want them backing me up anyway. There was about a three-month lull in recruitment." He also believed that the media helped the militia by scrutinizing them closely after the bombing: "What they really did, what most people don't realize is, they did the militia movement a big favor. Because what they did: they weeded out all the people who were just playing like they were in the militia, and what was left was the solid ones."

Second, the publicity of the Oklahoma City bombing pushed some of the most dangerous people involved away from the movement or towards action. A number of people who discovered militias were reacting to the media's coverage. When they found that the militia in their area was not like the media's created image, they left the movement. Other people saw the heightened attention as an opportunity to make a public statement, demonstrating their resolve and their commitment to their ideology. Still others, however, simply moved away from the militia movement or decided to go underground to get out of the spotlight.

Three types of militia groups have emerged. First, many groups are organized, above-ground militias, generally open to the public and willing to respond to requests for information. Interviewees talked about their role in the community, which includes participating in service activities as well as informing the citizens about political issues. One militia leader justified his decision to organize an above-ground militia: "I determined first of all that the militia was going to be public, open and visible. If we were going to have our legitimacy and credibility, we had to have visibility. Because each one of those are interrelated. In other words, you cannot have legitimacy and credibility if you're hiding away someplace in the woods." Second, some groups are organized as secret or underground militias. One militia leader said, "Another group left and went underground. They didn't want to be visible anymore. 'I don't want my face in the cameras'; 'I don't want to talk to any of those journalist reporters'; 'No, no, no, they're not going to come after me in the middle of the night.'" They knew that the publicity was going to bring an increased law enforcement presence in their lives and, thus, wanted to protect themselves from the resulting scrutiny and informant infiltration. They disappeared into other, less scrutinized extremist groups or into secret cells. One militia member discussed how the bombing affected other groups in the state where his group was operating:

> There were some militia groups that publicly disbanded when it happened. And the reason they publicly disbanded is because they realized that the whole thing was a setup and that they were going to be victimized. So what they did—they publicly disbanded and then quietly formed again back underground. What they did is they got rid of anybody that they didn't have absolute confidence in and went ahead and reformed. But that was in response to the fact that, when they saw the kind of news media that came out and so forth like that—the news coverage—they realized that they were being set up. We all did, in fact.

Third, some groups adopted a hybrid version of the previous two types of militia. These groups had units that communicated with the public and other militias, but they also had secret, tactical units. If people asked to join the militia, they would get access to the public unit, but the tactical unit would be confidential. Only individuals who could be trusted would be invited to join the tactical unit. Another militia leader offered a slight variation of the hybrid model when describing the importance of having secret cells. When I asked him how these secret cells could coordinate activities or get in touch when necessary, he suggested that each group could select one trusted representative to be the point of contact or public representative to interact with other groups.

Marketplace Hangover: The Disappearance of Militias from the Social-Problem Marketplace

Groups, special interests, and policymakers are constantly responding to some social problem, but the work is mostly done below the public's radar screen. Other problems are responded to as crises when celebrated cases require policy changes. These cases, when they raise a policy issue consistent with the frames of debate in society, force a reconfiguration of community boundaries. Moreover, the social-control responses that take effect, including the changes of policy, the creation of task forces, and the addition of bureaucratic resources, are far removed from the objective realities of the problem because perceptions of a threat always elicit a response more effectively than does the reality of the problem.

The length of time that a social problem remains competitive because of a celebrated case occupying a significant portion of public, political, and media conversation varies considerably, but that length corresponds directly to the media's interest in the problem. The news media play an important role in describing social problems, highlighting the need for a societal response, and monitoring how social-control organizations respond. Once the expectations of how society should respond to such threats have been met, the ceremonies used to process events have been concluded, and the standard operating procedures used in exhausting the public's insatiable appetite for a celebrated case have run their course, a social problem will move rapidly towards invisibility.

The public's understanding of militias, then, was developed in 1995 after the media decided to use militias as part of the explanation for the Oklahoma City bombing. The quantitative media analysis presented earlier indicates that peak attention to militias occurred in 1995, but a significant number of newspaper articles were presented in the year following the bombing. Table 3.1 also indicates that the militias' decline from being competitive in the social-problems marketplace was slow, but nevertheless militias are no longer an issue of significant media concern. The intensity of coverage has waned, the story has been told, and the media have moved on to focus on other problems and concerns.

The media's interest in militias was exhausted, in fact, after about two years. In the year following the Oklahoma City bombing, media coverage focused on describing militia presence in the United States. Many of the stories were investigative exposés, attempting to highlight the ideology, strategies, and size of the militia movement. The bombing was used to illustrate the need to cover this issue and to highlight militias as legitimate threats. The militia threat then evolved into a broader concern about domestic terrorism. The news media discovered that a number of far-right groups exist on the boundaries of society, and because of the media tendency to paint problems using broad brushstrokes, militias became indistinguishable from these other groups. The media went on to explore broader issues related to domestic terrorism, and media personnel searched for other potential domestic terrorist groups. Stories about the Christian Identity movement, Sovereign Citizens, Freemen, Skinheads, Tax Protestors, and the Aryan Brotherhood were all constructed within this larger framework as extremists who pose a significant threat to society.

The running theme of domestic terrorism was by now well established, and any crime incident involving a member of a militia group took on added national news importance. News organizations covered the processing of various militia groups by the criminal justice system. Other celebrated militia cases, such as the Viper Militia, the Washington State Militia, and the West Virginia Mountaineer Militia, provided numerous opportunities to revisit militias as a social problem and were newsworthy because of the wave of publicity accorded the militia movement. Similar activities uncovered after the interest in militias started to fade, however, received little or no attention. For example, one of my informants was surprised how little media interest there was in the Brad Glover case. Glover and seven others planned to attack Fort Hood in Kansas and other military installations in order to eradicate Chinese troops who had taken residence there. "This case was probably one of the biggest things since Oklahoma City, but only a bare handful of newspapers covered it."

The media also lost interest in the militia threat as the political and bureaucratic responses to this threat were gradually exhausted. Media routines coincide with the rituals of criminal justice and governmental decision making. The processing of McVeigh and Nichols by the criminal justice system provided opportunities to revisit the story and analyze their motives. For example, McVeigh's trial allowed the media to revisit the militia and extremist threat. But once he was convicted, the news value of the Oklahoma City bombing diminished significantly. The appeals, executions, and stories of McVeigh and Nichols did continue to be important news events, but media interest in militias has already been exhausted. Politicians also exhausted their opportunities to respond to terrorism generally and militias specifically. They responded quickly by holding specific hearings on the militia movement in the United States, and broad legislation on terrorism was introduced and passed in late 1996. Media personnel had numerous opportunities to highlight the movement of this legislation, discuss the obstacles it faced, and editorialize about why it was necessary. But when the legislation passed, the opportunities to revisit terrorism were reduced.

One of the reporters I interviewed was again having difficulty generating support for continuing to write stories about militias and the far Right. I spoke with him on several occasions between 1997 and 1999. At each interview, he said he was working on fewer and fewer stories, although he was keeping track of the various movements and waiting for the interest in the far Right to increase again. The last time I spoke with him in fall 1999, he was doing a story about what extremists were planning for December 31, 1999. He told me that his editors were interested in his story pitch, but he was also disappointed because he was not having much luck producing a good story. He thought it would be the last story that he did on the far Right for a while and that antigovernment groups are again below the media's radar screen. He also said, however, that militias and extremist groups would remain invisible only "until the next big boom. All of it will remain below the radar until something horrific happens. They will remain below the press radar as well as that of citizens."

Voices of Good and Evil

M any militia-related incidents were publicized in the media only because of the publicity momentum from the Oklahoma City bombing. The most celebrated of these incidents was the arrest of members of the Arizona Viper Militia. A discussion of the Viper case demonstrates how celebrated cases affect the construction of social problems in three important ways. It demonstrates how ordinary events can become celebrated simply because of the wave of publicity given to a social problem that is dominating the marketplace. It shows how authoritative claims-makers are able to capitalize on media coverage of such events, and it illustrates how the publicity often has unintended consequences.[1]

In late 1995, a hunter reported to authorities that a group of heavily armed men in camouflage prevented him from using a road in the Tonto National Forest in Arizona. The public learned later that these men were part of a group that authorities would refer to as the Viper Militia. Federal authorities, who had already invested significant resources to infiltrate militia groups in the wake of the Oklahoma City bombing, decided that the Vipers were a legitimate threat and targeted them for investigation. Drew Nolan, a gun-shop employee turned confidential informant for the BATF, and John Schultz, an Arizona game warden, were able to join the group, working undercover for over six months. Fearing the group was about to unleash a plot to blow up federal buildings, police departments, military headquarters, and a local media station, the BATF arrested twelve members of the group on July 1, 1996. It was reported in the news that agents seized over seventy machine guns, hundreds of other weapons, several thousand rounds of ammunition, blasting cord and caps, booby traps, and several tons of explosive materials such as ammonium nitrate (the fertilizer used in Oklahoma City), lead picric, nitro methane, and lead azide.

Since this arrest occurred when news focus on militias and domestic terrorism was high, the case became a celebrated news event, accounting for over half of the articles about militias indexed in NewsBank from July to December 1996. The Viper Militia case was an exclamation point on the previous fifteen months of news coverage highlighting the dangers of the militia movement. Diane Wagner, writing for the *Arizona Republic*, reported that "news media outlets across the country dutifully topped front pages and newscasts with a story on the biggest militia bust in U.S. History."[2] A *Newsweek* story entitled " 'Vipers' in the 'Burbs," discussed how the militia members "all looked ordinary, but harbored an obsession with guns—and possibly terror. The Feds may have busted them just in time." The *Newsweek* reporters hypothesized that the "Phoenix Suburbanites who played guerrilla games in their spare time may have considered much, much worse." They reported that this group had a long "history of talking dangerously tough," and it was believed that they "posed a significant terrorist threat."[3] Another reporter called the arrests a "Victory in [the] Domestic Terrorism War."[4] Television showed video of the targeted buildings and footage of the group setting off bombs, constructing the event in such a way that it seemed the investigation had prevented another Oklahoma City bombing. As the evidence against the group was presented, however, it was clear that the Viper threat was exaggerated and, had it not been for the publicity and concern conjured up by the news media around the militia movement, the case would never have received national notoriety. Alan Bock notes that members of the group were not even charged with threatening to blow up federal buildings. He concludes: "Judging by the currently available evidence, the Vipers were inaccurately and unfairly demonized as terrorists. Lacking proof of an actual plot to blow up anything, the government covered itself by charging the defendants with teaching and learning about explosives. . . . It was not so much what they did as what they said that bothered the ATF."[5] Federal agents admitted that the group was not planning to blow up any buildings, and a judge, when assessing if they were dangerous, released half of the Vipers without requiring them to post any bond. When members of the group were convicted, most were sentenced to relatively short terms of imprisonment.

The arrests of the Viper militia presented an opportunity for key claims-makers to highlight their ability to effectively respond to public enemies. Indeed, Alan Bock argues that both the BATF and Janet Napolitano, U.S. attorney for Arizona, overlooked problems with the Viper case in order to get good press. It is common for federal law-enforcement officials to promote such high-profile arrests as ceremonial victories in the war on crime or as evidence of effective responses to some significant social problem. The U.S. attorney general and the U.S. attorney for Arizona embraced the arrests as significant law-enforcement victories. Janet Reno, for example, discussed how BATF agents saved the public from "a potentially dangerous situation." Attorney Janet Napolitano staged a news conference to promote the "victory" and discuss how a significant public threat was extinguished. Representatives of the Treasury Department described the group as a major threat that was planning significant public harm. Joseph Roy, the director of the Militia Task Force based in Alabama, said that if the explosives had gone off, "the destruction would have been phenomenal."[6]

I arranged a series of interviews with several members of a militia group attending a gun shoot. Most militia groups camped relatively close to the shooting range, but this group decided to stay at a nearby motel. Three members of the group were willing to discuss their concerns. My discussion with them demonstrates the impact that media coverage can have on its implicated targets. They used aspects of the Viper case as examples of many of their concerns, and it was clear that media coverage fueled their anxiety and strengthened their commitment to their cause. They thought that the federal government concocted the arrest of the Vipers to justify continuing an assault on law-abiding gun owners, militias, and citizens' individual rights. It seemed to them that the media emphasized the arrests but ignored the case when information was released showing that the Vipers were not as dangerous as first portrayed. They thought that this bias in coverage was evidence of a larger conspiracy to paint militias as terrorists and hide any truth that was contrary to this claim.

The media's coverage of the Viper arrests confirmed to this group what other militia members believe—that the news media are a central force in a great conspiracy to establish a New World Order. The Viper case also fanned militias' fears that innocent people were going to be eradicated in a government crackdown on militia groups and gun owners. "They didn't consider themselves a militia, I don't believe," said one militia leader. "Everything I've read indicated that they were closer to a motorcycle club or a gun club." It is true that the media and the BATF changed the name of this group from "Team Viper" to "Viper Militia," although many of its major concerns were consistent with the primary fears of most militia groups. But the media and the BATF recognized the value in referring to the group as a militia, and people involved in the movement reacted by believing that the group had been dubbed a militia to justify a broader crackdown.

The Vipers were arrested through the activities of undercover agents. For one militia member, the Viper case confirmed his fears about the possibility of infiltration.

> In this case, paid informants came into their group, convinced them to do what they ultimately did that got them in a bind, [and] supplied the material. Now, I don't have much sympathy for the guys. I think they should have stuck to their principles, but in all likelihood [they] would not have been involved in what they were involved in that got them in a problem had not the government paid somebody and convinced them to do it. And I think that's an issue. In all of the national coverage of this group and these individuals, it's rarely mentioned that agent provocateurs convinced them to do what they did, and if they'd just been left alone, they probably wouldn't have bothered anybody.

It would have been better if law-enforcement officers had treated the Vipers case as a "typical militia bust"—a response to a common scenario: "Individuals have illegal weapons or illegal explosives. They are planning to use them at some future date in some weird, defensive capacity when the government comes to confiscate the guns, when UN troops leap out of the national parks, when the economy collapses, or when the blacks come out of the cities." Following this scenario, law enforcement has been able to respond to several groups before their activities escalated into something more serious. David Neiwert, in a discussion of the activities of far-right extremism in the Pacific Northwest, discusses how the Washington State Militia was closely monitored by law enforcement and infiltrated by an undercover agent; members were arrested for weapons, bomb making, and conspiracy charges before they could use any of the explosive material.[7]

The Viper case backfired when reporters decided that politicians and high-ranking law-enforcement officials were attempting to make political hay out of a typical event. At first, the news media did not question the legitimacy of the claim that this group was a significant threat because it was provided by key claims-makers. But the framing of the case changed when the evidence was inconsistent with initial reports. One informant told me that

> The media focused on the more sensationalistic stories. The media painted the Viper militia as going out to bomb all these government buildings in Phoenix. Well, actually, no. The Vipers militia was not planning on blowing up Phoenix. Eventually some reporters noticed that they were only charged with weapons and explosive violations, and there was no conspiracy to blow up Phoenix. This created a big backlash, where even Ted Koppel got into the act. And they chided law enforcement for that. The Viper militia ended up being a fiasco.

This "fiasco" contributed to the demise of the militia movement's reign as an important social problem, as media interest decreased dramatically after the Viper case had run its course.

Using Claims-makers to Explain Events

A feature of the mechanical processes used to construct media events is a reliance on willing claims-makers to provide information. Since journalists have to select and process a large number of news events daily, news organizations are forced to create an efficient news-construction process. The need for efficiency shapes the structure of media organizations, the expectations of reporters and editors, and the working routines of reporters. Perhaps the most studied aspect of these working routines is reporters' use of influential sources to construct events. Although journalists cite documents, records, and other archival sources of data, their primary source is attributable quotes, usually provided by institutionally affiliated claims-makers. Public organizations that are funded by taxpayers and that operate in the interests of public safety are vital to the presentation of crime and justice news. Crime-fighting institutions not only determine the best social-control strategies for responding to crime but also are afforded a public forum in which to explain and justify their actions. Crime inherently opens up important public conversations about morality, ethics, and community values—what is right and wrong, and how to behave in society. Public organizations direct the flow of these conversations through the media's coverage of crime. These claims-makers provide the facts, descriptions, summaries, and opinions that allow reporters to construct events.

Research shows the relationship between journalists and claims-makers as symbiotic and mutually beneficial. Organizational efficiency is the primary force that creates and sustains this relationship, as social-control organizations are burdened with the expectation of being efficient with limited resources. Efficiency issues shape all aspects and functions of these organizations, including how to respond to crime, how to interact with the public, how to collect and store information, and how to make information available to the public. Discretion is necessary to carry out organizational mandates—developing shortcuts and routines to manage these demands, and adopting stereotypes to speed up decision-making processes. All such decisions, however, are hidden from public view. Efficiency concerns also drive the decision-making processes of the news media. News space is limited, the number of events far exceeds the space available, and fresh news content must be created every day. Media organizations are able to manage these workload demands by instituting routines and processes that increase the efficiency and consistency of news production. News and public organizations alike benefit from the development of a cordial and working relationship in the interests of satisfying the workload concerns of both organizations. Public organizations do not provide unlimited access to documents and personnel, allowing only enough access to satisfy media demands. News personnel also have adopted convenient shorthands, frames, and a cultural nomenclature that increase the production capacity of media organizations but unfortunately provide a narrow vision of the realities of crime and deviance to be shared with the public. Journalists carefully manage their relationship with claims-makers so as to ensure that they have the requisite access to key definers of social issues; claims-makers benefit because they have a public forum in which to sway public opinion toward their preferred meanings of events.[8]

Although this relationship is generally known through the work of a number of scholars, it is important to note here that two characteristics of it enhance the media's role in defining community boundaries. First, media biases in the news-construction process result in policies, crime incidents, and claims-makers being represented in contrasting extremes. Despite a vast range of opinions, ideas, approaches, exceptions, and motivations, as well as conflicting data, media examination of crime policy can decide whether to label strategic responses as appropriate or unrealistic, the individuals involved in an event as victims or victimizers, and the definers of both events and solutions to crime as community representatives or outsiders. The representatives of the community promote appropriate policy and legitimize the role of the victim and victimizer in society. Community voices, such as representatives of social-control organizations, are used to reaffirm the public's commitment to the core interests and values of society. These individuals are asked to provide their knowledge about threats, explain the causes and extent of such threats, and offer response options. These voices have exalted status in our culture; their approaches and suggestions are automatically assumed to be right, or at least within the boundaries of appropriate action. The complexities and limitations of formulating such responses are ignored because clear boundaries are preferred. The perception that these voices are authority figures also helps convince others to bring their individual consciences in line with the moral core presented. Deviant voices, however, live in staunch opposition to this core set of values, and describing them as examples of life outside the norms of society solidifies their status as deviants. Deviants rarely have direct access to the public culture because of their conflicting viewpoints, low position in society, and resistance from the media. Gateways open only during moral panics, when their role is simply to inject the appearance of truth by affirming that a threat really exists. This contrast between community and deviant voices illuminates the moral boundaries of community life.

Second, the relationship between reporters and sources induces community boundary defining because of the symbolic power accrued not by the individuals involved but by the institutions they represent. Power flows from institutional status. The power of institutions in society is hierarchally structured, and thus individuals representing the highest-placed institutions are oracles of that power. For example, it is rare for the president to comment on a specific case, as Clinton did in response to the Viper arrest. Although mid-level law-enforcement officials tried to downplay the significance of the Viper arrest, reporters ignored their warnings because an institution with significantly more power was defining the arrests as a major victory. This demonstration of power is self-affirming. Individuals are asked to comment on significant social problems because they are positioned in an institution that is expected to respond. Stating that the problem is legitimate and worthy of a response confirms the status and powerful position of the institution. The irony is that by relying on a process that reaffirms the power of relationships in the existing society, it is ensured that outsiders will become more firmly entrenched in their ideology and that the public will always marginalize the opinions of deviant groups. In the case of militias, key community voices promoted policy responses to the militias, contributed to public fear by stating their concerns, and exacerbated the hatred for such organizations. A consequence of these activities was that they isolated militias from the mass public and drove the individuals who believed most deeply in conspiracies far underground.

COMMUNITY AND DEVIANT VOICES

Table 4.1 lists the primary categories of claims-makers used to represent communities and deviants in the public culture. Representatives of social control, experts on specific issues, and others are generally used to represent the core values of society. *Representatives of Social-Control Institutions* are those that society has come to expect will respond to its greatest threats. Politicians and criminal justice bureaucrats are expected to devise and implement strategies for responding to crime. What these claims-makers offer as the nature of the crime problem in society, its causes, and appropriate solutions are what the public has come to accept as being appropriate and effective. *Experts on Specific Issues* are also frequently asked to assess the nature of a social problem. These experts prowl along the fringe of the public culture waiting for a case or panic to occur, so that they have the opportunity to generate support, influence how the problem is framed, suggest solutions, and generally stabilize their position as experts. Finally, the *Individual* category includes citizens and victims reporting on the harm or fears associated with a threat. Involving the voices of victims and citizens proves that the marginalized group has affected the core of society and that the public needs to show support and compassion.

Three broad categories of deviant voices are frequently used to define and describe social problems in the public culture. *Celebrity Figures* are those individuals whom the media portray as national leaders representing a deviant group. Social movements may have many leaders and organizers who could effectively represent the concerns of the group.

Table 4.1 Categories of Claims-makers

	Community Voices	Deviant Voices
	Representatives of Social Control	Celebrity Figures
	Experts on Specific Issues	Examples
	Individuals	Dissenters

But once a social problem becomes a significant concern, the media rely primarily on a small group of individuals who come to represent the ideas, values, and concerns of all groups. The opinions, ideas, and ideology of this small group of celebrity figures, regardless of how representative their views might be, inform the way in which the public views the marginalized group. *Examples* are individuals who are processed by the criminal justice system during a moral panic and labeled as belonging to the marginalized group—either members of a local group or supporters of such a group. For example, gun violations, weapons charges, and cases involving explosives are frequently processed by the criminal justice system, but the media generally do not consider such cases newsworthy. Once a person is afforded the additional stigma of being a militia member, however, the case is worthy of coverage and the defendant may be invited to explain his or her involvement to the press. Such defendants become symbols of the threat, and thus the news media and other institutions handle their cases differently. Furthermore, most journalists are concerned about generating stories with a local flavor. In order to prove that the threat is not only widespread but also lurking nearby, journalists describe the activities of groups within or near the market area of the media organization. The local groups who are portrayed are those that most closely resemble the descriptions of the nationally marginalized group promoted by the media as celebrity figures. *Dissenters* are opposed to the celebrity figures of the movement and may be labeled as members of a marginalized group, even though they support strategies and ideologies different from those that have been presented in public culture as representative of that group. This category also includes mainstream groups who have ties to the targeted group but who distance themselves from or reject the ideology of the targeted group. For example, military organizations, religious groups, and the National Rifle Association had to publicly renounce the activities of militias to avoid negative publicity.

The Representation of Claims-makers in Militia Stories

There were 230 stories in the collected sample of newspaper stories focusing primarily on militias, the militia movement, or militia activity from 1994 to 1998. On average, six different claims-makers were cited in each story, with a range of one to seventeen. The average number of claims-makers cited is large and corresponds to the salience of the topic (discussed in Chapter 3) and the length of the stories. Newspaper reporters were afforded unusually large amounts of space to explore this topic. The 230 articles presented in the NewsBank database totaled over 290,000 words, with an average story length above 1,200 words. Although newspapers did cover specific crime incidents involving militia members, this type of story represented only 24 percent of the total number of stories in the sample; 76 percent of the stories in the sample were policy related and investigative. Reporters did discuss specific incidents involving militias, using such incidents to exemplify a particular point, but most of the coverage focused on broader analysis of the ideology, beliefs, and concerns of people involved in the militia movement.

Table 4.2 presents data on the representation of the six categories of claims-makers presented in this sample of newspaper stories. The results indicate that the total number of community voices only slightly outnumbers the number of deviant voices. Approximately 60 percent of the attributed sources in stories about militias represented community voices. Social-control representatives and experts on specific issues were the types of claims-makers most frequently used. Reporters rarely consulted individual sources such as victims and citizens. It is somewhat surprising that the deviant voices accounted for such a high percentage of claims-maker attributions. Combined, the three categories of deviant sources account for almost 40 percent. This result is noteworthy because it is often assumed that deviant voices such as representatives of extremist groups and individuals arrested for committing crimes have very limited access to the public culture controlled by the media and are accorded limited credibility by reporters. Yet reporters frequently used these claims-makers to write stories about militias. The Example category, consisting primarily of representatives of local groups, accounted for just over 21 percent of source attributions. Celebrity figures were used approximately 13 percent of the time and dissenters just above 8 percent.

Table 4.3 compares the representation of these claims-makers in different types of stories. First, it examines the representation in policy stories—investigative pieces that described the militia movement, its

Table 4.2 The Representation of Claims-makers in All Stories

Community Voices	%	Deviant Voices	%
Representatives of Social Control	27.4	Celebrity Figures	13.6
Experts on Specific Issues	25.1	Examples	21.4
Individuals	4.0	Dissenters	8.4

Note: Totals in this and subsequent tables may not equal exactly 100%, due to rounding.

Community Voices	Policy (%)	Incident (%)	Deviant Voices	Policy (%)	Incident (%)
Representatives of Social Control	20.7	54.0	Celebrity Figures	15.2	7.7
Experts on Specific Issues	29.2	7.3	Examples	20.7	25.4
Individuals	3.9	4.7	Dissenters	10.4	0.9

size, ideology, and policy options. Second, Table 4.3 also includes data on the representation of claims-makers in incident stories—essentially routine crime stories involving militia members. When a member of a militia group was arrested or on trial for a criminal offense, reporters described these incidents as they would any other crime story but also emphasized the defendant's link to a militia group. The representation of claims-makers in these types of story is different. In particular, as one might expect, representatives of social-control institutions, especially law-enforcement officials, were significantly more likely to be represented in incident stories than they were in policy stories. Experts on specific issues were infrequently cited in incident stories but were the most likely claims-makers contributing to policy stories. Celebrity and dissenter militia figures were more likely to be presented in policy stories than in incident stories.

SOCIAL-CONTROL INSTITUTIONS AS CLAIMS-MAKERS

Representatives of social-control institutions have embraced the opportunity to manufacture support for their policy preferences in the news media. Their efforts can be seen in the large number of institutions that funnel information through spokespersons, the attempts made to limit media access to certain types of information, and the willingness to answer questions posed by reporters. Representatives of these institutions have intricate understandings of the needs and desires of media workers, and they provide information in a way that is consistent with how the media construct events, thus increasing the efficiency of the news-production process.

Celebrated cases provide unique opportunities for these claims-makers to capitalize on public concerns and legitimize their role as important definers of the moral values of society. Yet social-control representatives can also view these cases as threatening because a wide variety of media organizations become involved, and the broad interest causes reporters to dig deep into a case and its connected issues to explore broader ramifications. These cases are usually seen as valuable opportunities to gain ownership of the problem and direct public discussions about it. Joseph Gusfield's analysis of drunk driving is illustrative. Gusfield acknowledges that social problems are not equal and will "wax and wane in public attention." He finds that claims-makers jockey for position following heightened attention to a social problem, and describes "the structure of public problems" as "an arena of conflict in which a set of groups and institutions, often including governmental agencies, compete and struggle over ownership and disownership, the acceptance of causal theories, and the fixation [fixing] of responsibility." The winners of this conflict have the opportunity to define the nature of a problem and its appropriate solutions.

> Public consciousness is then drawn into the actions of policymakers, experts, and journalists. . . . In their behavior in the public arena they create the order and consistency with which "society" is endowed. Public authority is engaged in preserving the illusion of a predictable, consistent, and morally controlled universe, one in which the facts about drinking and driving are clear. Consensus exists about heroes and villains.[9]

Representatives of social-control institutions are the most frequently cited source about militias when the entire sample of stories is examined. Moreover, their contribution to public discussions of militias can also be seen in their representing over half of the attributions to claims-makers in incident stories. It is clear that these sources saw value in attempting to be at least part-owners of this newly discovered social problem and worked at playing a role in defining the nature of the problem and offering appropriate solutions.

Representatives of government and law-enforcement agencies have contributed significantly to the dominance of the social-control category. Government officials, mostly federal and state politicians, were active contributors to the public debate about militias. Although these officials were involved in defining the nature of the social problem, their primary contribution came in making recommendations on how to respond to militias. Their concerns about militias and the discussion of appropriate responses were layered into the debates about domestic terrorism policy, which had consumed a large part of the national legislative agenda for the year following the Oklahoma City bombing. Although that case created the momentum for new federal legislation about this issue to be considered immediately, policy changes were slowed by some policymakers, gun enthusiasts, and civil libertarians. The debates concluded in 1996 with the passage of federal legislation that increased the power of law-enforcement officials to investigate terrorist groups and provided the resources to expand their manpower and technology. However, the legislation eliminated or narrowed some of the broad surveillance "wish list" items initially introduced. The attacks of September 11 helped reintroduce many items from this list, as President Bush's antiterrorism legislation attempts to significantly expand the surveillance capacity of law enforcement at home and abroad.

President Clinton's use of the Oklahoma City bombing, the militia movement, and the Viper arrest are good examples of how politicians can manipulate media coverage of celebrated cases. Clinton's leadership on these issues helped to shift the momentum of his presidency and carry him to victory in his reelection bid in 1996. When Clinton became president in 1992, the media environment was changing and expanding dramatically. The Internet, multiple twenty-four-hour cable news networks, talk radio, and political chat shows increased the competition for attention as actions and activities of the president were no longer always considered priority news items. When he first took office, President Clinton and his staff were learning how to manipulate this environment and some of their strategies worked, but others failed and the White House suffered serious setbacks in trying to create a positive presidential image.

During his two-term presidency, however, Clinton and his staff perfected their ability to manipulate the media. How was he able to achieve outstanding approval ratings and reelection despite Whitewater, Travelgate, Filegate, a campaign finance scandal, and multiple extramarital and sexual harassment scandals? Howard Kurtz, in *Spin Cycle: Inside the Clinton Propaganda Machine*, argues that much of Clinton's success was tied to his access to the media. Kurtz describes many strategies that were effective, including building relationships with a large number of reporters representing diverse media outlets, leaking stories to the press corps when a reporter had an exclusive, using newspapers to break scandal stories, and aggressively attacking his enemies in the media.[10]

In 1995, there was concern not only that Clinton might not be reelected but also that he would be challenged and lose the Democratic nomination. Hohenberg argues that the Oklahoma City bombing provided Clinton an opportunity to remake himself and overcome the mistakes the White House had made as he "steadily moved away from the Left and, in his words, 'back to the vital center.'"[11] In the weeks following the Oklahoma City bombing, he frequently discussed the bombing and used it to promote legislation to fight militias and domestic terrorists. He was going to get tough on terrorism. Clinton's first public statement about the bombing occurred at 5:30 P.M. on April 19, and he promised justice: "I will not allow the people of this country to be intimidated. Let there be no room for doubt: We will find the people who did this. When we do, justice will be swift, certain, and severe."[12] Clinton held another press conference after McVeigh was arrested for the bombing, appeared with the children of federal workers on television in lieu of his Saturday radio address, planted a dogwood in the White House lawn in honor of the victims on Sunday morning, and attended a memorial service in Oklahoma City on Sunday afternoon. On Sunday night, he appeared on *60 Minutes*. Clinton reacted to the anger of militia members, discussing Waco and Ruby Ridge and using them to outline his proposal to fight terrorism. He was incredibly visible in the time period following the bombing, and he frequently went on the offensive against the militia movement. For example, when delivering the commencement address at Michigan State University on May 5, 1995, he stated: "So I say this to the militias and all others who believe that the greatest threat to freedom comes from the government instead of from those who would take away our freedom: If you say violence is an acceptable way to make change, you are wrong. If you say that government is in a conspiracy to take your freedom away, you are plain wrong."[13] When members of the Viper militia were arrested in 1996, he had another opportunity to highlight the need for a broad federal response to terrorist groups. Clinton reacted immediately in ceremonial fashion on the White House lawn, "saluting the enforcement officers who made the arrests in Arizona yesterday to avert a terrible terrorist attack," and remarking that "their dedication and hard work over the last six months may have saved many lives."[14]

Members of the militia movement—strong conservatives who hated Clinton for his support of gun-control initiatives and also for his refusal to take responsibility for what occurred at Waco—were infuriated that he used the Oklahoma City bombing and the Viper case to get reelected. One member of a militia group believed that the Oklahoma City bombing, the emphasis on the militia movement, and the Viper arrests all seemed to be part of a larger conspiracy:

You've got to remember that if the feds didn't blow up the Federal Building, they certainly made hay with the issue as if they had. Let's set the stage. Bill Clinton admitted that he was in deep, deep trouble until Oklahoma City. I think in his words he said, "Oklahoma City broke the spell." Remember what the whole milieu of the country was like at the time of Oklahoma City? Clinton—at the time people were arguing about whether or not he was relevant, whether or not the president was relevant. The Republicans were resurgent—I mean, those of us like myself who had really busted our butts to get the Republicans [elected] in '94 had done so. We were motivated because of the assault weapons ban and the Brady Bill, and we had been promised by the Republicans that they would "cut, gut, and de-nut" the ATF—that they were going full tilt with investigations of Waco and Ruby Ridge, and that they fully intended to de-fund the ATF and deliver on the campaign promises that they had made. So, immediately prior to the bombing, everything was going very badly for the Clintons. After the bombing, Clinton took immediate advantage of it—painted along with his willing handmaidens in the media that the militias were setting up this "climate of hate." And so they exploited the situation—absolutely perfectly. After Clinton was reelected, he was quite candid about saying that Oklahoma City had been the turning point of his presidency—which was in the sewer—until the building blew up. Now, if you're a suspicious person, as many people in the militia movement are, because they don't trust this guy farther than they can throw him, the question then becomes—well, you know: was it deliberate or not? And a lot of folks came to the conclusion that, well, maybe it was deliberate.

Law-enforcement officials were also cited frequently in news stories about the militia movement, accounting for nearly half of the attributions to the social-control category. Overall, 10 percent of the claims-makers cited in stories about militias were officials working in some law enforcement capacity, and their frequency of representation increases when the sample is divided into different types of stories. The overall frequency of the use of law-enforcement officials as claims-makers was somewhat less than expected, but they still clearly played an important role in describing the militia movement. Law-enforcement officials were included in newspaper stories about militias in three different ways.

First, these officials played their typical role as the predominant source to describe the criminal activity associated with specific cases. Federal law-enforcement officials took advantage of their access to the media and were very active in describing the facts and investigative strategies used in responding to specific high-profile cases, such as the Viper Militia, the Olympic Park bombing, the Freemen standoff, the

Good Ol' Boys Roundup case, the West Virginia Mountaineer Militia, and the Washington State Militia. Although a few of these cases had only ancillary or unconfirmed militia involvement, reporters decided to explore potential linkages to militia, and law-enforcement officials were asked to comment. For example, militias actually received some positive publicity when the Gadsden Minutemen, an Alabama-based militia group, made national headlines when they released photographs and a videotape after they infiltrated the Good Ol' Boys Roundup—what was then an annual gathering of law-enforcement agents that took place between 1980 and 1995. The militia discovered that guests attending the roundup had to go through a "nigger check point" and could buy a "nigger hunting license" or a T-shirt with Martin Luther King's face painted behind a target. The "entertainment included a skit entitled 'Birth of the Black Race,' in which a watermelon was broken open and a black doll extracted from it."[15] The media coverage of the event resulted in congressional hearings in July 1995. Such positive coverage was rare, and even the militia involved in this case was later criticized when federal law-enforcement agents reported that they questioned members about the bombing that occurred at Centennial Park during the Olympics.[16] Although the investigation did not prove that they were involved, the fact that they were questioned inferred that they were like any other militia and thus were threatening to public safety.

Second, when newspapers explored the activities of rural militias, reporters relied on sheriff's departments' officials for a law-enforcement perspective. It was an interesting dynamic because sheriffs were generally sympathetic to the militia movement's position on gun control, individual rights, and the overwhelming presence of the federal government in their lives. Sheriffs often knew the people involved in or affiliated with militia groups, and supporting sheriffs was consistent with militia beliefs. "Our local sheriff and I went to school together. I've known him all my life, and he's a great guy and good sheriff," said one militia leader. "He speaks to me on the streets. He waves to me when he drives by. We've spent a lot of time talking. We share information and learn a little more about each other." On the other hand, sheriffs were frequently the targets of death threats and paper-terrorism strategies by some militia groups and other extremist groups falling under the Patriot umbrella, forcing them to tread lightly when talking about the movement in the media.

Third, federal law-enforcement officers attempted to use their access to the media to diffuse the anger of militia members. To illustrate this anger, one militia member said:

> These guys [federal law enforcement] are supposed to be heroes. Ah, I don't call that law enforcement. If and when we are ever forced to go [into] combat mode, they'll never know what hit them. They have to live in the cities. They have to live in homes. They're trying to enjoy the American way of life, just like we do. I've got news. They don't have an exclusive on dynamic entries. They don't have an exclusive on a lot of the things they assume that they have. I'm telling you, it's become an "us against them" society. They've got laws to protect federal agents that do not apply to the average citizen. And they're protecting agents of a law-enforcement agency, a federal law-enforcement agency, that under constitutional rules is not supposed to exist. Now these people are involved in the militia movement for exactly the same reasons I stated, and that is: American citizens are being killed, and the crimes are being covered up—by federal agents, mostly. And it's just an unacceptable situation.

Some federal law-enforcement officials attempted to diffuse such anger by publicly stating that militia groups had the right to organize and hold meetings and would be ignored until it was known they were involved in criminal activity. These officials also used their constraint as an opportunity to discuss how the law restricts their ability to investigate such groups. Louis Freeh, director of the Federal Bureau of Investigation, said, "For two decades, the FBI has been at an extreme disadvantage with regard to domestic groups that advocate violence. We have no intelligence or background information on them until their violent talk becomes deadly action."[17] In addition, to placate their critics, federal law enforcement also began taking a more passive approach to standoffs because of what happened at Ruby Ridge and Waco, patiently responding to the Freemen standoff in 1996 and allowing it to diffuse with time and negotiation. Militia members noticed the difference in response.

> The Freemen situation was extremely well handled. I mean the FBI went out of their way to let us know: "hey look, we're not going to have a problem here, we want to keep everything in order." So they extended a peace branch and said "look, you know, don't get excited about this— these people have done something that's wrong." And I think most militia members, after looking at what the Freemen were up to, would agree that

these guys were a criminal organization and they needed to be stopped. They were victimizing innocent people. You can't believe in the Constitution of the United States and turn around and say its OK to put a lien on somebody's house and get cash to go buy a truck.

Experts on Specific Issues as Claims-makers

Reporters rarely consult experts when producing routine crime stories. Rather, they simplify the production of routine stories by relying almost exclusively on criminal justice sources, victims, and defendants to reconstruct specific incidents, emphasizing the characteristics of the crime, victim, and defendant in a style that closely resembles police and court reports. These events are presented as independent occurrences, and thus there is no need, or desire, to explore causal explanations, general patterns, or the broader implications of crime for society. Such investigative analysis does occur, but producing articles about it is difficult. Following celebrated events, however, news organizations are willing to provide the space, time, and resources necessary to produce investigative and research-oriented pieces, expanding the list of claims-makers consulted by the media. The militia movement was the most popular of the many research-oriented issues pursued following the Oklahoma City bombing. The interest in the topic, and more importantly the concern for explaining what drives individuals or groups to commit such horrible acts, opened a window of opportunity for these experts to define the scope and nature of the militia problem in the United States.

This category of claims-maker includes a selection of characters who are perceived as being able to provide an intellectual perspective about a particular social problem. These experts are valuable commodities in the construction of social problems because they can support their claims with science, historical perspective, anecdotes, and experience. Reporters consulted a wide variety of professionals for these perspectives about the militia movement, including academics, research associates, policy analysts, journalists, abortion activists, and representatives from extremist watchdog organizations. These experts were the second most frequently used claims-makers, and at least one expert was included in *over 65 percent* of all newspaper stories about militias. Although this category includes many different types of expert, it is important to note that representatives from three specific organizations accounted for over half of the attributions. Over 30 percent of the attributions were to experts from the Southern Poverty Law Center (SPLC) or the Anti-Defamation League (ADL), two of the most widely recognized antihate watchdog organizations. Both were actively involved in describing and defining the scope and intentions of the militia movement. The third organization active in describing the militia movement was Political Research Associates (PRA), a Boston-based organization that monitors the political and extremist right. Chip Berlet, who is a senior research analyst for PRA and has published extensively, was the most frequently cited individual expert on specific issues.

From the perspective of a reporter constructing a story about the militia movement, the claims-makers representing these organizations were logical choices for several reasons. The first reason is their general credibility among media workers and the public. Reporters do not have the time to establish or refute the credentials of experts. Although there clearly is significant variation in the expertise of experts, reporters are concerned solely with the organizational tie of the expert and, if that can be established, credibility is assumed. Reporters do not question the opinions or conclusions provided by experts, but rather are primarily interested in deciding whether what they said is newsworthy.

The second reason for the frequent reliance on experts is their accessibility. One of my informants discussed why certain experts are consistently chosen to critique the militia movement.

> Reporters are essentially lazy creatures, and most of their inability to get things right, particularly about movements that they don't understand, comes from their use of self-appointed experts who also either don't know what they're doing or have an agenda. It is not some sort of conspiracy to not print the truth, but they are on a deadline. They want to be able to make one phone call for any given story—whether it's the Freemen incident, the Republic of Texas, or whatever. They want to be able to put together a story that has the experts they recognize as experts, because reporters are lazy and editors are very cautious and careful critters. And so they tend to fall back on what they know. For example, in their Rolodex under militias, they have the Southern Poverty Law Center. The Southern Poverty Law Center has presented themselves over the years as the recognized experts in the area of militias.

A reporter said that the SPLC "are good sources for me. Their research is impressive. Some reporters are afraid that they sensationalize too much, but most of their stuff they back up pretty well." The reporters interviewed discussed how easy it is to get information from these organizations or from other organizations providing data on the Web. For example, the "Militia Watchdog" Web site, created and maintained by Mark Pitcavage, was incredibly useful to reporters, law enforcement, and attorneys.[18] At the peak of the militia scare, this Web site was probably getting over 5,000 hits a month. Similar to how militia groups attempted to use the World Wide Web to disseminate their ideology and recruit members, the "Militia Watchdog" site was a hub of background information, scholarship, and the activities of key militia figures. The Web sites maintained by SPLC and ADL also had extensive data and contact information that was used frequently by reporters.

The expert representatives from the SPLC, ADL, and PRA were used frequently to define the militia movement. Journalists have a tendency to indirectly share sources, and a specific source can gain momentum as reporters read through existing coverage to identify a point of contact. Reporters use the Web and databases to retrieve stories published by other journalists. Experts from the ADL, SPLC, and PRA, and the militia members that became celebrity figures, were associated and assumed to be good sources of information early in the coverage of the militia movement. Other journalists noted such use, and the influence of these sources snowballed as they were given numerous opportunities to shape public understanding of the social problem.

A third reason for the reliance on these experts is that they were ahead of the panic curve about militias. Due to their efforts to monitor extremism and because of the frequent overlap between extremist groups, these watchdog organizations had seen and heard about militias well before even the earliest media reports came out in 1994. Although they were not able to generate public concern or media interest about militias during that time, they recognized that they needed to collect and compile data about militia groups. When the momentum shifted and media attention was high, these organizations could obviously provide a historical perspective and relate militias to other extremist groups; they also had a foundational understanding of the movement and some data. The data may have been limited, but no other organization could supply any. Law enforcement does not generally collect data on such movements, and thus the only source that could estimate the size and strength of the movement using data were representatives from these watchdog organizations.

Being an authority on a high profile issue, such as the militia movement, has various benefits to the contributing organization. One benefit is that experts on specific issues recognize the importance of public-relations propaganda to their causes. Like law enforcement and other government sources, many of these experts are motivated to participate in the construction of a social problem because it provides an opportunity to shape news coverage. Organizations can emphasize certain aspects of a social problem and encourage reporters to ignore other aspects. These organizations create documents and press releases, as well as make spokespersons available, to take advantage of heightened attention to an issue and define it in a way consistent with their goals. A member of a monitoring organization talked about how they package their data for reporters and law enforcement: "Well, you know, we cover everything. We give them as much background information as they need to do their jobs. We have our reports that we share with them which basically run down the kinds of information that we've developed, so that they will get a good sense of the problem and it will include everything they need."

Being an authority on a high-profile issue helps generate funds for some organizations as they directly solicit money for programs that respond to particular issues, and it also helps sell their books, videos, and pamphlets. It is easier to convince people to donate to an organization when it is working to eliminate a significant threat. Many militia members were highly critical of media coverage of the movement because of the reliance on these expert sources and their efforts to "demonize for dollars." One militia member stated, "if you really get into their finances, all the SPLC has to do is come up with some kind of threat—someone is threatening you—and we can stop that if you give us money." Several cited a series of *Montgomery Advertiser* articles critical of the Southern Poverty Law Center and Morris Dees. One militia member stated, "Although they don't see things from our point of view, they've done a series of stories on Morris, matter of fact, one was called 'Marketing the Militias.' It talks about how he used the Oklahoma City tragedy to pump for money, and you know the *Montgomery Advertiser* is not a pro-militia sheet by any means." Other reporters, as well as activists, have been critical of the fund-raising tactics of the SPLC. Silverstein reports: "News of a declining Klan does not make for inclining donations to Morris Dees and Co., which is why the SPLC honors nearly every nationally covered 'hate crime' with direct-mail alarums full of nightmarish invocations of 'armed Klan paramilitary forces' and 'violent neo-Nazi extremists.'"[19]

Experts on specific issues produced some of the first books on the militia movement, depicting it as a growing and alarming threat.[20] These books were incredibly influential in shaping news coverage of the militia movement. Stern's *A Force Upon the Plain* and Dees and Corcoran's *Gathering Storm* were both published in 1996, and a book tour to promote the latter overlapped the Oklahoma City bombing anniversary.[21] Dees and Corcoran note at the beginning of their book: "This is the story of a very dangerous movement, one the public knows almost nothing about. To some it might read like fiction, but, unfortunately, it is all true. . . . It is a continuing threat that promises to cause further destruction." They also discuss how assessing the threat posed by militias "is a bit like gauging the risk to shipping posed by icebergs. The number that can be seen is important, but the real danger lies beneath the surface. From the tips of the icebergs that we can see, it's clear that the militia threat is quite extensive."[22]

Reporters writing stories about the militia movement routinely ignored academics. This is a curious finding because there are many scholars who have done excellent research in this area and could have provided a broad context for a better understanding of the militia movement, as well as an added perspective on the cited data about the size of the movement. However, academics were ignored for many of the same reasons that experts from the SPLC, ADL, and PRA were emphasized. First, most reporters have a limited knowledge of the key academics to contact for information about such movements. Although it would probably take only a couple of telephone calls to discover the leading academic authorities on domestic terrorism, it is easier simply to contact representatives from well-known activist organizations. Second, some of the reporters I interviewed discussed the frustration they have experienced coaxing useable quotations from academic sources. The information academics provide is not neatly packaged and often is not consistent with what the reporter needs to publish a story. Finally, although there are some exceptions, academics generally are less motivated than other sources to participate in the news-production process. A reporter who wrote a large number of stories on the militia movement described how she was encouraged to use a wide range of experts. "My editor said, 'Why don't you find somebody else to quote?' We try not to have the same people all the time but once in a while you need to do that because there are not many people close to the issue. When you're on a deadline, especially if your story is due tomorrow, its whoever calls you back the quickest that gets in there."

Neighbors, victims, and other citizens were rarely cited in stories about militias. This result is in part tied to the type of story represented in the sample. Policy stories accounted for most of the stories presented, and victims and other voices of the community are outside the typical routines used by reporters to construct such stories. Moreover, these individuals are generally not readily accessible and are difficult to contact. Because what they could provide was only of peripheral interest, reporters decided that their inclusion was not essential. As we have seen, when a reporter writes a policy story, the focus is on identifying accepted public experts who can define the nature and the extent of the problem, or opposition figures able to refute, reject, or oppose such claims. If the number of crime incidents had accounted for a larger part of the sample, the number of individuals cited would have increased because including citizen and victim reaction to high-profile crimes is consistent with the standard routines of crime-story construction. Since crime stories were infrequently presented in the sample, and many of the incidents that were covered involved planning but not completing serious crimes, there were few victims or specific harms to describe.

Most of the crimes cited in the stories examined were not violent offenses but related to weapons or explosives, obstruction of justice, or conspiracy charges. The actions of law-enforcement agencies generally prevented these relatively minor crimes from escalating into major crime events. For example, one of the high-profile arrests receiving national news attention in late 1996 involved the West Virginia Mountaineer Militia. Media reports indicated that Floyd Looker, the leader of this militia group, was arrested after being paid 50,000 dollars for providing photographs and blueprints of a federal building to an FBI agent posing as a representative of a Middle Eastern terrorist organization.[23] Other members of the West Virginia Mountaineer Militia were arrested and charged with various explosives-related offenses. Since federal investigators were able to make these arrests before this group was able to carry out any plans, reporters relied primarily on law-enforcement sources to reconstruct the facts as a media story. Since there was no individual harm, it was not necessary for reporters to think about other potential sources that could be integrated into this story.

A related reason for the limited involvement of individuals in the construction of news stories is that the type of harm that such sources could describe or confirm was not a particularly important element of how militias were being described for public consumption. Individual harm was of limited concern because the broader emphasis was on how such groups posed a threat to the entire community. Militia groups were an undefined threat and a relatively unknown representative of deviance prior to the Oklahoma City bombing. When the bombing occurred, the press and the American public interpreted it as a crime against the United States. The choice of target sent a chilling message throughout the country, and McVeigh's revenge against the government highlighted our vulnerability to such attacks. The crime defined as a "Terror in the Heartland," to borrow from CBS's overarching theme of its coverage of the bombing, created widespread fear. When militias were linked to McVeigh, the potential they posed for harm became evident, and it then became more important to rely on sources who could explain the nature and significance of the threat to the entire community.

CELEBRITY FIGURES AS CLAIMS-MAKERS

When examining how social problems are presented in the media, it is important to consider how representatives of deviant groups achieve access to publicity about their concerns. In general, outsider claims-makers have limited access to the public through mainstream media sources. Thus, their role in shaping the contours of a social problem is overlooked in research describing social-construction processes. Representatives of the militia movement, however, appear to have been highly successful in achieving coverage for their concerns, using both traditional (mainstream news) resources and nontraditional ones (the World Wide Web). The celebrity figures of the movement, local examples, and dissenters accounted for 40 percent of the sources cited about the militia movement. Because of the frequent use of these claims-makers by the news media, it is important to develop an understanding of the characteristics of each of the different categories used to represent deviant voices in the news media.

The media frequently used celebrity figures to portray militia concerns and ideology.[24] These claims-makers were honored by the media as the deviant group's national representatives, and they became the people whom the public, the media, and other claims-makers most closely associated with the militia movement. The individuals listed in Table 4.4 were cited in at least one of the militia stories in the sample and were coded as celebrity figures. The importance of these celebrities

Table 4.4 Celebrity Figures and Affiliations

Celebrity Figure	Affiliation
John Trochmann, Randy Trochmann, and Bob Fletcher	Militia of Montana. Note that John Trochmann was by far the most visible and continues to be so. Fletcher and John Trochmann testified at the 1995 Senate hearings on the militia movement.
Bo Gritz	Not a representative of any militia group, but well known for his involvement at Ruby Ridge and the Freemen case and speaks frequently at public gatherings
Jack McLamb	Former police officer known for his *Operation Vampire Killer* publications and shortwave radio program
Sam Sherwood	United States Militia Association
John Parsons	Tri-States Militia—a national umbrella group
Dave Rydel	United States Theater Command—a national umbrella group
Linda Thompson	Leader of the Unorganized Militia of the United States and creator of the videotapes *Waco, The Big Lie* and *Waco II: The Big Lie Continues*
Norm Olson, Ray Southwell, and Ken Adams	Affiliated with the Michigan Militia at one time. Olson and Adams testified at the Senate hearings.
William Cooper	Author of a very popular extremist publication and shortwave radio program
James "J. J." Johnson	Ohio Unorganized Militia. He testified at the 1995 Senate hearings.
Mark Koernke	"Mark From Michigan"
Mike Kemp and Jeff Randall	Gadsden Minutemen. They were responsible for exposing the racist Good Ol' Boys Roundup.

is confirmed by two characteristics of their media coverage. First, when considering only national stories focused on general concerns about militias, celebrity figures were the top representative of deviant voices presented. Second, a relatively small number of individuals accounted for most of the media's use of these sources, whereas attributions to the other categories of deviant voices were dispersed across many different individuals.

These celebrity figures were frequently presented in the news for several reasons. First, they made themselves accessible. One of the celebrity figures of the militia movement whom I interviewed discussed how he thought he was exploiting media attention for his cause.

We found the means whereby the world would know who we are and what we are doing. We prostituted the militia in the media, using them as our mules to carry our message around the world. They cooperated because they understood: even though they didn't know what I was doing to them, they understood the symbiotic relationship. In other words, we certainly gave them the message so that they could market the product. You know, they'd have their mini-cam films at 11, and they could market the newspapers and whatever else they wanted. But in return, they would also be carrying our message everywhere. We had no radio stations, no television stations—we had no way to get the word out except through the existing media. And so we prostituted. We put on the dog-and-pony shows, training in the woods, the guns—all of that file footage using it. We did that, we put on a whole display for the media, and the media came running. They loved it.

After the Oklahoma City bombing, this celebrity figure said he was interviewed by journalists all over the world. "They were coming in from Japan, Germany, Brazil—every continent was sending media, and I had them in my house every week. They understand what's going on in America." He also discussed how he accommodated the journalists: "We had a little place where they actually set up, when they would come in, told here's your socket, here's your setup, here's your backdrops, and go ahead and arrange whatever it is you want to do."

Second, the dominance of these celebrity figures reflects their ability to contort their message in a way directly consistent with the intricacies of the news-construction process.[25] For example, Todd Gitlin examined the activities of Students for a Democratic Society (SDS)—an antiwar, antigovernment group prominent in the 1960s and 1970s—concluding that the news media played a central role in promoting and eventually demoting the claims of this group. He found that the media's coverage of the protests and positions of this group helped increase its significance by attracting new members and legitimizing its claims. But the media also forced SDS members to make their message conform to traditional ideologies promoted by standard media frames. The media relied on a limited range of activities and celebrity members of the group because they were most consistent with the "implicit rules of news-making."[26]

An interview with a militia supporter and former reporter demonstrates how Gitlin's conclusions can also be applied to media coverage of the militia movement.

The news tends to find the most radical, and that make the best news and the most sensational news. They leave the mainline people out because they are not news. In other words, my estimation is that there are probably 5 million people that are aligned with the militias, whether they are extreme members, part-time members, or whatever. It is quite a lot. Our Senate says 5 million, and you can darn near double it—who knows? Most of these people are not radicals. It is my estimation that news reporters keep a file on the most newsworthy. People like Wayne in Michigan and different guys are not newsworthy. They should be, but they are not. . . . I wrote a 5,000-word article for a newspaper, and they commissioned me to write it. I went out and talked to militia people, and that was years ago in Michigan when the thing was first starting. Three or four people I spoke with were just normal guys, but they don't get the press.

Gitlin's conclusions are also supported by the large number of militia members who discussed how reporters would simply ignore the information or materials provided to them when it was inconsistent with media expectations about what a militia and a militia leader should be.

The media considered these celebrity figures to be perfect, credible representatives of militias. And in reading the coverage, it became clear why certain individuals were preferred by what was highlighted about their backgrounds. For example, Norm Olson, along with Ray Southwell, became the primary media representatives of the Michigan Militia, even though both were ostracized by this group. The media usually noted that Norm Olson was a gun-shop owner and was wearing fatigues during the interview. Bo Gritz was described as a Vietnam War hero, a former presidential candidate, the negotiator of the surrender of Randy Weaver, and a person who liked to burn a United Nations flag at public-speaking engagements. The media also emphasized John Trochmann's friendship with Randy Weaver and Trochmann's attendance at events at the Aryan Nations' compound; but more importantly, he was the voice of the Militia of Montana. Linda Thompson was highlighted as creating the *Big Lie* videotapes and attempting to march a force of armed patriots on Washington, D.C. J. J. Johnson was an African American who was described as a leader of the national militia movement. Others like "Mark from Michigan," former police officer Jack McLamb, and William Cooper were noted as pushing New World Order conspiracies and sharing their views with thousands through shortwave radio programs.

These figures were also desirable because they were willing to make statements on the record. I asked a member of a county group about national news coverage and its emphasis on certain sources.

Oh, yeah. You'll always see John Trochmann. You'll always see the raving loonies. It is Koernke, Linda Thompson, and the Trochmanns. It's the people like Norm Olson. Oh, man! Good ol' Normy. You know there's no one in the country besides the press that pays the least bit of attention to what

Norm Olson says, and hasn't been for quite a few years now. When Norm announced after the Oklahoma City bombing that the Japanese government was responsible, he was finished.[27] Despite what the press might think, the constitutional militia movement is not made up of a whole bunch of raving loonies, and almost everyone, universally, when he came out with that, said, "Well, that's the end of Norm Olson." Well, it would have been, except for the press. Do you blame people for thinking that militia people are raving loonies—when that's the only kind of militia person that you see in the media? I don't really blame them.

In interviews, several celebrity figures of the movement clearly promoted an image that would make a reporter salivate. For example, one of these figures said:

Well, sure, the power brokers are the ones that are really controlling the government. I am sure that Janet Reno and Bill Clinton and others are merely puppets. Who are the people behind them? Well, if you look at it historically, the old money, the new money, the CIA, the old European bankers: you can make a lot of theory to try to find an answer. I don't know, but I do know this—that this long period of tyranny and oppression seems to be linked quite a bit with the World Bank. Money is behind it. Of course, money is power, and if you control the banking system, you can control the people. So, yeah, I think that's probably where the real power is—in the banking system.

Another celebrity figure confirmed these fears about the threat of a New World Order.

Now, we have foreign troops stationed in this country. In the past, we've only had foreign troops here for training purposes. We never had units under foreign command in this country. We do now. There is a feeling out there that there is a one-world order, one New World Order. With that comes a one-world government. There are people that believe that they should form a one-world government and they should disarm the government and they should disarm the public—citizens of all countries—and then if that's done no one has any means to fight and everyone's going to live happily ever after. What they're trying to do is disarm the people, come up with a one-world church.

These celebrity figures were very influential in three ways. First, they influenced public understanding of the militia movement. The ideas and claims of the few celebrities who dominated national debate *became* the militia movement. The public inferred that all militia members were like John Trochmann, Linda Thompson, Norm Olson, and the other celebrity figures of the movement. Second, they impacted media decision making. Reporters preferred these sources when describing the militia movement, and in most cases they were able to locate and use them. Once these celebrities had been identified with the movement, other reporters recognized them as key claims-makers, and so their involvement in the news process gained momentum. The coverage of these celebrity figures also influenced news coverage of local militia groups. Reporters assigned to these stories ventured out looking for any militia groups whose ideologies resembled what these national figures were promoting, ignoring any different groups. Finally, these celebrity figures impacted people active in the movement. People who joined or organized militias after Oklahoma City used aspects of the blueprint provided by celebrities in the media. These celebrity figures influenced the growth and direction of the movement by being willing to interact with the media. The coverage they achieved also gave them the requisite credibility to recommend to local militia groups how they should organize and in what manner. For example, the Militia of Montana distributed vast amounts of literature, including information on how to organize, and visited groups across the country to promote its vision of the movement. Celebrity figures were also used to attract people to preparedness expositions. Bo Gritz, Jack McLamb, John Trochmann, and other celebrities traveled across the country to sell literature and make presentations that promoted their views.

EXAMPLES AS CLAIMS-MAKERS

Examples are the deviant source most frequently cited when all stories in the sample are analyzed. The prevalence of this category is tied to the range of sizes of newspapers indexed in NewsBank. This finding demonstrates how a celebrated case can echo through newsrooms across the country. The facts, conjectures, and reactions to the Oklahoma City bombing had national and international news value. Moreover, when coverage of the case included an extensive examination of the militia movement, media organizations searched for a way to tie national concern to a local threat. Reporters were asked to describe the local militia presence in their community, and they were obviously successful in locating the groups in question. It is clear that the bombing impacted the public consciousness. But when the focus of concern expanded to include militia groups, reporters throughout the country identified and described a local presence. The threat was found to be close to home, and fear grew with each story.

News stories describing these local groups, although published in newspapers in different regions of the country, were similar in tone, description, and conclusions. Reporters tapped into an existing mold to find, investigate, and describe a local militia group. First, they relied on existing partnerships with federal and local law-enforcement sources to find local militia groups. After the bombing, federal law enforcement was actively locating various groups. Local law-enforcement agencies were not generally concerned about militias, but their officers knew of existing groups because of smaller jurisdictional boundaries. Reporters used their standing relationships with all these sources to discover whether a group worth covering existed nearby. In addition, reporters often "discovered" a local militia group and did a descriptive story about them following an incident in which members were arrested. Second, they investigated these groups by arranging interviews with members, although they preferred to attend meetings or training exercises. Finally, local stories describing militia groups followed a similar pattern. Reporters reminded readers about the Oklahoma City bombing and the antigovernment and hateful views of Timothy McVeigh. They then described the local groups by giving an overview of their sizes or describing the backgrounds of a few members—construction workers, electricians, bankers, police officers, and factory workers. Whether the size or the members were described, the message was the same: the threat was large and militia members were lurking everywhere. Reporters then explored what motivated these individuals to join and provided brief synopses of Ruby Ridge and Waco. Reporters further examined whether the ideology of the local group was consistent with national coverage, highlighting the local militia's concerns about the government and the United Nations. Newspaper reporters also frequently described the physical characteristics of the individuals interviewed, especially when they appeared wearing camouflage and sidearms. These descriptive stories typically concluded with a statistical estimate provided from another source about the overall size and scope of the militia movement.

I interviewed a leader who discussed the concerns of his militia group and his efforts to respond to inaccurate media coverage. A local newspaper reporter had done a series of articles about the militia following the

Oklahoma City bombing and relied primarily on information provided by the Southern Poverty Law Center. This militia member was so angry about the coverage that he contacted the reporter and had others contact him to complain. His primary complaint was with the emphasis on racism in militias.

> We don't have anything for racists. Even in the Patriot Movement the black people seem to be or want to be separated from the white people. Now why this is, I don't have any idea. I've never researched it. But now we've got a unit [of blacks] up north that consists of over a hundred members. A couple of their COs—they come down to the house here and they talk to me all the time. And shoot, I've had some of them over for supper, lunch, sit around and talk half the night. Right here in my home. So there's no way that they're going to get away with calling us a racist. That just won't fly here in this state. And it's our belief that blood flows the same color in all of our veins: the color of skin pigmentation has nothing whatsoever to do with what's inside. And as far as I'm concerned, any man who would be willing to put his life on the line for his country: by golly, he's OK in my book.

From the media's perspective, this leader of a local group should have been contacted because he would have been an excellent example of how the thinking of a local group was consistent with the conspiracy thinking being emphasized in national coverage, but the media also could have highlighted the inconsistencies between his statements and public beliefs. For example, this leader described how he thought that the news media were controlled by the Rockefellers and the Rothschilds, and was also involved in promulgating lies about the Oklahoma City bombing.

> Ammonia nitrate didn't blow that building. I don't think anybody in his right mind would believe that. If it had, there would have been so many people running around puking their guts up from the dust and ammonia-cyanide and stuff that would have been left over from that there wouldn't have been nobody on the street. They all would have been lying down in the street. I read an explanation for probably what happened, and the fact that they did move other explosives from the inside of the building out. So somebody done something wrong there, and I don't think it was all Timothy McVeigh.

He also talked about the United Nations establishing a New World Order and money being controlled by an elite group of international bankers.

The International Monetary Fund, that's the biggest bunch of scam artists. These guys, believe it or not and I've done some of the research on it, existed 540 B.C. You know, these same yo-yos we see now in current days. And what they've done is take all the gold and given us a bunch of paper because it's easier to handle. And of course, the people eat that up and they think it's so cool and of course we're going to have a dual-tier money system. They're already using some of this New-Age technology.

DISSENTERS AS CLAIMS-MAKERS

The final category of claims-makers used by the news media is dissenters, who attempt to counter the dominant imagery of militias in the news media. They recognize that the media play an important role in influencing public opinion about militias and are motivated to contradict what they perceive as demonization of the movement. Several of the interviewees discussed how the media have hurt their cause because of who and what were emphasized in the aftermath of the bombing. As standing members started to leave the movement, some groups and individuals decided to initiate public-relations campaigns to combat media images. There were two general types of dissenters presenting different oppositional viewpoints. First, individuals involved in the movement attempted to counter the dominant frames being presented about militias by offering themselves as examples not fitting the media's mold. Second, other groups sharing policy or political concerns with militias disassociated themselves from the militia and attempted to explain why their ideas were not like the militia ideology being presented in the press. The military, the National Rifle Association, and conservative religious groups described how they were different from militias, thus eliminating existing and potential allies.

Not surprisingly, this category of deviant claims-makers was used least frequently by reporters. Dissenters are moderates, and they do not make good press. It was apparent that reporters quickly developed a general understanding of how militias should be presented to the public and then went after the story. When they were confronted by groups who did not conform to these images, however, reporters chose to ignore or downplay their influence. Several militia members described situations in which reporters solicited interviews and their group was willing to provide information, yet information was never published. One leader said a television reporter came to a meeting a couple of months after the bombing. The reporter was surprised when most of the audience was not wearing camouflage, and she was disappointed when she discovered they had no plans to do any firearms training. Although she did some interviews and videotaped the meeting, the story was aired without the material she collected from them.

Another interviewee described how he was now the public information officer for a militia group of which he was a founding member in November 1994. His primary responsibility was main contact person for the press, but he also described other strategies he used to combat the negative images being presented about militias in the news media.

> Well, every year we have a table at the gun show. We have a piece of the highway, [as part of] the Adopt-A-Highway Program, where we're out picking up trash three times a day. We have a food pantry that anytime we hear about a local that needs assistance, we do that a little bit. We've got a class for ham operators. In fact, we also train people to be ham operators. We have a newsletter and send the newsletter to politicians and the news media. We also have a Web page. We do recognize that we need to be out there presenting our group as mainstream. But it's slow. We've offered our services to law enforcement. We've never been used, but we're ready. We've got military as well as police people who are trained in search and rescue. We'll keep offering, because we do recognize we need to change the image of the militia and we need to educate people too. I think that most people just think of us as a threat.

We discussed whether militias are dangerous, and he conceded that serious threats do exist in the movement. "The militia movement, like any other, has a wide spectrum of people in it. Our group is different than the weirdos that get in the news—people like Mark Koernke and those other guys in Michigan. Those guys are on the other end of the spectrum. A reporter came in and wrote an article pretty much about those other people we call wingnuts, but they don't represent us." He described his militia's position on the major issues emphasized in the news media.

> All our meetings are open to the public, to the press, to the police, to anybody who wants to come. There's nothing illegal going on, there's no

racism going on—we have people who represent many, many religions. Our battalion commander—the third highest rank individual in our militia—is a black guy. We're just out there doing what we think needs to be done, and we're very open about it. There's nothing clandestine or anything else about our group. There's nothing sinister or anything like that. Historically, militias have taken care of themselves, of their own families, their own communities. So that's our emphasis. We feel like there are enough problems we can lay our hands on right here. We're not worried about the UN. I'm certainly not worried about UN soldiers coming down the highway. It's never going to happen. Black helicopters don't particularly bother me. In fact, they don't bother me at all.

He talked about how surprised and frustrated the militia is with media coverage. He described several incidents in which he would spend a significant amount of time with a newspaper or television reporter, and then nothing, or next to nothing, would be published. "What we do isn't very exciting. When the local people show up and want a story about our group, I say, 'Well, you know, we can talk about it all day, but we're not going to build one bomb, so there's no headline here, it's just working Americans who feel like they need to move the country towards the original documents and the original philosophy you know, and this is the vehicle we use.'" He said local reporters just stopped requesting interviews, and he also criticized national coverage of militias. He described a situation in which a reporter from a national television news station interviewed him and a few other members from his group for an Oklahoma City anniversary story. The interview lasted over two hours. He said the story was edited down to less than two minutes and used less than fifteen seconds of what they said, instead relying on other sources and emphasizing hate and racism in militias.

Another type of dissenter cited in news stories about militias was representatives from organizations attempting to distance themselves from the militia movement. For example, reporters assumed that members of militia groups had extensive military service. McVeigh served in the army and was considered a model soldier; Bo Gritz, a celebrity figure of the movement, was a highly decorated Vietnam War veteran. Many militia groups train as paramilitary units, and training exercises became mandatory footage for television news coverage. Two lines of inquiry flowed from the ties between militias and the military: Did military service push Timothy McVeigh to terrorism? How extensively have militias infiltrated the military?

Public officials were asked to answer both questions, and they were quick to distance the military from McVeigh and militias. Art Pine, writing for the *Los Angeles Times*, stated that the circumstantial link between the army and the bombing "has tarnished the Army's image and sent senior military officials scurrying to limit the damage." He reported that Defense Secretary William Perry issued a reminder about regulations prohibiting enlistees from participating in extremist groups, and that a National Guard base prohibited a local militia group from using its firing range. Other officials were cited as stating that the link between the militias and the military was spurious. "Army officials investigating whether militias have been seeking to recruit active-duty soldiers at Ft. Riley have found no evidence that the groups have even tried to do so. The Army said there are no links between the two Oklahoma City suspects and GIs now on active duty at Ft. Riley."[28]

The National Rifle Association (NRA) also tried to distance the organization and its cause from the militia movement. It was difficult to do because of the militia movement's close alignment with the NRA's position on guns and federal law enforcement. The NRA and militias were strongly in favor of repealing the assault weapons ban that was passed in 1994, and the repeal in Congress probably would have succeeded if the Oklahoma City bombing had not occurred. The NRA was also criticized for a fund-raising letter calling BATF agents, "jack-booted government thugs," and for wearing "Nazi bucket helmets and black storm trooper uniforms," echoing many of the concerns being publicly attributed to militia members. There was clearly a lot of dissension among the NRA leaders about the strategic direction of the organization. In general, the NRA took a hands-off approach to militias, for fear of alienating potential supporters. When attending a gun show soon after the Oklahoma City bombing, I discussed the NRA's position on militias with a man working at their booth. He said he usually just avoided answering questions about the relationship. Some of the NRA's leadership, however, felt pressured to make some type of public response to the concern about militias. Writing for the *Washington Post*, Kim Masters quoted sources from within the NRA who stated that "there have been internal discussions for some months over the embarrassment that could result if the organization were perceived to be linked even peripherally to the paramilitary 'militia' movement." She also described a memorandum from the NRA president cautioning "that the association must avoid entanglements with such groups."[29]

CHAPTER FIVE

Terrorists and Outsiders

Reporters react to celebrated cases with anticipation and excitement. Their adrenaline rush is mirrored by chaos in newsrooms across the country. Daily routines are abandoned or ignored as media personnel contemplate how a celebrated case should be packaged for public consumption, what angles of the story need to be pursued, and what information is available. Packaging decisions are critical because these preliminary, definitional decisions inhibit later efforts to correct any misconceptions that are generated about a case. The packaging of a celebrated case is influenced by how it has been presented by other media organizations, the internal dialogue occurring at all levels of the organization, and the familiar processing routines invoked in response to such cases. Although celebrated cases are rare, they occur with enough frequency that shared understandings of the appropriate ways to process and present these events are institutionalized. These understandings are shaped not only by practice but also by informal commentaries that evaluate the nature of the coverage. Media coverage of celebrated cases is often fodder for the critic's pen, and the debate is replayed in coffee rooms, newsroom hallways, editorial meetings, bars, lunch counters, and interactions with frequently used sources. Even rookie reporters, who may not yet have newsroom experience with a celebrated case, are taught, encouraged, or scolded by veteran reporters and media managers to adapt specific frameworks.

Although understanding the individuals and institutions who are provided frequent access to the public via the news media is an important first step in documenting why social problems are constructed in certain ways, there is equal value in determining what is said by these sources. Having access to the social-problems marketplace is often assumed to provide opportunities for claims-makers to promote certain meanings, deconstruct alternative viewpoints, and suggest or support their preferred policy initiatives. But it is necessary to explore whether these assumptions are supported by data. For example, one could conclude that militias influenced media coverage significantly because the news media frequently relied on sources affiliated with militia groups. Yet this conclusion is contrary to what was expected, considering the large body of research emphasizing the dominance of official, institutionally affiliated sources.[1] The problem with assuming that equal access results in social problems being represented objectively is that it discounts the reality that cases, events, and issues can be reproduced in a number of different ways. The sources cited in media stories may give symbolic legitimacy to the content provided in news stories, but how media workers and claims-makers frame issues also has a significant influence on the public's understanding of social problems.

It is possible that the celebrity figures of a movement and other sources relied on to represent a deviant group's ideology may reaffirm the ideas being provided by other authoritative sources. Media workers seek out sources willing to support such frameworks, and militia personnel may unwittingly give credibility to them by participating in the established news-production process. This finding would be consistent with the analysis by Todd Gitlin of the framing of SDS activities discussed briefly in Chapter 4.[2] Other researchers, however, have found that deviant sources have had success in altering the media landscape. Valerie Jenness examined the claims-making activities of the prostitutes' rights organization Call Off Your Old Tired Ethics (COYOTE). COYOTE had tremendous success in getting public attention for its efforts, and more importantly, was able to reshape the symbolic claims made by law-enforcement officials and moral entrepreneurs. This group was able to generate media attention by using high-profile celebrities, staged events, and controversial issues. Unlike the SDS, whom Gitlin found to have made their message conform to dominant media frames, COYOTE was able to "reshape the symbolic landscape by reframing prostitution as a women's and civil rights issue."[3]

To see whether militia sources reproduced dominant frameworks or altered the media landscape, I examine how militias were framed in the news media. Three questions are addressed in this chapter:

- What frameworks were used by news organizations to describe militias?
- What claims-makers promoted these frameworks?
- Were militias able to shape how their movement was presented in the news by being accessible to reporters?

FRAME ANALYSIS

In order to understand how militias were presented in the news media, it is necessary to do a qualitative analysis of media texts. Here, I describe how the news media and sources framed militias as a deviant group. Since an overwhelming number of events and ideas are floating around chaotically in the modern world, frames inject order and predictability into our daily interpretations of social reality. Media workers, sources, and the news-consuming public rely on shorthand reference schemes that make reality seem consistent with existing conceptions. The frames used to describe events and groups are conceptualized here as organizing devices.[4] For example, Erving Goffman describes frames as "schemata of interpretation that enable individuals to locate, perceive, identify, and label" events. Similarly, Gitlin writes that media frames, which "are largely unspoken and unacknowledged, organize the world both for journalists who report it and, in some important degree, for us who rely on their reports." Others describe frames as "unifying devices" or "conceptual tools" that provide meaning to events, organize experiences, influence the interpretation of events, and guide responsive actions.[5]

The significance of these frames is in the acknowledgment that there are multiple, competing ways to frame events, and claims-makers work to sponsor and then promote preferred meanings. Reporters are selective in deciding how to portray an event and obviously prefer some interpretations to other equally plausible ones. Robert Entman notes that frames "select some aspects of a perceived reality and make them more salient in a communicating text, in such a way as to promote a particular problem definition, causal interpretation, moral evaluation, and/or treatment recommendation." Michael Parenti points out that the civil-rights movement and the student antiwar movement could have been framed as "movements for peace," but instead the CBS evening news preferred calling them the "civil disturbances of the sixties" and emphasized the rare violent protest. Doing so created a very different reading of the purpose and activities of this movement. Similarly, Katherine Beckett and Theodore Sasson argue that the media has presented and thus promoted "law-and-order" frames to fight crime and drugs, largely ignoring other possibilities such as "social welfare" frames. Because specific frames are selected and promoted at the expense of other interpretations, the framing of events has inherent ideological power.[6]

Consider the results of an interesting study done by William Lofquist. Lofquist compares the coverage of two independent media events that occurred around the same time in Rochester, New York. One of these events was the disappearance of a young girl; the other, the collapse of a salt mine. Lofquist argues that these events could have been framed in similar ways: as accidents, as instances of neglect, or as crimes. The disappearance of the girl, however, was immediately framed by the news media as a stranger abduction, and the mine disaster was interpreted as an accident. There was no evidence to support how either of these events should have been framed, and other explanations were equally plausible, but the media refused to consider any. Police officials, community members, and experts from the National Center for Missing and Exploited Children were used to support the abduction scenario, and officials representing the mine were used by the media to explain that the disaster was an accident.[7]

The frames used to define and interpret events and influence public thinking and policy making in reaction to social problems are influenced by many different forces, including the organizational routines of newsmaking and existing cultural concerns. News personnel work in a world that is dominated by interactions with other like-minded media workers. One could argue that media workers are part of a loosely linked fraternity solidified by their common experiences. In general, media workers have similar educational and job training, are of a similar demographic makeup, and share common professional experiences. Their experiences may include working a specific news beat or subject area, being pressured by editors to produce stories consistent with the priorities of the news organization, feeling alienated from upper-level management and its economic priorities, facing on-the-job ethical dilemmas, having sources refuse to comment or not being able to get the story because of time or access limitations, and attempting to manage sources who are working to manipulate them. Media personnel are socialized into this community by such experiences, and adherence to its written and unwritten directives determines whether a reporter is rejected or accepted. Through these experiences, reporters come to develop an appreciation for the preferred ways to frame media events.

Specific frames are constructed and reinforced by the organizational processes of news organizations, but these frames are also influenced by the larger historical and cultural themes at work. Many scholars argue that some frames are particularly significant and strike a "responsive chord" when they are able to resonate with larger cultural frames that exist in society.[8] Amy Binder posits that "a frame has a much greater chance of success if it draws on some conscious or subconscious, unified or disorganized belief held in the culture at large," and Beckett, in her analysis of how state and media claims-making influences public concern about crime and drugs, finds that "state actors' success in mobilizing public concern around these particular issues was not inevitable, and must be explained in terms of the resonance of the construction of the crime and drug issues with particular themes in American political culture." Similarly, William Swart discusses how a "frame is thus defined by its resonance with the cultural, political, or historical milieu in which it emerges" and argues that "claims-makers' rhetoric must match" the cultural context or people "will ignore the claims." These cultural themes seep into various aspects of the construction of events, influencing whether events are covered, how they are presented, and how much cultural capital is expended. The public will identify and react favorably to those events that are most consistent with existing cultural myths.[9]

FRAME METHODOLOGY

This chapter analyzes how militias were framed in the news media from 1994 (the first year in which an article about militias appeared in one of the newspapers indexed by NewsBank) to 1998. Each newspaper article was read and coded for descriptive information (reporter's name, newspaper source, date, number of words), type of crime information (if applicable), source information (discussed in Chapter 4), group information (what militia groups were mentioned; what other extremist groups were mentioned), and celebrated case information (what cases like the Oklahoma City bombing case, Ruby Ridge, Waco, and Viper were mentioned in the article). These coding categories provide quantitative information about the representation of militias in the news media. Two other coders and I read an article, and then noted what, if any, information about each category was included. For example, data were collected on any extremist group mentioned, in order to examine how frequently militias were tied to these other groups. The Ku Klux Klan and other white supremacist groups, the John Birch Society, Posse Comitatus, Tax Protestors, Freemen, and constitutionalists were mentioned frequently in articles that *focused* on the militia movement. At least one other extremist group was mentioned in just over 30 percent of the articles in the sample, illustrating how difficult it was for reporters to make distinctions between these groups and how much value reporters saw in linking them together.

Finally, a coding scheme to capture the frames emphasized was applied to each article. To develop the frame coding categories, I read newspaper articles, political speeches, scholarly articles, militia literature, and militia Web sites. The reading of these materials generated approximately seventy relevant categories. These categories were then collapsed into the nine frames provided in Table 5.1, as described in more detail below. The analysis of frames represents a qualitative analysis of media texts, and it focuses on two different levels of analysis. First, the dominant frames promoted in each article were identified. The results of this analysis provide an understanding of the dominant frames used by the news media to describe the militia movement during the 1990s. The second analysis, although overlapping the first in several respects, attempted to link claims-makers to specific frames. Thus, after reading each article, the coder was asked to evaluate what he or she thought were the dominant frames being promoted in that article. When this exercise was completed, the coder went back to the article and broke down each attribution to a claims-maker to determine which, if any, of the frame categories applied.

FINDINGS

Table 5.2 provides the results for the dominant frames used to describe militia groups in the media. The first seven can be considered antimilitia frames in that they raise concerns about the people involved in the movement, their beliefs, and their future plans. The last two frames are promilitia frames in direct contradiction to the other frames. Overall, the number of antimilitia frames presented in the news far out-

Table 5.1 The Frames Used to Describe Militias in the News Media

Frame	Samples of Phrases Classified
1. Threat–Terrorist	He feels he's only safe insofar as he can kill.
	There's going to be bloodshed.
	We are concerned about the threats to law-enforcement officers.
2. Threat–Growing Movement	We are getting ready for war.
	Each person recruits five other people. In a time of crisis, I can count on 200 people immediately and we can have 25,000 people together within three hours.
	The number has increased from 224 active militia organizations in 39 states two years ago to 858 active groups in 50 states this year.
3. Outsider	We are like two separate towns.
	They have an us v. them mentality.
	Militias prefer to withdraw from the civic process.
4. Conspiracy	The United Nations is leading a conspiracy to enslave the United States.
	I'm on a list to be enslaved in a concentration camp.
	Unmarked black helicopters hover in the skies over our country, a menacing prelude to the day when the United States falls under "One World Government" control.
5. Gun Policy	They're using the incident to disarm citizens.
	Our concern is with federal officials overturning the Second Amendment's right to bear arms.
6. Racist	Militia leaders have backgrounds in white supremacist groups.
	When you look at the leaders in the militia and Aryan Nations and other white supremacy groups, the same names keep coming up.
	Most of the people it investigated have past or present racist ties.
7. Religious	He believes he is a prophet of god.
	We're devoted to biblical principles.
	Groups are using claims of faith and religious conviction for an armed rebellion.
8. No Threat	We are real, average, everyday people.
	The threat is highly exaggerated.
9. Legitimate Concerns	Corporations are buying up, getting bigger and bigger, cutting back on the quality of goods, on work conditions, on jobs and raising prices.
	Their enemy is industries that rape the land for monetary gain.

Table 5.2 The Representation of Militia Frames in All Stories

Frame	Percentage
1. Threat–Terrorist	17.2
2. Threat–Growing Movement	20.2
3. Outsider	20.0
4. Conspiracy	11.3
5. Gun Policy	6.0
6. Racist	6.7
7. Religious	1.7
8. No Threat	13.1
9. Legitimate Concerns	3.8

numbers the promilitia frames. Approximately 80 percent of the frames captured in news stories about militias were classified into one of the seven antimilitia frame categories.

It is not surprising that the two threat frames, Terrorist and Growing Movement, were frequently used by reporters to describe militias. Indeed, these two frames combined accounted for nearly 40 percent of the media frames captured in newspaper articles about militias. The core feature of both of these frames is that militia groups are dangerous. Militias were portrayed as a threat in two different ways. First, the Terrorist frame focuses on the violent nature of individuals involved in the movement. Militia members were described as being angry, crazy, paranoid, violent, and malicious. Second, militia members were not only described as a direct threat to public safety but also were of concern because they were part of a larger movement organizing to overthrow the government. The Growing Movement frame was the most frequently portrayed in stories about the militia movement. The media emphasized the activities and strategies that militia groups used to grow, highlighting organizing, recruitment, and planning strategies. The threat emphasis here is on the size and scope of the militia movement and its activities.

Being defined as a threat is one way in which the media highlighted preferred behaviors of the community. Any legitimate issue, idea, or concern that militias may have had was lost or minimized because they were threatening. The media also illuminated community boundaries more directly by defining militias as community and political outsiders. The Outsider frame accounted for 20 percent of the total number of frames captured in stories about the militia movement. The focus of this frame is in highlighting how militias are outside the legitimate boundaries of community life.

The Conspiracy frame accounted for approximately 11 percent of the frames presented in the media. The core issue of this frame is the emphasis on unknown, dark enemies working to accomplish a one-world government. There are many versions of the one-world government conspiracy, but the media's coverage of the conspiracy thinking of the militia movement focused on their belief about a New World Order controlled by the United Nations. There were other conspiracies that the media emphasized in its coverage of the militia movement, including several related to the Oklahoma City bombing. For example, reporters described how some militia members believed that McVeigh was just another Lee Harvey Oswald—a dupe for a larger conspiracy working to demonize the militia movement.

The other antimilitia frames were less frequently captured in militia stories. The Racist frame accounted for nearly 7 percent of the total frames captured in this analysis. The central concern of this frame is whether the anger of militia members is directed at any specific groups, and reporters generally focused on the racist and anti-Semitic tendencies of the militia. The Gun Policy frame accounted for 6 percent of the total captured. Supporters of gun control promoted this frame, arguing that the stockpiling of weapons and explosives provided justification for passing and enforcing gun-control legislation. Gun enthusiasts, including militia members, attempted to counter these claims and argue against gun-control legislation. The Religious frame accounted for fewer than 2 percent of the frames captured.

There were two counterframes used to describe militias in the news media. The No Threat and Legitimate Concern frames are both promilitia and captured contrasting viewpoints in two ways. First, the No Threat frame, accounting for approximately 13 percent of the total number of frames captured, emphasizes that militia members are not a threat to citizen safety, but rather have been portrayed as a threat. The core issue with this frame is the demonization of militias by exaggerating their threat. Instead of being portrayed as threatening to citizens, militias are described as good citizens or patriots wanting to protect society. Second, the Legitimate Concerns frame (3.8 percent) captures the major social, economic, and political concerns of people involved in the militia movement.

Threat—Terrorist

The media's coverage of crime—from which crimes are selected and how much space is provided to whether an incident becomes celebrated and evolves into a moral panic—is determined in large measure by the threat associated with the offending individual or group. The legitimacy of a threat depends only on the *perception* that the target is extremely dangerous to the security and stability of society. Thus a threat is successful when it produces fear. Fear is a vitally important cultural commodity that helps to justify the demonization of individuals and groups by people in power. The news media contribute directly to this demonization by sustaining and feeding off of the public's fears. The news media intensify their coverage when a threat is thought to be significant, but in doing so, they promote and aggravate the corresponding fear. It is difficult to break this tautological chain because the ceremonies invoked in response to a threat also validate and sustain the threat (see Chapter 6).

Table 5.3 presents data illustrating the frames emphasized by the six categories of claims-makers discussed in the previous chapter. The three community-voice representatives were significantly more likely to provide the Terrorist and Growing Movement threat frames. These frames accounted for nearly 50 percent of the frames extracted from the facts and opinions provided by representatives of social-control institutions. These frames were also frequently attributed to the experts of specific issues used by the news media, although these claims-makers emphasized the Growing Movement frame more than the Terrorist frame. This difference is attributable to how these experts became the primary source of information on the size of the militia movement. It is clear that social-control representatives and experts on specific issues saw the symbolic and concrete benefits of promoting the Threat frame. Framing militias as threatening helped to dehumanize members of the movement, validate any planned responses by these agencies, justify the need for additional resources to respond to these groups, and diminish the credibility of the beliefs and concerns of the targeted group.

The media and claims-makers sought to demonstrate that militias were a threat worthy of attention in two overlapping ways. First, militias were portrayed as terrorists, tapping into a shared cultural understanding of the dangers and violent natures of groups that were driven by their hate for the United States government. The media portrayed militia members as willing to do whatever was necessary, including taking a massive number of casualities, to demonstrate a commitment to their

Table 5.3 The Representation of Frames by Claims-makers

Frame	Representatives of Social-Control	Experts on Specific Issues	Individuals	Celebrity Figures	Examples	Dissenters
1. Terrorist	27.1%	15.4%	17.7%	11.2%	10.3%	6.4%
2. Threat–Growing Movement	21.9	24.0	11.5	12.9	16.7	10.3
3. Outsider	19.4	21.2	29.2	12.6	16.7	11.3
4. Conspiracy	6.6	9.9	7.3	26.6	16.5	7.9
5. Gun Policy	4.6	4.6	6.3	5.6	6.6	8.4
6. Racist	4.6	14.9	1.0	3.9	4.1	7.9
7. Religious	1.1	2.0	3.1	2.5	1.9	1.5
8. No Threat	10.7	5.5	11.5	19.3	21.2	39.4
9. Legitimate Concerns	3.9	2.6	12.5	5.3	5.8	6.9

beliefs. International terrorism had been a priority news and popular culture topic for a long time. For example, Bethami Dobkin, in an examination of television news coverage of terrorism during Ronald Reagan's tenure as president, argues that the media devoted considerable attention to the topic and that the president used the media to generate support for harsh policies by selling terrorism as an attack on American values.[10] The intense coverage of international terrorism continued through the late 1980s and early 1990s, focusing on such celebrated events as the bombing of a Pan Am flight over Lockerbie, Scotland, and the World Trade Center bombing of 1993. The entertainment media have also helped to create public imagery about terrorist threats by using the international terrorist frequently as a legitimate enemy (discussed in more detail in Chapter 7).

The Terrorist Threat frame was frequently invoked in the news media's coverage of militias and had a powerful influence on the public's understanding of militias because it conjured up existing terrorist images from the public culture. It was inevitable that militias would be framed in this manner because of the route through which they entered the social-problems marketplace. Tim McVeigh, to borrow from Lou Michel and Dan Herbeck's 2001 book title, was the "American terrorist." This label was not inappropriate. It followed, however, that since McVeigh was initially presented in the news as an active militia member, all militia members must also be terrorists. Militia members were dangerous, plotting to overthrow the government using whatever tactics or weapons, especially bombs, were necessary. Like other terrorists, militia members were presented as casting a wide net to achieve their goals. The public was vulnerable, and it was inevitable that innocent people would be caught in traps set by these terrorists. The news media emphasized the militia movement's deep commitment to their beliefs, their unwillingness to compromise or negotiate a middle ground, and their willingness to take whatever steps, including using violence, that were necessary to achieve their goals. This frame was frequently invoked and it persisted because of the coupling between McVeigh and militias. When the Terrorist frame was determined to be an appropriate way to describe militia members, reporters relied on preexisting terrorist imagery that solidified their status as a significant threat. Moreover, the persistence of this frame made it difficult for the public to call upon any images inconsistent with it.

Once the media recognized that McVeigh's link to militias was loose, there were several other celebrity militia faces and cases who filled the terrorist void. One of the celebrity figures I interviewed, who estimated that he has been interviewed by 500 other reporters, demonstrated his willingness to confirm the threat frame—which also helps explain why he was so sought after by the media.

> Patrick Henry was in fact correct when he said that guns are the teeth of liberty and that we must stand in the face of tyranny, yet armed and looking dangerous. You bet we're dangerous. We're dangerous people when it comes to the abuses of a tyrannical and oppressive government, and we will stand in defiance of those people. Does the public want to protect themselves? Do they want their own countrymen, their own patriot countrymen to be their guardians of life, liberty, and the pursuit of happiness? Well, history will show that you cannot entrust those sacred rights that we have enumerated for us in the Bill of Rights—you cannot trust that to government. These things must be inalienable. These things must be held by the people, and we must put severe restrictions and reins upon government. Why? Because history again shows governments tend to consolidate, condense, and centralize their power and become absolutely corrupted and tyrannical. And history also shows that no government is ever self-correcting—that eventually there will be revolution. Or it will become absolutely despotic and totalitarian—one or the other. But I know this: if the present course of this country does not change dramatically, we are going toward armed revolution.

Linda Thompson was another celebrity figure who immediately helped to fill the void for reporters looking for good threats to emphasize.[11] Although I was not able to interview her, I have read some of her work and am aware of how others describe her contributions to the militia movement. Thompson had a relatively short tenure as a celebrity figure of the movement, disappearing from public view in late 1995. But her short stint as one of the anointed leaders had a tremendous effect on public understanding of the militia movement. Thompson was first linked to the militia movement during the Waco siege, but she had been pushing conspiracy theories prior to 1993. For example, one of the reporters I interviewed discussed her conversations with Thompson in the early 1990s.

> When she came out with her Waco video, I said that name is so familiar, I know I've heard about it before. Well, it turns out that back in 1991 when we had Operation Rescue abortion protests, she called me. She was an

attorney for an abortion doctor. And now she has totally switched sides. She's gone just the opposite now. She was telling me about a conspiracy involving the protestors and they were trying to kill this doctor.

Thompson called herself the "Acting Adjunct General" of the "Unorganized Militia of the United States." There were several reasons why Thompson became such a media darling. She created two popular videos about the Waco incident that were widely circulated among militia groups. Jason Vest, writing about Thompson for the *Washington Post*, reported that McVeigh watched one of these videos, *Waco: The Big Lie*, before bombing the Murrah building. Thompson was well known for planning a militia march on Washington, D.C., in 1994. The ADL's summary of the planned march states that Thompson "ordered all participants to come armed and in uniform," and "they [the militia] would arrest congressmen who have failed to uphold their oaths of office." She was also in Waco for the Branch Davidian's standoff with law enforcement, and she tried to incite a militia protest. She faxed a message, titled "Waco: Time for the Militia," to thousands of "Patriot" fax machines. In this message she states: "The Unorganized Militia of the United States of America will assemble with long arms, vehicles (including tracked and armored), aircraft, and any available gear, for inspection for fitness and use in a well-regulated militia, at 9:00 a.m. on Saturday, April 3, 1993, on Northcrest Drive, off I–35, going east on Northcrest Drive off the interstate in Waco, Texas."[12] Reporters also found it easy to define her as a threat because she was usually confrontational when approached by reporters. In an article titled "The Spooky World of Linda Thompson," Jason Vest reported that "her voice screeches from the pay phone receiver," she "slams down the phone," and then "a man in an olive green T-shirt bursts through the door, takes a camera from his pickup truck and begins snapping pictures of a reporter's car." He writes, "Suspicion is Linda Thompson's business."[13] A reporter that I interviewed wrote a story about Tim McVeigh's telephone records and reported that McVeigh called Thompson. After the story was published, Thompson called this reporter, threatened to sue, and warned that the reporter would have to give a deposition. When Thompson agreed to an interview, or reporters were able to obtain information from her World Wide Web site or her other writings, she accentuated many of the dominant frames being used to describe militias. Examples include her call to respond to the armies of a One World Government, her repeated sightings of black helicopters and United Nations troops and military equipment, and her alternative explanations for what occurred in Waco. For example, the following excerpts are taken from one of Thompson's publications, "Waco: Another Perspective."[14]

> We have three confirmed reported citings of trainloads of U.N. tanks going into Portland, Oregon, over the past few weeks, and troop movements of unmarked military vehicles across the nation. Perhaps you might want to ponder the significance of these events.

> The Waco massacre has awakened Americans all across the nation to what is horribly wrong in this country. A voice of unity is being heard, growing louder each day.

> And each of them, Bill Clinton, Janet Reno, William Sessions, and Lloyd Bentsen, are murderers.

> A one world government where, in order to put the new government in place, we must all be disarmed first.

> Americans, my fellow patriots, we have cold-blooded killers running our country. Isn't it about time you put down your beer, get up off the sofa, and do something about it?

Threat—Growing Movement

The second way in which the media demonstrated that militias were a threat was by highlighting the organization and strength of the militia movement. The media's focus on militias would have dwindled much more rapidly, or would never have intensified, had McVeigh been portrayed in the news as a "Lone Wolf." Once it was assumed that the act was not an isolated incident, however, it was important to describe the organizational tactics of the movement and substantiate claims about the size of the threat with data. The structure and tactics emphasized in the news made it appear as if the militia movement were preparing for war and the Oklahoma City bombing was only the beginning of that war. Tom Toles's editorial cartoon published in May 1995 captures this frame effectively. (See Figure 2.)

Media emphasized the paramilitary structure adopted by many militias, the public appearances made in camouflage with sidearms, and the training exercises in remote locations. The news media also highlighted

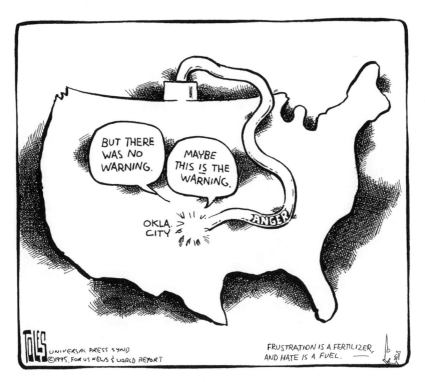

2. *Tom Toles, Growing Anger. TOLES © 1995 The Buffalo News. Reprinted with permission of UNIVERSAL PRESS SYNDICATE. All Rights Reserved.*

the secretive nature of many groups, describing the cell structure adopted by some groups that would allow them to avoid detection and infiltration by government agents. Although these groups were secretive and independent, the media often described how the groups were linked via modern technologies and would be able to mobilize quickly if necessary. There was clear overlap here between the images of the United States military and of militia organizations. Many militia groups are indeed highly militarized, adopting hierarchical command structures, participating in military training exercises, and marching in military formation. This overlap forced many reporters to explore the military's influence and presence in the militia movement.

Statistics are also an effective way to demonstrate that a movement is threatening. It is important that anecdotal evidence, which alone can be a powerful way to justify public concern, is also legitimated with data. The news media use statistics frequently when describing the extent or size of a social problem. The public tends to accept statistical claims uncritically, assuming that those who provide such numbers are authorities on an issue. Our culture assumes that constructed "scientific" facts are truths, and thus it is important that numbers be used to illustrate the significance of a problem. Statistics can easily be gleaned from bureaucratic reports, press releases, or data presented on the World Wide Web by these agencies. Organizations collect, process, and make data available to news media in a way that increases their likelihood of presentation. Claims-makers recognize the value of using numbers to substantiate claims about the size of a movement. Joel Best discusses how statistics result from a social process. "Statistics shape our sense of a problem's urgency, which in turn affects policy. Claimsmakers use statistics to persuade; their numbers need to be understood for what they are—part of the rhetoric of claimsmaking." Dobkin came to a similar conclusion when examining international terrorism: "Through the use of statistics, both journalists and politicians added legitimacy to the significance of terrorism as an object of discourse and as constituting a threat of crisis proportions." The media rarely collect independent data, relying instead on statistics from these agencies. Moreover, when the attention to a social problem is intense, as during a moral panic, reporters do not have the time or the desire to question the reliability of the figures provided.[15]

Statistical data about the size of the movement were provided in 35 percent of the stories in the sample, focusing primarily on the number of groups, the number of states with a militia presence, or the number of individuals actively involved in the militia movement. Over 50 percent of the statistics provided were about the number of groups in the United States or in a specific state. Twenty-two percent of the articles with statistical data included the number of states with militias, and 19 percent reported the number of individuals involved in the movement. Other types of statistical data provided in stories about the militia movement included data on the number of bombings in the United States and the number of gun shows per year. The two major sources of all statistical estimates reported in militia stories were experts and militia members. Approximately 50 percent of the statistical estimates provided in stories about the militia movement were provided by experts from either the Southern Poverty Law Center or the Anti-Defamation League. Over 20 percent of the statistical data were provided by militia members asked to estimate the size of the movement. Representatives of social-control institutions, usually law-enforcement officials, accounted for about 10 percent of the statistical estimates provided in these stories. In addition, a large percentage of the statistical estimates, nearly 19 percent, were provided in the news media without specific attribution to any source.

The number of groups active in the militia movement was important, but it was also effective to show that the threat was increasing. For example, in the newspaper articles published prior to the Oklahoma City bombing and in the period immediately following, articles describing the size of the movement relied primarily on data provided by the Anti-Defamation League. On May 4, 1995, Tom Kenworthy and George Lardner published an article in the *Washington Post* on the militia movement. Using data cited by the Anti-Defamation League in a report titled "Armed and Dangerous: Militias Take Aim at the Federal Government," they state: "Bands of armed militants, most calling themselves militias, are cropping up across the country. They have no centralized structure, but there are links among some of them, largely the sharing of propaganda material and speakers. A survey conducted by the Anti-Defamation League of B'Nai B'rith found evidence of their activity in 13 states." In this same article, Chip Berlet of Political Research Associates "estimated that out of the tens of millions of populist middle-class voters, about five million consider themselves 'patriots,' convinced that the federal government is corrupt and moving toward tyranny. Perhaps 40,000 have taken the next step and joined armed militias." In a July 1995 *Washington Post* article, Serge Kovaleski reported that the movement had grown significantly. "Citizen militias have been among the main disseminators of the theories, and a recent Anti-Defamation League report found that these groups now operate in at least 40 U.S. states, compared with only 13 last fall, and have added about 5,000 members."[16]

The Southern Poverty Law Center (SPLC) also contributed frequently with estimates of the size of the militia movement. These figures were typically attributed to its Klanwatch Intelligence Project—an intelligence operation used to monitor extremism. Morris Dees and James Corcoran in their book *Gathering Storm: America's Militia Threat*, describe how the Klanwatch Project gathers its data, noting that the "investigative staff gathers its information from public sources, recorded speeches and publications of the leaders and groups we monitor, law-enforcement sources, court depositions, Internet postings, informers, and, in some cases, carefully conducted undercover operations."[17] Some of the SPLC's estimates, published in various newspapers, on the size of the militia movement are provided in Table 5.4. These data show that claims

Table 5.4 Number of Militias Estimated by the Southern Poverty Law Center

Date	Number of Militias Estimated	Newspaper (Reporter)
3/19/95	in 20 States	*St. Louis Post-Dispatch* (Holleman)
6/18/95	224 groups/39 States	*Los Angeles Times* (Feldman)
9/2/95	340 groups	*Chicago Tribune* (Worthington)
10/15/95	400 units/42 States	*Dallas Morning News* (Watts)
7/2/96	800 militias	*Knight-Ridder News Service* (Cannon and Edna)
12/15/96	950 units/50 States	*Dallas Morning News* (Watts)
3/30/97	858 active patriot groups	*Times-Herald* (Follick)
9/29/97	858 militias/50 States	*The Arizona Republic* (Shaffer)
2/13/98	858 militia-type operations	*Rocky Mountain News* (Sanko)

about the militia threat grew dramatically in a relatively short period of time. Prior to the Oklahoma City bombing, the SPLC estimated that there was an active militia movement in twenty states. After the bombing, the estimate grew to 224 groups in 39 states by June and 340 groups by September. In October, the number increased to 400, and militia organizations were called "units" rather than "groups." Watts states that "One militia monitor, Klanwatch of the Southern Poverty Law Center in Alabama, counts more than 400 units in 42 states, and officials say new ones are popping up regularly. That is nearly double the number identified by Klanwatch last summer." By mid-1996, the media reported that SPLC data indicated that 800 militias existed, and the number grew to 950 in all 50 states by the end of the year. SPLC's estimates declined to 858 in 1997 and held steady at this number for over a year. More recently, the SPLC stated on their Web site that the number of militia groups "has dwindled to fewer than 200."[18]

A militia informant told a story that illustrates how law-enforcement officers had limited information about the militia movement and relied on the data provided by these expert organizations. The anecdote also illustrates how militias reacted to the media's reliance on such sources. Most importantly, it illustrates the importance of having large numbers and creating the perception of increased growth to substantiate claims that such groups are threatening. I asked him about the estimates being provided in the news media about the size of the movement.

> Now, I can give you some examples of how that's played out to the detriment of the truth, but I think one of the most outstanding ones is the Mormon Militia Battalion in Salt Lake. Sounds pretty scary, doesn't it? After Oklahoma City there was an AP reporter in Salt Lake whose editor said, "Well look, you know, looks like the militias are being tied to this bombing—get me a story about all the mad dog militias in Utah." So he

called up a source of his at the ATF [Bureau of Alcohol, Tobacco, and Firearms]. The ATF gave him a list of these mad dog militias in Utah, including a group called the Mormon Militia Battalion. Well, he wrote the story and almost immediately got a phone call from a guy named George Bascomb. Now George is, I guess, [in his] 60s pushing 70s, and he's the leader of the Mormon Militia Battalion, which happens to be a historical preservation group. That to the Mormons is very much like the Sons of Confederate Veterans. They honor the memory of the original Mormon militia battalion that blazed a trail across the West in 1846 for the federal government. The only gun they own is a restored 1827 flintlock musket. They are mainly made up of old geezers who go around and mark graves and work with Boy Scout troops who go around and mark the path of the original Mormon militia battalion. Well, this story appears in the paper, and all of a sudden, poor Mr. Bascombs's phone starts ringing off the hook, with all of these Boy Scout troops—"You know, we can't deal/work with you guys if you're involved in blowing up buildings and things like that." I mean, this is the tenor of the times. Well, Mr. Bascomb did the only thing he knew to do, which is to call the reporter and try to set him straight. And after a long conversation, he persuaded the guy to come out to some of his meetings and sure enough, Mr. Bascomb's group was exactly what he presented it to be. So the AP reporter called his source at the ATF and said, "Hey look, you know, where did you get this stuff? These guys are just historical preservationists." And the ATF guy said, "Yeah, you know, we investigated those guys and they're OK." He says, "Where did you get their names from?" He says, "Well, we got it from this list. It comes from this place in the south—Southern Poverty Law Center, in Montgomery, Alabama." Now mind you, he already admitted that they investigated these guys, so here's sloppy scholarship on the part of the SPLC. But unfortunately, in the newsrooms of America's newspapers and television studios, when you bring up Morris, you're talking about St. Morris of Montgomery. He can do no wrong. And obviously he's the expert.

Militia members furnished 20 percent of the statistical estimates provided in newspaper stories. Numbers provided by organizations such as the SPLC or ADL are assumed to be credible because of the authoritative position of these organizations in society. Estimates provided by deviants are also credible because of their insider status. Since they are part of the movement, they are assumed to have enough access to be able to estimate its size. Local leaders were asked to estimate the size of their group and the number of groups present in a specific state. Celebrity figures also promoted the Threat–Growing Movement frame by providing estimates of the number of people in the movement, often significantly eclipsing any organizational estimates. For example, Mark Koernke estimated that there were 4.5 million active members of the militia movement when interviewed by a reporter in 1995.[19]

Outsider

The emphasis of the Outsider frame is on how the beliefs, concerns, and activities of individuals involved in the militia movement are not appropriate. The pattern of specific claims-makers who invoked this frame is similar to the Threat frames (see Table 5.3). Sixty to 80 percent of the frames promoted by social-control representatives and experts emphasized the Threat or Outsider frames. These community voices used the Outsider frame to demonstrate that militia behavior and ideology did not belong in society and would not be tolerated. The Individual category also invoked this frame frequently. Reporters used individuals—like neighbors, business owners, or victims of militia activity—infrequently as sources, but when they were consulted, reporters often emphasized how they described militia members as "outsiders." Using individuals to support this claim effectively relegated militia members to the outer boundaries of society. Many of these neighbors and citizens discussed how they, like members of militia groups, had concerns about the government and could relate to the militias' activism, but the individuals would usually go on to conclude that the militia went far beyond their own concerns.

Maureen Haydeen, writing about a case that received national news coverage in late 1995, provides a good example of how a social-control representative promoted the Outsider frame. Joe Holland founded the Indiana North American Volunteer Militia in 1993, although he had been active in other antigovernment movements in the 1980s.[20] He was a pig farmer who refused to pay taxes and used Freemen-like paper-terrorism strategies. After the Internal Revenue Service seized his farm, Holland was directly and indirectly involved in a number of fraudulent scams. He also partnered with a like-minded resident of Darby, Montana, by the name of Cal Greenup. Greenup, like Holland, refused to pay taxes, believed the government and its environmental regulations were to blame for his misfortunes, and threatened to use violence to protect his interests. Greenup formed a chapter of Holland's North American Volunteer Militia. The partnership quickly dissolved because both men came under the scrutiny of federal and local law-enforcement officials for a variety of crimes, including bank fraud, bankruptcy fraud, security fraud, and tax evasion. Mark Pitcavage describes how their activities went well beyond economic offenses: "Holland and Greenup were calling for the establishment of vigilante 'common law courts' that would try public officials for 'treason,' then hang or shoot them. Authorities became particularly worried in late March 1995, when Greenup—already charged with tax evasion but refusing to turn himself in—told a bail bondsman that a common-law court had met and threatened to hang Ravalli District Judge Jeffrey Langton, and to shoot Sheriff Jay Printz, County Attorney George Corn, and deputy county attorney Mike Reardon."

Montana sheriff Jay Printz is highly respected by members and supporters of the militia movement because he shares many of their views. Haydeen reported that "the sheriff is somewhat sympathetic to anti-government views of militia members. An avid gun-control opponent, he has joined three other sheriffs in the nation to sue the federal government over the Brady Law. Printz contends the federal government can't force him to enforce gun-control provisions." Printz and his colleagues took issue with the provision that a local law-enforcement official had to conduct the background check on a handgun purchaser, and they eventually won their lawsuit contesting the law.[21] Despite sharing some of Holland and Greenup's concerns about the federal government, Printz was quick to point out that what Holland was doing was unacceptable. Haydeen reported that Printz said: "We had a very volatile situation here and Joe Holland was a man who with his rhetoric fanned the flames. . . . There was gas all over the place out here and he was sitting back in Indiana throwing matches at us." Later, he is quoted in this newspaper article as saying: "This community is a very tolerant community. But we decided enough is enough when they threaten to kill judges and sheriffs."[22]

Another way that the media presented militias as outsiders was to describe how different they were from other people in society. The media emphasized that militia members preferred to be isolated from others in the community; they home-schooled their children, stockpiled food and supplies in order to be prepared for disaster, spent their weekend leisure time in the woods training in weapons and paramilitary maneuvers, and practiced nontraditional religions. "By filming us in camos," said one militia member, "they can easily differentiate us from the rest of society." The media portrayed these activities as being strange, and the public had a difficult time accepting the idea that there might be a need for preparedness. One militia member described how surprised and disappointed he was with how other citizens reacted to his preparedness efforts.

We do a lot in the area for community disaster preparedness. We work with State Emergency. There is always a potential for disasters that are not political or economic. The general mainstream population is comfortable and is not willing to admit that there could be a situation where you just can't hop into your car and drive a mile or two to the grocery store and get your dinner and come home and fix it. Nature is still out there. When I say I keep a month of food in my house in the form of emergency rations, to some people I'm written off as a wacky weirdo from that point on. Even to be that feebly prepared. Even the other day I was talking about a first aid kit that I carried in my car and somebody was saying how strange that was. People are so far removed from being self-sufficient, and that's a lot of what the militia movement is. In a nutshell we would say we don't want government taking care of us. We want to be able to take care of ourselves and the freedom to take care of ourselves and as well as our neighbors and families, and people are getting further and further removed from that. That's just unimaginable to many people that they would ever need a first aid kit in their car.

The Outsider frame also captures how the media portrayed militia members as refusing to participate in traditional democratic processes. Politicians frequently invoked the Outsider frame, stating that members of militias are antigovernment. Militia members themselves had a difficult time understanding how they could be portrayed as antigovernment because they view themselves as patriots, and questioning the legitimacy and policies of political leaders is at the core of the democratic process. They often link themselves to militias who played a critical role in the Revolutionary War and early American society. I interviewed a militia member who had been active for about three years.

Sometimes you'll hear people talk about the militia or ask a militia representative "Why do you want to overthrow the government?" Our response is to look dumbfounded and to say "What do you mean, overthrow the government?" We don't want to overthrow the government: we want to restore the government. What I feel like we're in is like a socialist liberal occupation by liberal judges that impose nonlegislated laws on us. We're in an occupation where people can't mind their own business and worry about what kind of gun I've got in my locker. Ted Kennedy's car has killed more people than my guns have. We're the one who are, like, leave us alone and we'll get along fine. They say people like us are extremists, we're dangerous. We can't have that. Park your butt in front of your TV, watch a sitcom, and drink a beer—damn it.

Conspiracy

The Conspiracy frame was promoted relatively frequently in the media's coverage of the militia movement. The primary conspiracy theory captured by this powerful frame is concern about a one-world government. Conspiracy thinking in general had strong cultural momentum in the 1990s because of the approaching new millennium and Americans' intrigue with such theories (explored in more detail in Chapter 7). Both news and entertainment media attempted to take full advantage of the public tension regarding end-of-the-world scenarios. Moreover, the most frequent frame provided by celebrity figures was the Conspiracy frame (see Table 5.3). Celebrity figures were willing to promote and defend their conspiracy theories in the news, even though it was impossible for reporters to fully explain these theories. Reporters would often mention a belief in a New World Order, black helicopters, international bankers, and government-controlled weather machines without providing any explanation of how these ideas fit under their conspiracy umbrella.

Antigovernment groups offer a variety of different conspiracy scenarios involving various groups or institutions through which this one-world government would occur. Their conspiracies are supported by picking and choosing anecdotal, fabricated, excerpted, or theorized evidence from speeches, media articles, political documents, myth, and mainstream and extremist publications. The media's coverage of conspiracy in relation to the militia movement focused on their concern that the United Nations was the evil force enlisting the help of international bankers, politicians, and journalists to overthrow the government. Reporters described how the United Nations (and its plans for a New World Order) was a great enemy of the militia movement and militia members feared that their guns would be confiscated as part of this conspiratorial plan and believed that black helicopters were patrolling the skies to monitor militias, foreign troops were based in the national parks, highway signs were being marked with barcodes to guide these troops, and abandoned missile sites were being prepared to imprison patriots.

For example, a multiple-county militia's public information specialist, an individual who claimed that he was interviewed frequently by the media, summarized his conspiracy beliefs in the following way:

The New World Order government—one-world order. It's being driven by the United Nations. They want a one-world government. They want to eliminate countries, boundaries, and citizenship. They want to eliminate all nationality feelings and become a "world citizen." The news media, the rich, the elite have been promised that they will participate in this New World Order. That they will not be subject to the same things that the ordinary citizen will be, like the mark of the beast, the microchip system, the cashless society, socialized medicine, problems with obtaining food, getting a decent job, problems with maintaining a household, and putting your kids in school—the things that everybody has to work hard to obtain. These people have been told that they will have no problem with this. They will be the elite. They will be the anointed. They will be given preferential treatment. That's why they're doing it. They've been lied to and they believe it.

He also elaborated on the media's role in establishing this New World Order.

Let me read you a quote. Now see there's so many: I can back up everything I'm saying with documentation, but I would have to send you an envelope the size of Mount Rushmore to put all this stuff in. That's why I have people come into my shop so I can educate them and show them in black and white what's going on. Listen to this quote. David Rockefeller gave this quote in 1991 in Baden-Baden, Germany. I quote:
   "We are grateful to *The Washington Post*, *The New York Times*, *Time Magazine* and other great publications whose directors have attended our meetings and respected their promises of discretion for almost 40 years. It would have been impossible for us to develop our plan for the world if we had been subject to the bright lights of publicity during those years. But the world is now more sophisticated and prepared to march towards a world government. The supernatural sovereignty of an intellectual elite and world bankers is surely preferable to the national auto-determination practiced in past centuries."

This New World Order has been planned and ordained for almost a hundred years. Minimum. The Federal Reserve System will implement it. We were the last major country on earth to establish a national bank or central bank. Through that, they have taken the wealth of this country. They have bankrupted this country. And that's only the tip of the iceberg. There are so many ways they are doing this that it's impossible for one person to understand everything. This is an ongoing, educational type of deal. You have to understand where it's coming from. The news media, television, the radio, all the news media, all the print. They are basically behind this new-world-order government. They are a party to it and a part of it. And these are the strategies that they're using. The media. All the media. They are telling the American people what they want them to hear, not what they should know.

The Rockefeller quote was taken verbatim from Jack McLamb's *Operation Vampire Killer 2000*, and the specialist's other ideas were also clearly influenced by extremist literature.[23] The conspiracy literature circulating among militia groups provided comfort to those members of the militia movement who felt the most politically and economically disenfranchised. They could identify closely with conspiracy theories, but their willingness to try to explain these conspiracies to reporters only exacerbated the appearance of the irrationality of the entire militia movement.

Gun Policy

There was intense discussion of guns and gun control in the news media in the decade prior to the beginning of the militia movement. Gun violence is one social problem that moves frequently in and out of the public culture and is consistently one of the more contentious issues that politicians must negotiate. There is often a celebrated case that pushes the issue into the marketplace, and policy changes are often debated following one of these events. Legislation is passed, but it is often watered down because of the very successful efforts of the National Rifle Association and other gun lobby groups. Gun-control legislation consumed a significant portion of policymakers' discretionary time in the 1980s, and militia members were angry about it.

The concern about gun control is demonstrated in the following interview with two leaders of an East Coast militia. Most of the interview focused on guns and politicians' response to guns. One of the leaders said:

Here we have an assault weapons ban, and we have heard about how dangerous they are. I'm trying to get the statistics for this. But I think more people die from lightning strikes than are killed by assault weapons. Probably a lot more. You have a better chance of winning the state lottery than being killed by an assault weapon. It is only, like, four or five people have been killed by assault weapons. It is so small. More people slip in their bathtubs than what is caused by these weapons. Reporters will not report that.

Both individuals discussed how the media demonized guns by making them appear evil, and then the other leader said:

The thing about guns and firearm ownership: I started to learn to shoot when I was eight with adult supervision. In the '60s, everybody in my neighborhood had a gun. Not one person I ever grew up with went to prison on a firearms charge. There has to be some other factor involved other than the gun. Back in the 1960s, I was fifteen years old, we all had .22s and shotguns. Nobody ever committed a crime. It is not all the gun's fault. None of us ever committed a violation. Under today's laws, I would be in jail because it has become so restrictive. Basically, the people haven't changed, but the laws have changed. I think that is one of the festering problems we got. Half of the guns we owned in the 1960s are illegal.

Gun-control legislation was a consistent sore spot for people involved in the militia movement, so it is surprising that the Gun Policy frame was rarely provided in the media. Occasionally, if an arrest involving weapons was covered, there would be a discussion on whether an individual could possess a large cache of weapons. Also, the gun-policy debate was tangled into the antiterrorism legislation introduced after the Oklahoma City bombing because there was some concern by progun advocates about the attempts to track explosives, and these concerns slowed the passage of the legislation. In general, however, the gun debate was absent in articles about the militia movement. Militias were certainly not a good opportunity for progun claims-makers to champion their cause, and it was illustrated in the previous chapter how groups such as the National Rifle Association decided to distance themselves from militia leaders and militia groups. The fact that militias were being framed as terrorists increased the urgency for groups such as the NRA to be distant. Finally, reporters are familiar with the format used to present the gun-control debate. In general, a case is discussed that raises some policy-relevant concern, and then supporters and opposition figures are asked for their opinions about the issue. The gun-control format was not consistent with how militias were being described.

Racist

It is surprising that the Racist frame was not more frequently used in stories about militias, even though it represents fewer than 7 percent of the total frames captured in these stories. There was some variation, however, in relation to the types of claims-makers promoting the frame, and it was one of the more dominant frames provided by experts—a finding that makes sense considering the involvement of the Anti-Defamation League and the Southern Poverty Law Center as important sources in this category. This frame is the second most frequently promoted, behind the Threat—Growing Movement frame, when sources representing only these two organizations are examined. The militia groups that these organizations were first exposed to were racist, so they assumed that all militias were racist. Both organizations had discovered militias prior to the Oklahoma City bombing through their monitoring of hate groups, and promoting this frame is consistent with their broader mandate.

The Racist frame primarily appeared in two ways in stories about the militia movement. First, reporters portrayed militias as racist by association. One militia member said, "[The media] linked us with the neo-Nazis, the skinheads, the Klan, and every other reprehensible group you can think of." Other hate groups, such as the Ku Klux Klan, are well known, and images of the Klan coexist with many racist symbols. Often reporters substantiated their claims of racism in the militia movement by simply noting the influence of racist groups like the Klan, the Aryan Brotherhood, or neo-Nazis on militia ideology and the people involved in the movement. Second, a discussion of racism in the militia movement often resulted when a reporter described the background of some of the celebrity figures of the movement.[24] John Trochmann is probably the best-recognized individual celebrity active in the militia movement. Trochmann is certainly considered one of the founding members of the 1990s militia movement, and his Militia of Montana was a model that reporters could cite when describing the strategies and concerns of the movement. Trochmann was quoted in a large number of articles because he usually provided interesting, newsworthy quotations. He is also a highly photogenic example of someone from a stereotyped rural lifestyle. When reporters explored deeper his background and history, they ultimately discovered and reported his friendship with Randy Weaver, as well as his ties to the Aryan Nations, including being a speaker at the Aryan Nations Congress in 1990. Reporters noted racist ties when describing Bo Gritz, another celebrity figure connected with the militia movement. Gritz was David Duke's running mate in the 1988 presidential election and also had ties to Christian Identity leaders. One of my interviewees, who attended a preparedness expo just to meet Gritz, was disappointed, remarking, "He's one of the spokespersons for the militia and he's one of the most racist persons you could ever meet. And that's the biggest problem. And he just went off on how Jewish people are controlling the government and stuff—and well, I was just, like, this is crazy."

Dissenter claims-makers tried to refute the claims about the racist influences on the militia movement. In the interviews, militia members often cited as evidence they were not racist that many of their members and individuals in leadership positions were minorities. "Our unit commander is a Spanish fellow, a Mexican," said the leader of a militia group, "and the meetings start with a prayer and the Pledge of Allegiance." I also interviewed several African Americans involved in the movement who disputed the racist images being promoted in the news. One African-American militia leader said:

> When I got involved in this, I had all intentions of going out and exposing the white supremacists out there. I found out what is going on is just the opposite. There are some out there, don't get me wrong, but no more than a general peppering—between 10 and 15 percent. Which, if you go down any street in this country and talk to a hundred people, at least 10 to 15 percent are going to be racist.

Other interviewees talked about how a militia group was responsible for exposing the racist activities taking place at the "Good Ol' Boys Roundup," and one talked about how one of his major objectives was confronting racists:

> I mean, if you look at the thrust of my work over the last two or three years, you'll find that I'm more hated by the neo-Nazis than is Morris Dees. And the reason is because I'm up in their face more and I know who they are and I'm constantly, me and my boys is constantly messing with them in a variety of ways. And the reason we do that is to put them

off balance, to make them hesitant, because we don't want these people responsible for any more terrorism outbreaks.

Religious

The Religious frame was infrequently captured in news stories about the militia movement. Religion is certainly an important aspect of the broad antigovernment movement, and there is a significant amount of extremist literature offering religious interpretations of a variety of different issues. For example, Joel Dyer, when examining all antigovernment groups, argues that, "In today's antigovernment movement, religion and conspiracy are inseparable." He states that, "with the help of the antigovernment movement, all the ingredients of the rural crisis—global economics, mental depression, corporate monopolies, and poorly planned government policies—are being passed through a sieve of religion, and this will ultimately determine the direction and intensity of the heartland war. At first glance, religion appears to be the driving force of the people in the antigovernment movement."[25] I also found some racism couched in religious rhetoric when interviewing militia members. One militia member stated:

This is a Christian nation. It was founded by Christians, and in a democracy the only way that you can have a free nation is through having some form of God in your life, because there is nobody watching you. I'm a Christian: I read the Bible every day. I really, really put faith in God that whatever he wants to do is fine with me, and everything since I've been doing that has come out just fine. I see people in the news media that talk about right-wing Christians and Christian extremists and all these extremists. I'm going—if you really read the Bible, you know there is right from wrong and there is black and white. Other than that, what would possibly be extreme about Christianity?

America was started as a Christian country, and that's why we've excelled. I'll give you a perfect "for instance." Look at Africa. Two and a half times the size of America, with every natural resource that you could possibly want. Why are they so dirt poor? Talk about a miserable, Godforsaken place. Why do you think that is? I have the theory it's because the people over there were not Christian. The one Christian nation over there was South Africa. It was a prosperous place. They talk about apartheid, and they needed a fence around South Africa. Not to keep the blacks in, but to keep the blacks out. If apartheid was so bad, how come blacks from all over the continent were immigrating there? It was the only Christian country. When you think about it, look at all the natural resources, all the mineral wealth, all the natural timber, the water, everything that they've got there. It's probably ten times what we have here on the continent of North America. Yet they're in squalor, horrible conditions—and why? They don't believe in God.

However, such views were not common among people involved in the militia movement. Militias were generally not radical enough to attract individuals interested in religious and racist views of Christian Identity theology. Many such individuals visited militias and may have been active for a short time, but they generally moved to other antigovernment groups because the militias were not extreme enough. Members of militia groups were dedicated Christians, but they were much more likely to rationalize their beliefs using the constitution than the Bible.

No Threat

Although counterclaims were significantly less likely to be presented in newspaper articles about the militia movement, two frames—No Threat and Legitimate Concerns—were offered in defense of people in the militia movement. Of these two counterclaims, the No Threat claim received a fair amount of coverage in the news media. All of the deviant voice claims-makers, including celebrity voices, examples, and dissenters, promoted this frame. It represents approximately 19 percent of the frames promoted by celebrity figures, 21 percent of the frames promoted by examples, and nearly 40 percent of the frames promoted by dissenters.

The Threat image was so powerful that many people in the movement stopped going to meetings because they felt pressure from friends, family members, and co-workers who had been influenced by the dominant imagery. The public assumed that all people in the movement were equally dangerous because the only image they had of militia members was that promoted in the news. Many people quit because they could not endure the media's microscope. Many who remained in the movement attempted to prove that they were not a threat. Dissenter claims-makers felt particularly strongly about the need to promote this counterclaim, using various strategies. First, they stressed that they simply existed to protect citizens in case of an emergency situation, their gatherings were peaceful, and they wanted to work within the system. Many of the interviewees emphasized that they were not threatening, usually explaining that their strategies and tactics were defensive. One of the interviewees said, "The entire function of the militia is defensive in nature. If you have a militia organization that is operating on an offensive nature, they're not a militia organization. They are something else. If they have a true militia intent, they have to be defensive in nature. The militia does not prepare for offensive strikes: it is defend, defend, defend." Another militia member also emphasized the defensive nature of the militia movement,

> Our belief is that militias are the protector of the people. That is the message we really want to get out. That is the whole purpose behind the militias. Our objective is to assist the sheriff, another is to defend against invasion, insurrection, and three is to protect against tyranny. The militias are entirely a protective and defensive force. That point has never been brought out in the media. The media is totally ignorant of our heritage— not just the media, but the people themselves.

He described how they often invited reporters to their meetings so that they could prove that they were not a threat. "They are usually bored because we are talking about a law or legislation or constitutional issue and it is not very exciting. No guns, no fertilizer bombs—there is nothing here. We talk about issues and bad law."

Second, militia claims-makers also argued that the threat was simply exaggerated. They believed that politicians and experts needed to justify their response to militias and did so by emphasizing the dangers of the movement. One militia leader said: "Why do these people who were working at mills, or sitting behind a desk, or out farming, or out logging, suddenly turn terrorist? That doesn't happen in America. Where did the media get this from? Probably Morris Dees or the ADL." These claims-makers also argued that the media was responsible for demonizing militias. An interviewee remarked: "The media is going to emphasize whatever is sensational. They want to see guns and uniforms and people training and faces painted. The implication is that here is these dangerous people training in our backyards, and they are going to come after us. And that is really not the case."

Legitimate Concerns

The Legitimate Concerns counterclaim was infrequently captured in articles about the militia movement even though militias asked hard questions of the policy decisions made by the federal government and federal law-enforcement officials. Policy decisions have both intended and unintended consequences, and militias raised concerns about how the unintended ones seemed to disproportionately impact their ability to make a good living. For example, this frame captures the economic concerns of militia members. Not all citizens have shared equally in the benefits of a global economy. Militia members believed that they were excluded because of unfair policies restricting their ability to cash in on economic growth. One of the reporters interviewed discussed how these issues were simply ignored by the news media: "Most coverage ignored some of the economic root causes of why people are susceptible to these groups and these theories. A lot of the people who subscribe to these notions now lost their farms, their ranches, their jobs, and became vulnerable and susceptible to some of these conspiricists." When I asked why the media seemed to ignore the underlying economic issues, he replied: "It's too complicated. It's much easier for the mainstream press to portray antigovernment groups and individuals in these movements as bubbas—as camouflage-clad hicks who have nothing better to do than play soldier in the woods."

Reporters generally did not have the time or desire to fully explore the legitimacy of the concerns of people involved in the militia movement. Instead, reporters had two easily identifiable reasons for militia anger—Ruby Ridge and Waco. In over half of the policy stories published about the militia movement, government excess in those incidents was given as the primary motivation for joining a militia. The incidents may have pushed individuals to action, but militia members were angry long before Ruby Ridge and Waco, and reporters made no attempt to understand why.

It is interesting that Legitimate Concerns accounted for nearly 13 percent of the frames provided by individual sources, but for only 5 percent of the frames provided by celebrity militia figures, 6 percent of the frames provided by examples, and 7 percent of the frames provided by dissenters. This finding is particularly important when linked to the heavy emphasis of the Outsider claim in the Individual category. The media acknowledged that there were problems and issues that should concern the community but emphasized that these concerns should be addressed in an appropriate way. Other individuals were portrayed as sharing many of the concerns of militia members, but they were not spending their weekends in the woods preparing for Armageddon. The tactics used by militias were thought to be inappropriate. Consider the following excerpts from a newspaper article titled, "Grass-Roots Rage: Below the Surface: Alienation Simmers in Corner of Mid-America."[26] Dale Russakoff interviews a large number of citizens, property owners, and business owners from Meadville, Pennsylvania. He describes Meadville as "no hotbed of anti-government extremism. In fact, the mindsets forming here are important largely because this community is so ordinary, a stand-in for countless towns across the nation's vast, still rural heartland." He describes how "Meadville inhabits a vast political zone located between the November election and the April bombing, a zone where violence against innocents is abhorrent, but where anger and alienation run much deeper than even last fall's dramatic election results revealed. If militias seem forbidding to most people here, the sentiments behind them are felt by many in the mainstream." The reporter quoted a state senator as saying, "These are good, honest, hardworking people who would be the first to volunteer if there was an external threat to our country . . . They are what you'd call red-blooded Americans." The reporter interviewed Daniel Leech, a sixty-eight-year-old business owner, who remarked of militias: "I don't want anything to do with them, but I think I understand their attitude. . . . If you ran a small business, you'd understand too. People are being squeezed more and more all the time." Leech apparently invited other business owners to talk with the reporter because they were much more "radical." Those people "said running businesses had radicalized them because regulations and taxes make it so hard to make money. Asked why they are different from Leech, a businessmen who at 68 still believes in working within the system, they said Leech's generation benefited for years from tax loopholes that now are closed." They then described their feelings about the Oklahoma City Bombing: "My reaction was: It's a damned good start. It's about time somebody took things into their own hands. If we think we'll take control of our own destinies without some bloodshed, that's pretty naïve thinking on our part. There's no peaceful solution to this problem. There are too many people living unfairly off the system. Every day I go to work to support people on welfare. The American dream they sold us was the American lie: they're waiting there to take it all away." Another man then responded: "he believed the federal government blew up its own building to create a crisis and suspend individual freedoms. He said he had seen right-wing videotapes warning of a New World Order in which every nation would cede sovereignty to the United Nations, and believed much of it." The man also said, "I'd just as soon go down the middle of the road myself," he said, "but to combat radicals like our government—the IRS, the EPA, OSHA, who come in our company like the Gestapo, picking on us because we generate money—you've got to have radicals like militias."

CONCLUSION

Although there was a heavy presence of militia members in constructing stories about the militia movement, these sources appear to have been employed because they generally confirmed the dominant frames being used by the news media. The media framed militias as being outsiders threatening to mainstream society. These frames worked well in the description of the movement because they have a long cultural history and the public identified closely with them. By being accessible to reporters, the militia members interviewed inadvertently confirmed that they were threatening, irrational, committed, and paranoid. Militia sources did promote promilitia frames more frequently than other sources, but they also frequently confirmed the Threat, Conspiracy, and Outsider frames.

Confirming the Threat

F or three days in April and three in October, gun enthusiasts
from across the country meet outside Fort Knox, Kentucky, to
attend the Knob Creek Machine Gun Shoot. I first heard of this
event from a militia member who described it in the following way:

> There are two outfits that hold it, the National Machine Gun Association,
> and there is some other automatic weapons association or something. It's
> a big, humongous militia rendezvous. There's thousands of people out
> there camping out and everything. And of course everybody brings wives
> or girlfriends and families, and it's just a big carnival. Everybody's wear-
> ing camouflage and packing automatic weapons and stuff like that. It's
> kind of like Woodstock with camouflage.

The gun enthusiasts, militia members, and others in attendance buy,
sell, and trade guns at this event, but the real attraction is that it provides the opportunity to shoot or see others shoot a wide variety of
machine guns and other weapons, including UZIs, AK47s, MAC10s,
M16s, cannons, and flamethrowers. "Everything in there is probably
from the Revolutionary War and up," said the same militia member.

> If you need a part for your military weapon of any kind, it's there. You
> need a barrel for your M1 carbine, they've got them out there. You need
> MREs, they've got them. You need ammunition, they've got it. You have

to wear earplugs, because they have every gun imaginable, from muzzle-loading Civil War cannons all the way up to Vulcan twenty-millimeter Gatling guns. It's a big valley and it's about 350 yards long, and they'll do stuff like put old cars or old refrigerators out there and they'll just decimate them with automatic weapons fire—especially from the .50 caliber and the .30 caliber machines guns and stuff like that. It's just a hoot.

Many militia groups attend this event to share their love for guns, but they also use it as an opportunity to discuss the strategies, concerns, philosophy, and tactics of the militia movement.

I attended the Machine Gun Shoot to make additional contacts and get a sense of how tightly groups involved in the militia movement were connected. Early media reports and several interviewees had stressed how militia groups were moving towards a national umbrella structure and were closely connected by modern technologies. Tom Kenworthy and George Lardner, in a *Washington Post* article that gave an overview of the militia movement, claimed that "the militias' use of computers, faxes and short-wave radios has given them the power to mobilize quickly in the face of even minor perceived threats."[1] One of the militia members I interviewed described a nationwide network of militia groups linked closely by the World Wide Web, fax machines, and other technologies.

Nothing, absolutely nothing can happen in this country that the militia doesn't find out about and flood the airwaves, the Internet, the phone lines, the faxes, beepers, cellular phones, two-meter band radio, short-wave—we flood the entire country with the information. Not a single thing escapes our knowledge. Not a single thing. If a helicopter takes off in California and flies over a patriot's house, we learn about it. If there's overt action, we know about it. If there's covert action, we find out about it. There's a lot of good people in the military, there's a lot of good people in the government, the FBI, the ATF, the IRS, there's a lot of good people that tell us what's going on. We have sources of information that are infinite.

The Machine Gun Shoot provided me the best opportunity to test whether the media and militia claims about technological connections translated into strategic and ideological cohesiveness.

It certainly became clear that informal connections between some groups are very strong. Several of the militia members I talked to had been attending twice a year for several years, and they used time away from the range to mingle with others in attendance and rekindle past friendships. Theories, ideas, and information were exchanged around campfires and at the dinner table, then individuals and groups would use technologies to sustain the relationships made at this event. One militia leader discussed how his group was able to build relationships at Knob Creek. He said, "It [Knob Creek] allows you to share information and to actually know that there are people out there that think the same way you do." But several attempts to formalize these connections under a national umbrella organization have been unsuccessful. At the Machine Gun Shoot in April 1998, the United States Theatre Command (USTC), a group based in Michigan, did attempt to unify the militia movement. They scheduled a meeting at a town hall in Shepardsville, Kentucky, relatively close to the shooting range, and sent out notices and invitations prior to the April gathering. I spoke with one of the leaders of USTC on the morning of this meeting, and he was clearly hopeful that at the end of the day "we will represent the largest national alliance of militias in the country." I asked him if I could sit in on the meeting, and he told me it would be up to the people who attended. I was in the audience and watched as about 200 militia members trickled into the meeting hall. I was sitting at a table with a group that was clearly upset about the meeting because they thought it was going to be a waste of time and they wanted to be back at the shooting range. Any hope that the USTC would be a unifying organization was quickly dashed when one of its leaders, whom some suspected of being a federal informant, got into a fight with the leader of another group.

When others separated the two men, the meeting was brought to order and the Pledge of Allegiance was recited. Several militia leaders asked whether the reporters in the audience could stay for the meeting. The crowd was strongly opposed. It was 1998, and most militias were fed up with media attention on their activities, expecting that any news coverage would simply add to the demonization of the movement. The reporters were therefore told to leave. Researchers were not held in any higher esteem, so I was also asked to leave after the USTC leader introduced me to the audience. But the reporters and I did not miss much. As I was talking to a reporter outside the meeting hall, a large group of militia members left the meeting and congregated outside. We joined the discussion and found out that the meeting was not going very well and there was a lot of dissension between groups. It was clear that the

USTC did not have the power to unify the movement and that the ideological differences between groups presented insurmountable obstacles.

Militia members from Indiana and Kentucky and I watched as a steady stream of people exited. We were joined by a celebrity who said that such a nationwide organization was not a good idea and did not make any sense in the first place. He suggested that groups needed to keep to themselves and work together in small, leaderless cells. He described how such a structure would protect against informants and agent provocateurs, and reminded us of what happened to the Arizona Vipers, the West Virginia Mountaineer Militia, and the Washington State Militia. After he left, others dispersed and headed back to the shooting range. I then joined a conversation between a group of militia members and a reporter from a national magazine. As we were talking in a parking lot, there was a car accident about 250 yards away from where we were standing. Militia members closest to the accident immediately ran to the scene and acted as first responders. Two others retrieved first-aid kits from the trunks of their cars, some called for emergency assistance, and some started to direct traffic away from the crash scene. It was an impressive response, and the situation was quickly under control. They comforted the victims of the crash and stayed until paramedics and police were at the scene. When the commotion was over, I headed back to the parking lot of the meeting hall, where the discussion had shifted to the status of the people involved in the accident. I asked the reporter from the national magazine whether he was going to cover the militia's response to the car crash. He had not even considered it until I mentioned it to him. He said that he was not in Kentucky to cover car crashes but was sent to evaluate the militia movement. He then said he was heading back to the shooting range because that was where he had hoped to find his story. The media's coverage of militias following the Oklahoma City bombing had created and confirmed a clear consensus about the militia movement. Militia members were not like the rest of mainstream society: their ideas, strategies, and lifestyle were marginalized and demonic. This reporter was searching for the opportunity to reproduce the frames that had dominated descriptions of militias for over three years, frames that were frequently legitimized by the many ceremonies invoked in response to celebrated cases.

SUSTAINING THE THREAT

Past research has focused on how and why certain social problems enter the social-problems marketplace, but less attention has been paid to understanding how long problems stay competitive and explaining why concern about a social problem disappears. Once the militia movement entered the social-problems marketplace, it stayed competitive for a long time because it provided an excellent opportunity to reaffirm the processes used by core social-control institutions to respond to society's greatest threats—and the militias' actions were certainly seen as threats. To justify being involved in the movement, militias had embraced some of the United States' most sacred symbols. They claimed they were patriots, comparing themselves to the founding fathers and some of history's other significant heroes. Militia members embraced the Constitution and the Bill of Rights, and sometimes shared their passion eloquently in public forums about their vision of the fight for freedom. "Yes, I am a patriot. I question my government's means, methods, and motives," said one militia leader, "and I intend to question them in public." Another militia member remarked, "We stand up in public and proclaim the Constitution and the Bill of Rights as our law, as our forefathers laid down for us, and they've [government officials] just totally ignored it. And if you're familiar with what's going on in the country, you know it's not just me saying this: this is spread clear across this nation." Some people in the movement have refused to accept the legitimacy of government and its restrictions, withholding taxes or ignoring the restrictions on gun ownership, driving without a license and license plates, and questioning the legal rights of the government to intervene in any aspect of its citizens' lives. Thus, it was particularly important for social-control institutions to intervene on behalf of mainstream society. Such challenges to the fundamental processes of a democracy made it urgent to respond to militias, and social-control representatives had access to public forums in which they could respond. Once militias were perceived as threatening, their concerns about the current state of government and their interpretations of history were effectively defused.

Militias also provided a good opportunity to reaffirm the role of social-control institutions because there was little conflict about these groups. If a problem produces conflict among people who have access to the arenas in which social problems are constructed, the process of demonization will be slow and less effective. Often success in sustaining interest in a social problem depends not on the realities of a public threat, but on a situation creating newsworthy demons that can be exploited for a large array of benefits. A problem becomes increasingly significant if the need for a response is consistent with collective concerns and the ideological battlefield is clearly marked. The existence of clear boundaries produces tremendous cultural capital and momentum for change. If the battlefield is not clearly marked, however, then resistance among claims-makers is greater, stifling change and progress.

The instability of the social-problems marketplace creates an opportunity to invoke similar patterns of response to very different social problems. The nature of the perceived threat to society is constantly changing, but the collective response to the highlighted threat follows a familiar pattern, invoking similar ritual ceremonies. Formal ceremonies, such as political hearings, criminal trials, dedications, memorials, support rallies, and vigils, are not just news events providing opportunities for media organizations to publish stories consistent with a running theme: they are mechanisms of legitimacy used to confirm the nature of the threat and to create and validate responses. Although a considerable quantity of public debate does occur, involving many different parties with opposing viewpoints, the individuals locked in battle do not question the legitimacy of the process used to respond to social problems but struggle over semantics and support responses that are always consistent with existing political and bureaucratic preferences. Thus, there is a control valve inherent in the public discussion of social problems that limits the scope of definition and response. The structure of public debate ensures that the social problems given serious consideration will eventually be defined and controlled by standard agencies and responded to in a way preferred by those agencies. Since the processes used are recognizable and respected, the public is willing to accept the results without question.

The ritual ceremonies initiated in response to celebrated cases both confirm and create group solidarity as well as confirm existing structures, authoritative positions, and existing patterns used to process deviants in society. Research by several scholars supports these conclusions. The important work of Katherine Bell on ritual practices concludes that they make beliefs and ideals "real" and provide a "collective confidence in the well-being of society." Daniel Dayan and Elihu Katz argue that ritual ceremonies celebrate the "rules of the game"—"the rules by which the system is governed, and in terms of which society reflects upon and evaluates itself." Such rules constrain the nature of the conflict, for it is within the boundaries constructed by these ceremonies that appropriate solutions will be searched for and found. Hans-Peter Muller argues that "we can infer from Durkheim's writings that a crisis of legitimacy always points to an underlying moral or value crisis and that this crisis is usually due to the gap between existing values and the social structure of society. What follows is obvious—this gap can be closed only by institutional reforms which can be vehicles for value realization; without such value reform, the social identity of a society as well as the social integration of its members into society will be threatened."[2]

Celebrated cases also contribute to the creation of group solidarity by adjusting the boundaries of society. Such events are unique in their ability to produce a common ground of beliefs among the diverse public. The public sets aside its differences because of the heightened state of panic caused by the event. One of the common denominators among the diverse groups is the belief in the authority of the rituals used to process deviants, and thus those rituals are effective mechanisms for showing that the targeted group is in conflict with the rest of society.

The most important public social-control ceremony in modern society is the criminal trial, which is formal and dramatic—unlike any other stage of the criminal-justice process. The ritualization of the trial, including the confluence of symbols, customs, and traditions associated with it, magnifies its power. Each trial ceremony follows specific formats and procedures, which help justify any decision made and the decision-making process itself. The trial is significant because of the public's role as the jury and the support of the decision by symbols and traditions. The construction and aesthetics of courthouses symbolize power, truth, and authority. The decor of a courtroom typically includes the great seal of the United States, the flag, and a representation of the scales of justice. The authority and objectivity of judges is represented by their presiding at a bench above and removed from the proceedings. The process is standardized, and deviation from the standards is quickly punished. The central point is that the institutionalized symbols, customs, traditions, and processes of these ceremonies are never in dispute but are assumed to represent fairness, equality, and justice. Any final outcome is therefore assumed to be just.

It is important to note that the trial is the only stage in the entire criminal justice process in which the public plays a direct role in the outcome by rendering a verdict. A trial is essentially a morality play, with forces of good attempting to bring to justice a citizen breaking established norms. Although the media and crime-control organizations play a significant role in determining which individuals and groups are defined as deviant, the definitional processes are given symbolic justification and reaffirmation through court processing. If the media portray individuals or groups as deviant, but they are later exonerated at trial, then the public is likely to be confused and disturbed by that portrayal. Trials are public events that provide perhaps the clearest statement of preferred norms and behaviors, so it is very important that trial decisions be perceived as fair and credible.[3] Decisions about offender processing and media presentation must be biased towards conviction for news organizations and other social-control organizations to maintain legitimacy. When the trial ceremony confirms what the media have already established and the public denounces the behavior as unacceptable, then the crisis of moral concern has passed and important new boundaries are legitimated.

This chapter examines several ceremonial processes that helped shape the view that militia members should be considered a priority threat. Since there was little specific knowledge of militias when media coverage of them burgeoned in 1995, the ceremonies invoked in response worked in combination with media constructions to create new community boundaries. Militias were first defined in the media as threatening outsiders, and ceremonies such as congressional hearings and high-profile trials stabilized that image. This chapter examines some of the key designation and reaffirmation ceremonies that created and solidified the public's understanding of militias. First, it examines the congressional hearings that were held in the months following the Oklahoma City bombing, emphasizing the investigation of the militia movement. Second, although the media covered a large number of high-profile cases involving militia members, the public trial of Willie Ray Lampley and his co-conspirators in Oklahoma and the trial of the Oklahoma City bomber were key boundary-defining ceremonies.

DESIGNATION CEREMONIES

The news media can ignite concern about a social problem through its sensational coverage of certain events. An important ingredient of the media's power as a social-control institution is its ability to begin constructing an event immediately after it occurs. Once an event is publicly known, the media have the capacity to be at the scene quickly, and twenty-four-hour news channels, the Internet, and wire services allow reports to circulate instantaneously. Important representatives of organizations who respond to events tailor their reactions to the formats preferred by the media. Moreover, all immediate reactions have to be filtered through the media, allowing their formats and interpretations to be the first public impressions of the event. One of the most powerful images of the Oklahoma City bombing was what remained of the Murrah building after the explosion. Pieces of wire, metal, and steel could be seen dangling in front of the corridors and cavities in what was left of the standing structure, and the mountain of concrete and debris remaining at the base of the building was an enduring symbol of the destruction. The media's social-control role is also heightened by its ability to conduct "research" into a newly discovered social problem—relying on existing data, sources, and archival materials. Its findings are presented as the result of an "investigation," a term that lends credibility to the results.

The beginning stages of the criminal justice system, including the investigation, arrest, and pretrial hearings, shape the continuing coverage of the event. These stages are far less significant than the criminal trial, however, because they are short, generally inaccessible, and inconclusive. Trials are dramatic and accessible. They also have a revered status in the culture as the vehicle for the appropriate exploration for truth. The problem is that cases come to trial slowly. The criminal justice system moves along at a snail's pace, especially when the case is high profile and a defendant has or is provided with the resources to take full advantage of pretrial hearing opportunities. The public is frustrated by the pace of justice, but their concerns about trial delays are diminished by the other formal social-control ceremonies that fill the time gap, including political events such as congressional hearings and formal and informal congressional investigations.

Political hearings provide a formal structure that can be initiated almost immediately in response to an issue that is causing significant concern. The U.S. Senate, for example, took less than ten days to hold terrorism hearings after the Oklahoma bombing. Such hearings are structured to control the nature and direction of public discussion about a concern. They are perceived as being like a trial; witnesses are sworn in before they testify, cross-examination occurs, and the verdict is usually rendered as a series of recommendations about new legislation. The congressional inquiries provoked by the Oklahoma bombing focused on defining the nature of the problem and proposing appropriate solutions. Furthermore, such hearings provide a platform for specific institutions to promote their preferences because they are called on as experts. Their testimony is considered "research evidence." Legislators, of course, have a significant impact on the direction that such hearings take because they convene the hearings, invite participants to testify, present testimony, and cross-examine witnesses. Congressional hearings involving crime control are also heavily influenced by law-enforcement officers, prosecutors, and other experts frequently called upon to provide their vision of the threat being explored. These hearings then determine what types of follow-up are necessary to better understand the nature of a threat or respond directly to that threat. Legislation and resources flow from or are supported in these hearings, and such immediate "action" gives the impression that the situation is under control.

Although numerous congressional hearings were held in response to this celebrated case, the discussion focuses on the following: "Terrorism in the United States: The Nature and Extent of the Threat and Possible Legislative Responses"; "The Militia Movement in the United States"; and the "Nature and Threat of Violent Anti-Government Groups in America." In addition, I briefly examine the informal hearings that were conducted about the militia movement by the Democratic Leadership in the House of Representatives in July 1995. These hearings were the key ceremonies that helped structure the political response to domestic terrorists and militia groups. They also helped solidify the images of militias being promoted in the news media.[4]

"TERRORISM IN THE UNITED STATES"

In reaction to the bombing, President Bill Clinton used the media to offer his and the country's support to the people of Oklahoma, but he also exploited it as a political opportunity. A few days after the bombing, Clinton sent his antiterrorism bill to Congress—a bill that would impact how law enforcement investigated foreign and domestic terrorist groups. On April 23, he announced his plan on the CBS news show *60 Minutes*. The plan emphasized two general types of response: providing additional resources to monitor terrorist groups and limiting individual rights. He called for more legislation, money, and personnel so that law enforcement could more effectively monitor and infiltrate suspected terrorist groups. He wanted to hire 1,000 new agents and spend over 1 billion dollars over a five-year period to fight terrorism. He proposed creating an FBI counterterrorism center to enhance law enforcement's intelligence-gathering capacity and to increase the federal government's jurisdiction over international terrorist attacks occurring in the United States so as to make it easier to deport alien terrorists. He also proposed increasing law enforcement's access to the financial reports of suspected terrorists and enhancing its ability to use electronic surveillance techniques.

The first day of terrorism hearings happened a few days later before the Judiciary Committee of the Senate. These hearings show how media coverage of a celebrated case immediately opens a "window of opportunity" for policymakers to exert their presence and authority on an issue.[5] They also show how the committee setting provides those with access the opportunity to push specific meanings and understandings of an issue as well as to advocate for solutions that support those understandings. The opening statement by Senator Orrin Hatch, chairman of the committee, is a good example of how such ceremonies allow those with access to shape political understandings of events. His statement focused on three issues. First, he pointed to the bombing as the event that ignited the need for such hearings, calling it "tragic beyond belief," and stating that the people who committed it were not Americans, whereas the people "working to bring order to the chaos in Oklahoma" and "share the same moral outrage" were true Americans. The link between the Oklahoma tragedy and the need for legislation was reinforced by every person who testified and was particularly emphasized by the involvement of the two Oklahoma senators as witnesses. Second, Hatch responded to the criticisms of the FBI by commending it for its work on the case and remarking that the "Bureau is as impressive as it has ever been." He also said that Louis Freeh, the director of the FBI, was the "best we have ever had." Freeh testified on behalf of the FBI at the hearing, discussing the hard work and successes of the Oklahoma City investigation. He also emphasized the need to expand the intelligence-gathering capacity of the FBI and supported various provisions of the legislation being considered, including the creation of the counterterrorism center, the allocation of resources to pay for better technology and more agents, sources, and informants, and the restriction of obstacles to investigating of terrorist groups. Third, Hatch called terrorism one of the greatest evils of our age. He then briefly described how, although the battles to pass legislation to fight terrorism had been going on for years, the leaders of the Democratic and Republican parties and the president needed to work together to pass antiterrorism legislation as quickly as possible. Jamie Gorelick, Department of Justice deputy attorney general, was one of the first people to testify and she pushed the bill supported by Clinton, outlining its major provisions.[6]

The final panel of experts, consisting of Morris Dees, Steve Emerson, Brian Jenkins, and Robert Kupperman, testified only briefly about what should be done about terrorism, concentrating on the nature of the terrorist threat in the United States. They tried to define the significance of the problem by discussing which groups needed to be more closely watched and monitored. Most panel members, in describing what they saw as the most significant terrorist threats, expressed concern about the thriving militia movement. Dees, director of the Southern Poverty Law Center, traced the roots of the 1990s militia movement to the activities of the Order, a violent paramilitary group that made headlines in the 1980s. He provided numerous examples of known criminal activity by militia members as anecdotal evidence of the looming threat. Dees reiterated SPLC's position on the heavy overlap between militia and white supremacist organizations, and then urged the senators to take a closer look at the violent activities of militias. Emerson, who is an expert on international terrorism, focused primarily on Middle Eastern threats to national security, but he also made the following remark about militias: "because of this new threat now in the United States from Oklahoma or other based extremist militias . . . the United States has to take a more proactive approach towards [extremist militias]."[7] Jenkins, a representative of an international intelligence and security agency, stressed that the militia threat was large and growing, and he discussed the existence of a powerful underground network of groups, linked by modern technologies, with a willingness to use violence against the government. Kupperman, the final panelist, was from the Center for Strategic and International Studies. Although he did not focus on militias per se, he stressed that we should be equally concerned about foreign and domestic terrorism.

Multiple legislative proposals on terrorism were introduced. What was eventually passed went through rounds of rigorous compromise, but it is interesting that the focus of media coverage was on the president's legislative package. Moreover, although the legislation had far-reaching implications and was directed at a broad range of targets, the media focused on what the final group of panelists had stressed—the need for legislation to effectively respond to militia groups.[8] The media described militias as "vigilante groups" and discussed how the needed legislation would "open militias to U.S. surveillance" and "give tools to target militias." Most of the media coverage supported the legislation, claiming that law enforcement was limited in its ability to track groups that were planning significant harm. The legislation was presented as providing the tools to overcome these limitations. The link between militias and the legislation sent to Congress by the president following the bombing impressed upon the public the idea that militias were indeed terrorists and needed to be more closely monitored because they were a significant threat. This theme was more closely examined in the Senate only weeks later.

"THE MILITIA MOVEMENT IN THE UNITED STATES"

Public debate about domestic terrorism focused almost solely on militias in the few months after the bombing. Media coverage strongly promoted this connection, and the activities of politicians and experts solidified it. The early concerns generated about militias created enough momentum to encourage additional congressional inquiry. In June 1995, less than two months after the bombing, the Senate Subcommittee on Terrorism, Technology, and Government Information held hearings on the militia movement.[9] The objectives of this hearing were to examine the scope of the militia movement, the nature of militia activities, the reasons for their existence, and the extent to which they posed a threat to citizens. But this hearing barely scratched the surface of any of these issues. Rather, it simply was another opportunity to confirm the dominant ways that militias were defined in the news media. It also strengthened the link between militias and McVeigh because almost all the witnesses made references to the Oklahoma bombing.

Politicians and a panel of law-enforcement officials who testified promoted an image of militia members as dangerous outsiders and part of a growing movement. Three states tightly tied to the discussion of militias from the outset were Michigan, Montana, and Arizona; and senators from both Michigan and Montana as well as law-enforcement officials from Montana and Arizona testified, and their presence confirmed reports that these states were core areas of militia activity. Both parties testified about the militia's "growing power," a "growing concern" for militia activity, and "the substantial number" of people involved in the movement. They also made claims about the "proliferation of militias," providing statistical estimates on the size of the movement that ranged from 224 active militias in 39 states, to groups in 40 states, and from 100,000 to several million members.[10]

Media reports supported the Outsider frame, quoting Arlen Specter as saying: "What I want to do is, I want to hear all your ideas, because I want your ideas compared to mine, and I want to let the American public judge whether you're right or I'm right," and when "more people hear what you say, the ranks of the militia will be reduced."[11] Militia members were also described as outsiders in the hearing testimony, as witnesses emphasized the "extreme positions of some militia members" and their "extreme rhetoric," claiming that they promoted far-reaching conspiracy theories. Militia members were dangerous in that they were "spreading a gospel of hate," carried a "deep strain of racism," had an "arsenal of weaponry," threatened people routinely, and were part of "an organized effort against law-enforcement officials." The significance of the militia threat was substantiated by anecdotal examples of events in Minnesota, Arizona, Michigan, Montana, and West Virginia. For example, three different witnesses discussed an incident in which three militia members had recently been arrested in Michigan for various offenses. Law-enforcement officials had stopped their car as the militia members were gathering intelligence about target locations such as police departments and communication centers. The testimony emphasized that they had a large cache of weapons and military gear, including AK-47s, armor-piercing bullets, gas masks, night vision goggles, and bayonets. Michigan senator Carl Levin, one of the witnesses who described this incident, discussed how the men skipped bail after being arrested but other camouflage-clad members of the Michigan Militia showed up to threaten the court and law-enforcement officials.[12]

The most surprising feature of this hearing was that militia members themselves appeared to testify on behalf of their movement. The final panel of witnesses consisted of some of the most celebrated militia figures: John Trochmann and Bob Fletcher of the Militia of Montana; Ken Adams and Norm Olson of the Michigan Militia; and J. J. Johnson of the Ohio Unorganized Militia. Allowing the targets of specific legislative efforts to defend their position is extremely rare, although not unprecedented.[13] Most hearings are dominated by representatives with a stake in how a problem is defined and an interest in recommending how it should be fixed—usually representatives of social-control organizations, experts, and other institutionally affiliated claims-makers. In these hearings, the militia figures did little to challenge the dominant frames being promoted in the news media. Instead, their testimony and their verbal banter with senators during the question-and-answer period served only to isolate further the militia from the mainstream. It appeared that these figures had been invited to the hearings because they had a large following and were "the leaders" of the militia movement. Their views, described extensively in the media following the hearing, were therefore presented as those of the entire movement. The ceremonial atmosphere of the hearings gave additional credibility to the images that they themselves were promoting.

The Democratic leadership from the House of Representatives convened informal hearings about the militia movement only a couple of weeks after the Senate hearings. The Democrats claimed that they called the hearings because of the limitations of the Senate's investigation. In Charles Schumer's opinion, "the hearing on the militia movement [had] quickly disintegrated into a soapbox for the wacky right, lending legitimacy and exposure to the militia movement generally." Militia members were not invited to participate in the new hearings. Witnesses instead told "their tales of threats, intimidation, and terror at the hands of armed militias." Several witnesses testified as victims of violence and intimidation, and an expert from the Anti-Defamation League provided a statistical overview of the size of the movement. Other witnesses said that citizens were becoming less willing to serve as public officials because of threats of violence, and others warned that the tactics of militia groups were seeping into the mainstream.[14] The criticisms directed at the Senate for allowing militia members to testify were off the mark. Ironically, both hearings focused public thinking on the fringe elements in the militia movement and its most dangerous aspects. Moreover, an examination of the news coverage of the Senate hearings involving militia members shows that the most extreme positions that had been promoted about the militia movement were confirmed, solidifying the public's belief that all militias were to be feared and that it was necessary to support legislation to fight them.

The involvement of the militia celebrity figures was the main reason why the Senate hearings were newsworthy and received significantly more coverage than any other hearings on terrorism or extremism. The importance of this event was also heightened because current technology permitted direct mass access to the nationally televised event. In general, congressional hearings receive little attention in the news. National newspapers, such as the *New York Times*, the *Washington Post*, and *USA Today*, have institutionalized routines to include coverage of congressional hearing activity, but most large city newspapers ignore such events. The senate militia hearings, however, were covered in most major city newspapers because of the involvement of celebrity figures. The *Atlanta Journal and Constitution*, the *Chicago Sun-Times*, the *Boston Herald*, the *New York Daily News*, the *Cleveland Plain Dealer*, the *St. Louis Post Dispatch*, the *Phoenix Gazette*, the *Denver Rocky Mountain News*, and the *Tampa Tribune* are just a few of the newspapers that provided coverage of the hearings.

The celebrity figures who testified on behalf of the militia movement were inherently newsworthy. Not only had these five individuals become the most identifiable members of the movement because of their aggressive involvement in construction activities after the bombing, but also their testimony created good media drama. It is significant that the media coverage of the hearings emphasized the sensational testimony of Trochmann, Olson, and Fletcher. It virtually ignored that of Adams and Johnson, who were uncontroversial, emphasizing that politicians needed to examine the nature of the concerns that were driving people to the militia. They also stressed that they would expose anybody involved in the movement who posed a threat to citizens or law enforcement. Johnson described how militia members were like mainstream society, and he testified that the movement was not just made up of groups of angry white males, thereby contradicting the image that militias were racist thugs.

The views of Trochmann, Olson, and Fletcher were accentuated in news coverage because their testimony was consistent with the most extreme images presented about the militia movement. Fletcher, who also appeared on *Good Morning America* on the day of the hearings, testified that there were two bombs that exploded in Oklahoma City and said other suspects were still at large. Most emphasized in the media was his belief that the government had the ability to control the weather using a device to further the interests of the New World Order: "Yes, sir, that is my belief, as bizarre as that sounds. If somebody had told me that that equipment even existed ten years ago, I would have thought they were nuts, sir; . . . And if you think that eighty-five tornadoes take place in the middle of our growing area by simultaneous accident, I am sorry." Trochmann tried to convince the Senate panel that the militia represents the views of a majority of society. He called the movement a "great neighborhood watch" and described it as watching out for problems: "when we encounter what we perceive as threats to a peaceful society, we do something about it." Asked if there is a time when people should take the law into their own hands, Trochmann responded, "When someone comes to destroy my family, I won't have a choice. If that were ever to happen, I would defend to the last drop of blood."[15] Dennis Roddy used Trochmann's appearance at the hearings as an opportunity to do a feature story on the leader of the Militia of Montana for the *Pittsburgh Post-Gazette*. Roddy wrote that Trochmann appeared to get increasingly angry at questions posed by the senators and pondered whether Trochmann "conceal[ed his] true colors." Roddy also spent a significant amount of time probing into Trochmann's ties to the Aryan Nations (which he denied having during his testimony).[16]

Olson's testimony was highlighted in most of the media coverage of the hearings because it confirmed the perceived threat and outsider status of militias. He was the only panelist to appear in camouflage, and the media emphasized this paramilitary attire. Olson was also quoted heavily because he said things such as the "government intrudes far too much in citizens' lives," "the Federal Government itself is the child of the armed citizen," "we the people are the parent of the child we call government," and "the Federal Government needs a good spanking to make it behave."[17] John Mintz, covering the hearing for the *Washington Post*, emphasized that militia members had to testify in the huge room under the colossal seal of the Senate, that Olson appeared in fatigues, and that there was hostility between the senators and the militia members. He characterized the hearings as a "war of words," using the following prolonged verbal exchange between Senator Arlen Specter and Olson as illustrative of the tension.

> Displaying skills from his time as Philadelphia's district attorney, Specter repeatedly asked Norman Olson, former head of a large Michigan militia, about statements to reporters that he could "understand" a justification for bombing the Oklahoma City federal building on April 19. "I understand the dynamic of retribution, sir . . . when justice is removed from the equation," replied Olson, wearing his Michigan militia military fatigues with a "commander" shoulder patch. His voice rising in anger, Olson said, "You're trying to make us out to be something we're not. We're opposed to racism and hatred. We stand against corruption. Many of us are coming to the conclusion you represent corruption and tyranny. . . . There is intelligent life west of the Alleghenies. . . . You're wasting precious time." "I don't take lightly your comment that I represent corruption," said Specter, who demanded proof of the claim—but received none.[18]

Olson also put forward his theory about who was responsible for the Oklahoma City bombing and charged that there had been a cover-up of the conspiracy behind the bombing. He testified that "the Central Intelligence Agency is probably the grandest conspirator behind all of this Government, and . . . perhaps the puppeteer strings of the CIA reach even into the . . . Senate of the United States of America"[19]

Militia members were irritated by the results of the hearings, the people chosen to represent the movement, and the way the media covered the event. One militia member told me that he really did not blame the public for fearing the militia because it was a belief promoted in the news media. "They think," he said, that people "like Norm Olson represent the majority . . . in the movement." This interviewee discussed how he was initially excited about the prospect of having militia members testify at the hearings because he thought it would be an opportunity to open a dialogue to combat what was being presented in the press about militias. Having seen who was asked to testify and what they said, he dubbed the proceeding the "farce that was the militia hearings." He found them "kind of funny in a tragic sort of way. We're watching this thing, and here's Normy talking about the Japanese blowing up Oklahoma City. And then there's the other guy, Fletcher from Militia of Montana, talking about the weather machine. And everybody is groaning and throwing stuff at the television and saying, 'Ah, man—do you believe that?'"

"Nature and Threat of Violent Anti-Government Groups in America"

During the terrorism hearings in April 1995, Senator Bob Dole testified, "Partisan politics will also stop at the evil's edge in our war against terrorism. . . . We also need to demonstrate to the American people that we are committed to a serious anti-terrorist blueprint." His public promise of bipartisan cooperation and quick action dissolved almost immediately. The scars of Oklahoma were not deep enough to allow the parties to forget the bitter partisan battles that had come to a boil during the 1994 congressional elections. Civil libertarians raised concerns about the legislation and its impact on individual rights. But the most controversial aspect of the antiterrorism legislation was using chemical markers so that law-enforcement officials could trace the source of explosives. This provision was strongly opposed by the National Rifle Association, whose lobbying efforts persuaded Republicans to slow the movement to pass this legislation. This legislative slowdown is a good example of how the media can help set the political agenda by its coverage of policy issues and celebrated cases, but the implementation of change ultimately depends on the dynamics of political power.[20]

The House of Representatives tried to nudge the legislation in late 1995 with its hearings on the "Nature and Threat of Violent Anti-Government Groups in America." The broader focus of these hearings was influenced in part by the expanded media investigations into extremist activity. The media's focus on the militia movement following the bombing had exposed reporters to a host of different extremist groups. The result was a broader coverage of extremism in America, in which militias were discussed in relation to the other groups. The House hearings were called to examine the activities of violent antigovernment groups, but again the best example given of "armed extremists" and "violent groups" was the militia. Chairman Bill McCollum talked about how he hoped "to sort out the confusion associated with the term militia." Senator Jerrold Nadler commended the committee "for holding this hearing today on the topic of militias" and remarked that the "use of armed force by self-appointed individuals . . . presents a clear and present danger to our preservation of our system of government." Senator Charles Schumer, who was instrumental in conducting the informal house hearings on the militias earlier in the year, remarked, "I support the right of grown men and women to dress up in war-like costumes, . . . But I absolutely deny their right to inflict violence." He also tried to push forward the antiterrorism legislation, stating, "It is time for every Member who opposes the terrorist bill to stand up in the light of day on the House floor and explain to the American people why he or she opposes it."[21]

Professors Brent Smith and John George, both well-known and respected terrorism researchers, testified on the first panel, providing an historical and contemporary overview of antigovernment groups in the United States. The second panel was stacked with representatives from antihate groups, including the Anti-Defamation League, the American Jewish Committee, the Southern Poverty Law Center, and the Simon Weisenthal Center. Michael Lieberman, testifying for the ADL, reported their findings on the strength and size of the militia movement. The gist of his position was that militias "present[ed] a serious potential for danger" and that there was "increasing membership in militia groups."[22] The other three members of this panel offered similar testimony, emphasizing the growth and threatening behavior of the militia. The third panel of experts consisted of law-enforcement and court officials, who stressed particular cases and their efforts to respond more effectively to militia groups. The final panel included representatives from the American Civil Liberties Union and the Independence Institute. They described their concerns about the terrorism legislation and addressed general obstacles to trying to respond legislatively to all kinds of terrorists.

The issue of terrorism was frequently presented in the news in the days following the hearing, but coverage focused on the ceremonial dedication of a memorial for victims of the terrorist bombing of Pan-Am Flight 103. For three reasons, the media virtually ignored the House hearing. First, the hearing could not compete with the coverage of the memorial. This terrorist bombing was a celebrated case involving international terrorists, and President Clinton attended the memorial service. Second, the media were less interested in this hearing because the interest in Oklahoma had waned, and the perpetrators were in custody awaiting trial. Third, this hearing was not nearly as dramatic as the Senate hearings involving militia members had been. The opportunities for political ceremonies about militias were fading, and the terrorism legislation introduced following the bombing was stalled in a sea of partisan conflict. Yet, just as general interest in the militia movement started to fade, a series of high-profile trials occurred that helped refocus and reaffirm concern about the militia movement.

WILLIE RAY LAMPLEY AND THE TRIAL OF THE OKLAHOMA CONSTITUTIONAL MILITIA

In November 1995, Willie Ray Lampley, his wife Cecilia, John Dare Baird, and Larry Wayne Crow were arrested for conspiracy to manufacture and possess a destructive device.[23] The arrests resulted from an investigation initiated after the Oklahoma City bombing to more closely monitor the militia movement. Richard Schrum, an undercover informant who volunteered to work for the Federal Bureau of Investigation after the bombing, infiltrated Lampley's militia and secretly recorded conversations. It was discovered that Lampley and the others planned on using ammonium nitrate fertilizer bombs to blow up offices of the Anti-Defamation League, the Southern Poverty Law Center, abortion clinics, civil rights offices, welfare offices, and gay bars. Law-enforcement officers also seized numerous guns and three semiautomatic weapons when making the arrests. The *Associated Press* hinted that the case might involve militias, reporting that these defendants were a significant threat to society. It was also reported that Lampley and his co-conspirators were planning to create problems for the government by constructing a fertilizer bomb.

There were a number of reasons why the arrest, arraignment, and trial of the Lampleys and their co-conspirators received extensive local and national news coverage. First, although there was no evidence that the Lampleys were linked to Timothy McVeigh and Terry Nichols, the media emphasized various connections to the Oklahoma City bombing. The arrests were made in Oklahoma, and federal law-enforcement officers recovered an ammonium-type bomb, like the one used to destroy the Murrah Federal Building. A reporter from the *Globe and Mail* wrote, "In a chilling echo of the mass murder that took place here seven months ago, an eastern Oklahoma prophet of doom and two others appear in court this week charged with conspiring to blow up numerous buildings with fertilizer bombs." One of the government informants was quoted in a newspaper article as saying that he "saved as many lives as what was lost in Oklahoma City," and that his job "was to monitor the militia situation, [including] anybody that might be a potential terrorist or anything that would cause a situation like Oklahoma City."[24] The case "carried eerie overtones of the April 19 bombing,"[25] including that one of the potential targets of the investigation was Elohim City—a known community of Christian Identity adherents. Readers were reminded that Tim McVeigh had telephoned Elohim City a few minutes after reserving the Ryder truck used in the bombing.

A second reason why this case received media publicity was that it provided an excellent way for law-enforcement and political officials to demonstrate how their efforts to monitor extremists more closely had prevented an act of domestic terrorism. It was reported that law enforcement had captured a very dangerous group of individuals and was increasingly successful in its efforts to monitor the militia situation, but it was also emphasized that they needed to continue their investigative efforts to search out similar threats. Media coverage stressed how law enforcement had been quick to respond and to control potentially dangerous situations involving extremists like the Lampleys. It was reported that law-enforcement officials had to learn antigovernment ideologies and were beginning to use what they learned to monitor and control such groups. *Newsweek* reporter Tom Morganthau wrote, "The rise of the US militia movement now confronts federal authorities with a plausible risk of terrorism from within. Worse, from the FBI's point of view, the American ultra-right has widely adopted the concept of 'leaderless resistance' which means its adherents organize themselves in tiny cells that are exceedingly difficult to detect or infiltrate. And there are numerous incidences of recent militia activity that give one pause." Morganthau used the Lampley case as an example.[26] Other authorities stated that the Lampley case demonstrated how terrorists are prepared to kill innocent bystanders and that early detection of terrorist activity is vital but challenging. Law-enforcement and watchdog groups used the Lampley case as evidence that there was no easy way to respond to such groups and that vigilance was necessary, but it was inevitable that some dangerous militia members would be overlooked.

Third, the Lampley case was important because it was linked to the Tri-States Militia, a South Dakota–based national "communication center" that claimed to be connected to 900 different militia groups in about 48 states. John Parsons, one of the members of this organization, ran the communication center, essentially taking calls from militias and investigating rumors and accusations of suspicious government activity. The media treated Parsons as a celebrity figure because it appeared that this organization was a national hub coordinating militia concerns and because he was willing to provide newsworthy ranting about a one-world government. He testified that Lampley and Crow asked him for his support to bomb several buildings: "We need to do four or five to create problems for the government," Crow was quoted as saying; "God won't be mad at us if we drop 4 or 5 buildings—he will probably reward us." Parsons's testimony also revealed, however, that the FBI paid him close to 2,000 dollars a month to funnel information to them about the militia movement. Although his testimony helped convict the defendants, it ruined his credibility and purged the Tri-States Militia from the movement. It also generated militia support for Lampley and anger towards the government and Parsons for their devious tactics.[27]

The trial of the Lampleys and Baird was more then a simple airing of the facts of this particular case.[28] Not only were these three defendants on trial—so were the militia movement, Tim McVeigh, and the government strategies for monitoring and investigating potential terrorist groups. It is particularly significant that the trial started in April 1996, coinciding with the one-year anniversary of the Oklahoma City bombing. During the trial, a memorial wreath was placed on the courthouse door and a memorial sign was placed in the window of a Federal Protective Service vehicle outside the courthouse. The United States Court of Appeals for the Tenth Circuit acknowledged that the jurors probably saw both memorials, and evidence admitted during the trial made both direct and indirect reference to the Oklahoma City bombing. These facts solidified the connections between this case and the bombing, increased national media interest in the case, and made it harder to conduct a fair trial.

This trial was also the first opportunity for the public to formally condemn the activities and ideology of the militia movement. The case provided an opportunity to revisit many of the dominant themes presented in the media, and it was used as confirming evidence that the militia threat was legitimate. The media reported that Lampley was affiliated with the Universal Church of God and was either the leader of a militia or a member of the Oklahoma Constitutional Militia. Although the backgrounds of all four defendants were described in the media, the press focused on Willie Ray Lampley. Media coverage depicted him as dangerous, unstable, wacky, and driven by a commitment to his beliefs. Lampley claimed that he was a religious prophet, had strong antigovernment beliefs, and was planning to use violence to accomplish his objectives. There was videotape of Lampley in military fatigues, and it was reported that Lampley believed that he was "the prophet of God, that he's going to die from all this, and [after] three days he will rise from the dead and inherit the earth"; that "the nation was about to be devastated—first by natural disasters and then foreign attack—because the government had turned away from God";[29] and that "if you want freedom in this country you are going to have to shed somebody's blood for it."[30] He also warned: "you need to read the Second Amendment. I have the right to bear it [a fertilizer bomb] as an arm."[31] It was also reported that he tested whether Schrum was an undercover agent by making him hold a "Yahweh" stick; if Schrum were lying he would drop dead after touching it.[32] He targeted gay bars, abortion clinics, and the offices of the Southern Poverty Law Center and the Anti-Defamation League, and he was the mastermind behind "Operation Super Glue"—a plot to glue the locks of the doors of such places.[33] Lampley also sent letters to government officials prophesying their deaths and a letter to President Clinton warning of an imminent invasion by United Nations troops; he claimed that troops would be used to control the United States by the New World Order.

These images and concerns about militia activity were highlighted during the trial. For example, during voir dire, jurors were asked about abortion, militias, the Second Amendment, and the government. Several media organizations reported that the courtroom reacted with laughter and applause when one potential juror said that he knew a militia member and thought he was a nut. The prosecution and the defense presented two very different stories to the jury. The prosecution's case was consistent with the majority of the media images of militias after the Oklahoma City bombing, and they effectively put the group and its beliefs on trial. They described how this group was a threat and planned to cause significant harm. Prosecutors emphasized Lampley's concerns about a New World Order—that the world would be controlled by a cartel of Jewish bankers—and his belief that violence had to be used to prevent this taking place. The defense focused on one of the central counterclaims being voiced by militia leaders and militia supporters—that the government works to entrap law-abiding citizens. Since the key witnesses for the prosecution were both undercover informants paid to infiltrate this group, defense attorneys attempted to show that the defendants were entrapped and would not have committed these acts if not for Schrum's prodding.

The type of bomb materials confiscated and the emphasis at trial on the defendants' antigovernment beliefs, coupled with the anniversary and the other reminders of the Oklahoma bombing, forced the jurors to think about and rule on these cases and issues simultaneously. The jurors were asked to rule on the facts presented about the case, but they had the additional burden of deciding whether the demonization of militias was justified and whether militia concerns about overzealous law enforcement were irrelevant. The jurors took less than five hours to convict. Prior to sentencing, the media frequently discussed the maximum punishments that could be given to the defendants, emphasizing that society will not tolerate such acts or the people who commit them. On July 11, a federal judge sentenced Lampley to eleven and a half years in prison and three years supervised release, Cecilia Lampley to four and a half years in prison and three years supervised release, and Baird to ten years imprisonment and supervised release. These harsh punishments were reported in the news, helping to stem the public's fears and concerns about similar types of activity and also reaffirming confidence in social-control institutions to take whatever steps are necessary to prevent similar crimes from occurring. Yet a more important test remained in the trial of Timothy McVeigh.

The Criminal Trial of Timothy McVeigh

Certain criminal cases involving militia members like the Lampleys were covered extensively in the news media. The investigative activities and general processing of these cases were covered directly and also were embedded within broader descriptions of the militia movement and extremist activity. The cases provided convincing evidence that fears about such groups were justified and that perseverance in investigating and monitoring such groups was essential for the public's safety. The amount and type of publicity generated specifically about these cases, however, were significantly different from the celebrated coverage of the processing of the Oklahoma City bombing by the criminal justice system. This case was probably the second most important media crime event of the 1990s, spurring in-depth coverage of all aspects of the trial and close examination of relevant policy issues. The criminal trial of Timothy McVeigh ranks among the top ones of the twentieth century. Reporters covering the trial estimated that over 2,000 media personnel were appointed to cover the trial, including representatives from every major news organization in the world. [34]

McVeigh's trial was a particularly high-stakes affair.[35] The government was under enormous pressure to extinguish this symbol of evil and hate by convincing a jury that he was guilty. Such a verdict would send a clear message to racists, terrorists, militia members, and other antigovernment zealots that such beliefs are not acceptable in this society. An important message could also be broadcast to the world: the United States has no tolerance for terrorist acts on its soil. In addition, the criminal justice system in general and the court system in particular had suffered significant blows to their legitimacy in the time period immediately before the trial. The Federal Bureau of Investigation, the once revered top law-enforcement agency of the federal government, was coming under increasingly frequent external attacks for foul-ups, mishaps, and cover-ups. The FBI's involvement in Ruby Ridge and Waco was replayed frequently in media coverage, investigative reports, and a string of congressional hearings. Its laboratory was heavily criticized for its prosecutorial bias in analyzing evidence. The Oklahoma City bombing site provided the opportunity to restore public confidence in the FBI because it was an enormously complicated scene with a vast amount of investigative data that had to be analyzed to prove guilt beyond a reasonable doubt. Although the defense tried to introduce the documented problems of the laboratory, the judge would not allow the FBI to be put on trial, and the analysis of the FBI evidence in this case is considered one of the great efforts in society's war on crime.

The McVeigh trial was also an important opportunity to prove that the court system had the capacity to process high-profile cases in a manner consistent with our ideal of justice. The coverage of the Oklahoma City bombing had from its very beginning overlapped with what was probably the century's top media crime event—the O. J. Simpson case. The Simpson trial began in January 1995, was in progress when the bombing occurred, and concluded in October a few weeks before the Lampleys were arrested. A racially divided public reacted very differently to the not-guilty Simpson verdict.[36] Some people viewed it as an indictment of a system that had long lost its purpose and legitimacy; others saw the verdict as showing that the burden of proof of the system, when having access to the resources to fully test the concept of "reasonable doubt," is a heavy and almost insurmountable obstacle. The case was considered an embarrassment by some and a triumph by others, but the important legitimacy question it raised was whether the criminal justice system was equipped to administer and process those rare cases that reach the pinnacle of publicity with fairness, dignity, and integrity.

The Simpson trial taught valuable lessons to all parties. First, the public consumed the trial from start to finish because cameras were allowed in the courtroom and several networks provided gavel-to-gavel coverage. The public's strong opinions about the case were therefore based on more than the media sound-bite summaries that generally constitute the sole source of reality construction for most cases. The public did have the usual media interpretations, commentaries, and editorials, but it was also part of the courtroom drama and could make independent evaluations. In contrast, such access was not provided to McVeigh's trial, or to either trial of Terry Nichols, and thus the media summaries of those trials informed how the public viewed them. Second, the Simpson trial was held in Los Angeles—a city with a long history of racial tension that had not recovered from the aftermath of riots following the acquittal of LAPD officers charged with the beating of Rodney King. McVeigh's trial was transferred from Oklahoma to Denver, making it easier to find jurors not linked to the bombing in some way and not influenced by the pretrial publicity. Although the defense motioned that McVeigh could not receive a fair trial anywhere because the entire country was prejudiced by media coverage—and using the O. J. Simpson case as evidence of the inherent prejudice of such high-profile cases—the trial judge went to great trouble to insure that the jury could be impartial by using lengthy voir dire to assess the bias of potential jurors. Third, the Simpson trial lasted nine months, with many witnesses testifying for several days. The McVeigh trial, however, was a model of efficiency, with only twenty-two days of witness testimony.[37]

U.S. district court judge Richard Matsch was the perfect representative of judicial objectivity. He had nearly thirty years experience as a federal court judge but looked more like a justice of the frontier West, with his graying hair, bushy mustache, and penchant for wearing a cowboy hat and boots outside the courtroom. His reputation was impeccable. It was reported that he preferred to eat alone at bar-association conventions to "avoid potential conflicts of interest," that he took a bus to work "so he could do paperwork on his way to the courthouse," and that he admired frontier men and women for their "gritty determination and unbowed discipline." It was also frequently reported that Judge Matsch went to great lengths to keep the trial under his control. Wayne Wicks, the media coordinator for the trial, stressed how Matsch did not want another "O. J. Circus" and promised "Denver Theater" rather than the spectacle that became the Simpson trial. Unlike the Simpson trial judge, who was enamored with the publicity and lost complete control of the prosecution and defense activity inside and outside the courtroom, Judge Matsch was clearly in charge and strictly disciplined anybody violating courtroom rules of decorum. His gag orders prevented the lawyers from grandstanding and attempting to spin facts to sway public opinion to their positions. The prosecution and defense teams were not allowed to become talk-show pundits, authors, and public personas like the celebrity lawyers of the Simpson case. Similarly, Judge Matsch protected the identities of jury members, including withholding personal information from the media and constructing a wall in the courtroom to shield the media from seeing jury members' faces. He made it clear that he intended for McVeigh to receive a fair trial and that he would not allow the media to a sensationalize it. Reporters were publicly critical about his restrictions, but many gave him high marks despite the draconian access restrictions. One reporter, for example, said, "If I'm ever on trial for murder, I would want him presiding over my case." In an editorial published in the *Denver Post*, the trial was called a "judicial tour de force" and highly praised: "given the enormity of the crime, the global spotlight focused on it and a scenario strewn with bizarre and sometimes unprecedented developments, attainment of the verdict in two months is a heartening fulfillment of the constitutional promise of a speedy and public trial." The *Post* credited Matsch for the effective and fair processing of this case.[38]

The opening statements of the criminal trial and the prosecutor's closing statement at the sentencing hearing effectively capture the full symbolic meanings of the McVeigh trial. When delivering the prosecution's opening statement, attorney Joseph Hartzler made several jury members and attorneys cry.[39] He told several powerful stories that captured the pain and suffering of the victims:

As Helena Garrett left the Murrah Federal Building to go to work across the street, she could look back up at the building; and there was a wall of plate glass windows on the second floor. You can look through those windows and see into the day-care center; and the children would run up to those windows and press their hands and faces to those windows to say goodbye to their parents. And standing on the sidewalk, it was almost as though you can reach up and touch the children there on the second floor. But none of the parents of any of the children that I just mentioned ever touched those children again while they were still alive.[40]

He also, of course, highlighted the prosecution's case against McVeigh, describing what type of evidence each witness would provide. He promised that the evidence would be brought together "like bricks building a brick wall" and that "we will build a solid wall of evidence against McVeigh."[41] This wall provided a cogent image that separated McVeigh from the rest of the community, and Hartzler accentuated McVeigh's outsider status by describing his hate for the government, the lengths to which he went in order to seek revenge for what happened at Waco, and his desire to start a violent revolution.

The opening statement by the defense only reaffirmed the outsider image stressed by the prosecution. After reading the names of all the victims of the bombing, Stephen Jones reminded the jury about the intense publicity and significance of the case, stating "that somewhere between 50 and 100 million people throughout the world, courtesy of CNN, watched physicians crawl through the rubble of the Murrah Building" and "The President of the United States and the Attorney General of the United States went on nationwide television within hours after the bombing." Jones did not disagree with the prosecution's characterization of McVeigh as antigovernment but explained that having such views was not a crime and that many people shared those views. One of the most critical errors, which only further isolated McVeigh from the rest of the community, was that Jones portrayed him in a way that was very similar to the media's take on militia members: he was angry at the federal government and motivated by Waco, Ruby Ridge, and the passage of the Brady bill.[42]

At the conclusion of the trial, the jury convicted McVeigh after deliberating for almost twenty-four hours over four days.[43] The guilty verdict was by far the most newsworthy stage of the criminal trial, receiving top-story placement in all different types of media. Reporters placed the verdict within the context of the entire event: they conjured up images of the initial impact, reminded consumers of the incredible losses suffered, described the arrest and investigation to link McVeigh to the bombing, then highlighted the evidence provided by key witnesses at the trial. Media organizations also relied heavily on their attorney consultants and other legal sources to critique all members of the courtroom workgroup. The verdict was described as a significant and far-reaching victory. Reporters wrote that the verdict would allow "healing" and "closure"; would send "a pointed message to would-be terrorists"; might "act as a deterrent to US-based extremist organizations" and return "the lost luster of the country's criminal justice system." The decision also "demonstrates the government was able to track down and prosecute one of the perpetrators of the nation's deadliest terrorist attack" and provided "a degree of solace to survivors."[44] The verdict etched the frames used to describe militia members more deeply into the public's psyche.

There was, however, one outstanding question to be answered—was the jury willing to sentence society's top criminal to its top punishment? Death-penalty cases are processed in the United States in two stages: once guilt is determined, an additional trial is held to weigh aggravating and mitigating factors to decide whether death is an appropriate sanction. The jury still had to decide whether McVeigh should be executed.

The sentencing phase lasted eight days, as the defense and prosecution presented evidence for and against aggravating or mitigating factors. The closing statement of this hearing again shows what the McVeigh trial had become. Beth Wilkinson delivered the closing statement, frequently reminding the jury that they represented the whole community—a community that needed a guilty verdict. She started her opening statement in the following way:

It's time for justice. A little over two years ago, Timothy McVeigh decided that he had no time for justice. He believed that it was his right to murder innocent women, men, and children. He believed that he could take the law into his own hands and declare war on his fellow Americans. He killed without regard to race, creed, color, or age. He destroyed the lives of families in Oklahoma City; also in Orlando, Florida; Fort Worth, Texas; Evergreen, Colorado; and everywhere else in the United States. Without even a nod to justice, he stole the innocence of our children who, like us, never believed that in America an American citizen would kill his own in the name of patriotism. . . . But today, despite his total disregard for life, liberty, and justice, we give the defendant what every person in this country deserves: Justice. Timothy McVeigh has been presumed innocent. He's had a public trial, and he has had citizens from his community consider all of the evidence before declaring him guilty beyond a reasonable doubt to every crime charged. Unlike his victims, Timothy McVeigh receives justice. But as you know, justice is not finished. There is one decision that you all must make as the conscience of the community.[45]

On several occasions, she stressed to the jury that they were the community's moral conscience: "The citizens of this country, the community whose conscience you now represent, have already determined that the death penalty is appropriate in certain cases." "Look into the eyes of a coward and tell him you will have courage. Tell him you will speak with one unified voice as the moral conscience of the community and tell him he is no patriot. He is a traitor and he deserves to die."[46] This was a theme emphasized within the national media's coverage of her closing statement.[47] Finally, after discussing the aggravating and mitigating factors raised during his sentencing hearing, she concluded:

In his opening statement to you, Mr. Jones recognized that the bombing at Oklahoma City was seared into the memory of our generation like the attack on Pearl Harbor was to the generation before us. Mr. Jones was right. Like the attack on Pearl Harbor, the bombing in Oklahoma City threatened our sense of security within our own borders; and this threat to our insecurity [sic] came from and was caused by Timothy McVeigh. He betrayed every American. He betrayed his fellow soldiers from the Persian Gulf. He betrayed his family and he betrayed you. He is a traitor who chose of his own volition to betray his country by murdering as many United States citizens as he could. No person, no government action, no second or third reality that Mr. Burr mentioned, made Timothy McVeigh murder 168 of his own people. As the moral conscience of the community, you must speak on behalf of all Americans who rightly refuse to accept any justification for this horrible crime. It is time for justice. It is time to impose the ultimate sanction on the man responsible for this terror. Serve justice, speak as the moral conscience of the community, and sentence Timothy McVeigh to death.[48]

On June 13, 1997, after carefully weighing the evidence provided at the sentencing hearing, a unanimous jury recommended that Timothy McVeigh be put to death. McVeigh's lead defense attorney, Stephen Jones, argued that the media produced the verdict and sentence—the intensity and scope of the coverage prevented McVeigh from receiving a fair trial. He blamed the media for publishing false, misleading, and sensational stories that prevented an objective public from weighing the facts of the case. The media, according to Jones, orchestrated the outcome by emphasizing certain negative characteristics about McVeigh and downplaying exculpatory evidence. He also concluded that the media helped create public acceptance of the verdict and sentence.[49]

After McVeigh left the courtroom knowing he was sentenced to death, Judge Matsch celebrated the judicial process by making the following remarks to the jury:

> I want to thank you on behalf of all of the people of the United States. You have served your country and you have served the system, as we've so often referred to it; but the system is really the democratic system that is our form of government, wherein people are brought together from all walks of life and background and given the responsibility for making the decision. And you have done that. Now it may be a matter for you now or at some later time to wonder: Did we do the right thing? The answer to that question is yes, you did the right thing, not because I believe it one way or the other but because you did it. And that is what we rely upon, 12 people coming together, hearing the evidence, following the law, and reaching the decision. So therefore, it is done. And you, as the jurors, are the final authority.[50]

With Judge Matsch's reaffirmation of faith in the legitimacy of the system and the public's role in the process, the first and most important stage of the Oklahoma City bombing case was complete. The sentence of death can also be considered a symbolic endpoint for the moral panic over the militia movement. Media coverage of the bombing, the militia movement, and the ensuing ceremonies initiated in response brought people together within a common framework to understand the issues. Militia groups were emphasized in news coverage, and although there were stories about other extremist activity, the public was forced to think about those groups in relation to what they had come to know as the militia movement. The brick wall that prosecutors used as a metaphor in McVeigh's trial was also an effective device for understanding that collective sentiments had taken on a new form. This wall articulated a clear boundary. Although McVeigh had long been disentangled from the militia movement, the early link between the two could not be completely erased from the public psyche. These events clearly illuminated

McVeigh as a symbol of evil and hate, and indirectly confirmed that other domestic terrorists, including militia members, were demons. Once these new boundaries were articulated and accepted, the panic about militias had no more momentum.

Maintenance Ceremonies

The political and criminal justice ceremonies discussed above helped define the scope of concern about the militia movement and provided the necessary environment of legitimacy to support responding to militias in a certain way. There were other ceremonies that helped maintain the image of militias, including Terry Nichols's trial. For his role in the Oklahoma City bombing, Nichols was convicted in a federal court in 1998 for conspiracy and manslaughter, and was sentenced to life imprisonment without the possibility of parole. The media were not nearly as interested in this trial as it had been with all aspects of the McVeigh case—for two reasons. Nichols's role and life were secondary in much of the coverage because it was apparent that McVeigh was the mastermind of the plan and it was easier to find many newsworthy examples of his hatred. Nichols's trial also lacked drama. The verdict in the McVeigh trial demonstrated that the government had a very good case against both defendants, and it was almost a foregone conclusion that Nichols's conviction would be forthcoming. The case therefore received far less national coverage than McVeigh's trial. (It did receive similar coverage in Oklahoma only because that state is pursuing state charges against Nichols to secure his death sentence.) By 1998 the news media had exhausted its coverage of the militia movement. Reporters continued to discuss the activities of specific groups or certain celebrity figures but such stories were presented as isolated incidents.

Popular Culture and Militias

Colonel James "Bo" Gritz is one of the most recognizable public figures linked to the militia movement. Gritz was already a high-profile figure before he achieved additional celebrity as a media-proclaimed militia leader.[1] The ex–Green Beret first gained fame as the most decorated veteran of the Vietnam War, receiving over sixty commendations for valor, and he used his connections and clout to organize numerous missions to Southeast Asia to search for American soldiers missing in action. Although these missions were unsuccessful, the efforts solidified Gritz's status as a hero to some people and an outsider to others. Gritz claimed that his efforts to save prisoners of war were deliberately thwarted by the government because it feared exposing the Central Intelligence Agency's involvement in drug smuggling during the war. He was also able to parlay the celebrity he achieved pursuing prisoners of war into political opportunity. Gritz was the Populist Party's vice-presidential running mate to former Ku Klux Klan leader David Duke in 1988, and was the party's presidential candidate in 1992. His 1992 political platform included the elimination of the federal income tax, the Internal Revenue Service, the United Nations, and the Federal Reserve. His campaign slogan, "If ballots don't do it in '92, bullets may have to in '96," resonated strongly with opponents of gun control and people holding antigovernment views. His presidential campaign also coincided with the Randy Weaver standoff. Negotiations between the FBI and Weaver were stalemated when Gritz visited Ruby Ridge in

August 1992 to offer his services to mediate the dispute. Weaver agreed to meet with Gritz, and over several days he and Jack McLamb, another celebrity figure of the militia movement, negotiated Weaver's surrender to law-enforcement authorities.

Although Gritz was not affiliated with any militia group, he was a perfect role model for militia members, and Valerie Alvord, a reporter for the *San Diego Union-Tribune,* called him the "godfather of the modern militias." Of all the figures who achieved celebrity status during the militia panic, Gritz was the most respected and admired by militia members themselves. When asked about Gritz's popularity, one militia sympathizer said, "He is a well-decorated veteran. He deserves it. When he speaks, he watches his words. I guess he is the only one that they can really put their finger on that has some authority to them." Gritz had a popular shortwave radio program and was one of the main reasons why many militia members attended preparedness expositions. For example, of the various speakers and seminar leaders at the Indianapolis Preparedness Exposition in 1997, Gritz, with his presentations, "The Heart of the Monster" and "Spike the New World Order," was the only one who attracted standing-room-only crowds. The publications, videos, and other materials he displayed at his booth sold well, and supporters, autograph-seekers, and others wanting to have their picture taken with him often surrounded him. Gritz encouraged people to join Jack McLamb and him in Kamiah, Idaho, at one of their Constitutional Covenant Communities he called "Almost Heaven." The literature promoting the development promised the opportunity to live a patriot lifestyle, "a place to go where like-minded people seek to live as free Americans," and claimed that such communities "may well be necessary if we are not successful in stopping the planned, socialist police state called the New World Order."

Gritz was the only high-profile leader of the militia movement who had experiential credibility. He was a war hero with firsthand experience that others could only imagine. One militia activist, who listened frequently to Gritz's shortwave radio program, said "You know, he is a sixth-degree black belt and he has killed several people using what he has learned when he was over in Vietnam." He was familiar with various operations that Gritz was involved in and discussed the training he has done. Thousands of militia members have participated in his SPIKE (Specially Prepared Individuals for Key Events) training events because Gritz has used such programs to train armies all over the world. Gritz's credibility was enhanced by his political résumé, affiliations with racist groups, and friendship with Randy Weaver. He was the presidential candidate of the Populist Party—a party founded by a leader of the anti-Semitic Liberty Lobby—and watchdog groups claimed he spoke at numerous Christian Identity events. Moreover, he was responsible for saving one of the movement's martyrs at Ruby Ridge. Gritz was a charismatic speaker who spoke about issues important to his audience. He shared his concerns and stories while wearing his decorated military uniform, and used language familiar to militia members, pushing anti-Semitic, antigovernment, and satanic ritual abuse conspiracies. In one of his lectures at the Indianapolis Preparedness Exposition, he focused on the fear of a one-world government run by the United Nations. He criticized the president of the United States and the director of the FBI, referred to Mikhail Gorbachev as the anti-Christ, and castigated the media's role in promoting the interest of elites. He also talked about the case in which he was arrested for attempting to kidnap a child on behalf of the mother (he was acquitted in 2000 of these charges). Linda Wiegand, who lost custody of her children but fled with her two boys and accused her husband of sexual abuse, attended the exposition and talked about her case during Gritz's presentation. She had been arrested and her children were returned to the father, but she claimed the father and the police officers who investigated the charges were involved in a satanic ritual abuse ring.

Gritz also became one of the most admired leaders of the militia movement because his autobiography and persona reminded people of a popular culture icon—John Rambo. Although he appeared in 1972 in Charles Morrell's novel *First Blood*, Rambo made a significant impact on public culture only when the film of the same name was released in 1982.[2] Sylvester Stallone played the main character—a Vietnam veteran unable to adjust to mainstream society, choosing instead to travel the countryside alone, searching for remnants of his heroic past. Early in the movie, however, he discovers that one of the few remaining members of his elite, specially trained military team has died—killed by cancer due to exposure to a deadly chemical used by the government during the war. Rambo's outsider status is vividly displayed when he stops for food in a small town called Hope but encounters its sheriff, who promptly escorts him to the town boundary. The sheriff tells Rambo that the people of his town do not like outsiders, considering them troublemakers, and he tries to convince Rambo to take a bath and realize that the war is over. The sheriff drives away, but Rambo rebels and begins to march back towards the town. The sheriff, getting a glimpse of the defiant menace through his rearview mirror, turns around and arrests him for vagrancy, disorderly conduct, and other misdemeanors.

Physical abuse by several deputies forces Rambo to demonstrate his hand-to-hand combat prowess, after which he manages to escape from the jail to the mountainous wilderness surrounding Hope. The rest of the movie focuses on the sheriff department's pursuit of the escaped prisoner. Rambo displays amazing survival skills. Armed at first only with his knife, he systematically puts his first wave of pursuers out of commission, killing the most ruthless deputy in self-defense. An army of police officers and military personnel is then brought in to continue the pursuit. They think they have successfully eliminated the threat by destroying the entrance to an abandoned mineshaft that Rambo has been using as a shelter. Rambo, however, again demonstrates his pre- paredness skills as he navigates through the heart of the mine to dis- cover another exit. Rambo unleashes his anger on the people of Hope, hijacking a military vehicle and using high-powered weapons to obliter- ate the town. He is eventually surrounded and certain to die in a show- down with the law, but instead is peacefully talked down from the confrontation by his commanding officer from Vietnam.

Several scholars of popular culture have emphasized the symbolic power of the Rambo character.[3] Carol Fry and Christopher Kemp, for example, describe how Rambo gives us "a modern champion . . . who in his agony provides a fantasy victory over cultural and historical forces which are beyond the power of the audience to control." Simi- larly, Frank Sweeney claims that Rambo "represent[s] the treatment of all veterans, . . . Alienated, he is unable to return to the country he loves and is destined to be forever on the move." Sweeney offers several ex- planations for the popularity of the character; the film taps into our natural desire for victims of injustice to seek revenge, it uses American frontier myth imagery, and the film provides an opportunity for the public to expunge its guilt about the war. Rambo rewrote history and allowed the public to redefine the Vietnam War as a victory.

The trilogy of movies based on the Rambo character (*First Blood*, *Rambo II*, *Rambo III*) was enormously popular. *Rambo II*, for example, made over 150 million dollars and planted "the image and persona of Rambo into cultural history."[4] The popularity of the character is demon- strated not only by the sequels that saw Rambo rescuing forgotten American POWs (*Rambo II*) and fighting Russians (*Rambo III*) but also by how it was used in other popular-culture outlets, including cartoons, toys, candy bars, videogames, and comic books.[5] Moreover, the persona of the character endures: Hollywood hopes to put out a fourth Rambo movie. In 1997, *People Magazine* reported that Miramax was starting production of a picture in which Rambo stops a militia group from blowing up a building in the Midwest—a plot that "was definitely inspired by the Timothy McVeigh case."[6]

Bo Gritz claimed that he was the inspiration for the Rambo character.[7] Whether or not this is true, it is certain that his popularity among militia members and his status as a media militia celebrity were linked to the similarities between his real life and the fictional life of John Rambo. The character was an unappreciated hero of the war. His flashbacks to Vietnam in the first movie and the rescue missions of POWs in the second movie substantiate Rambo's personal pain and sacrifice for the country. His ability to achieve victory, even when significantly outmatched in manpower and weaponry, is a credit to his skills as a soldier. Gritz's distinguished service record was well publicized; one can imagine the pain and suffering he endured and the Rambo-like skills he used to receive his honors. The similarity between Gritz and Rambo is also strengthened by their outsider status, their victimization by government cover-up and conspiracy, and their willingness to stand up to authority. For example, Gritz's claim that the government successfully thwarted his efforts to bring home American POWs is consistent with the exploitation of Rambo by the government. In *Rambo II*, particularly, the government is depicted as going to great lengths to ensure that his mission is unsuccessful because it does not want the public to know the real truth about Americans lost in action. Finally, Gritz's hero status among militia members was linked to his role as negotiator in the Weaver case. The media's depiction of the conclusion of the siege, where Gritz walks out of the cabin with Weaver, was very similar to the concluding scene of *First Blood*, in which Rambo's colonel, the only man he can trust, escorts him from a surrounded building.

Once the militia movement became an important social problem, the media frequently invoked the popular imagery of the Rambo character when describing other militia members. Rambo became a quick and vivid way to convey understanding to the public about the physical appearance and threatening nature of militia members. Aline McKenzie described how the Georgia State Defense Force and other state-sanctioned militias, groups that perform mostly community service and National Guard support activities, were under attack because the public assumed that they were like antigovernment citizen militias. Members from such groups in different states described how people harassed them for the same reason. They themselves described antigovernment militias as "kooks," "thugs," and "renegades," and their recruitment procedures focused on screening out anyone interested "in being Rambo." Similarly, a newspaper article that focused on the similarities between citizen militias and a group called the Environmental Rangers was titled "Green Rambos," and McVeigh was called a "Rambo-like guy that liked guns." As the prosecutor made clear during the opening statement of his criminal trial, McVeigh justified his actions the way Rambo did—because the government drew "First Blood." The prosecuting attorney stated:

> But the tragedy at Waco really sparked his anger; and as time passed, he became more and more and more outraged at the government, which he held responsible for the deaths at Waco. And he told people that the federal government had intentionally murdered people at Waco: they murdered the Davidians at Waco. He described the incident as the government's declaration of war against the American people. He wrote letters declaring that the government had drawn, quote, "first blood," unquote, at Waco; and he predicted there would be a violent revolution against the American government. As he put it, blood would flow in the streets.[8]

Even militia members referred to the fringe contingents of their own movement by using the characterization of Rambo in a derogatory way. For example, an operations plan called "Project Worst Nightmare," which included bombing federal buildings on the one-year anniversary of the Oklahoma City bombing, was circulated, but militia members reacted by saying that there was nothing to it: it was simply created by "somebody wanting to play Rambo."[9]

THE RELATIONSHIP BETWEEN NEWS AND POPULAR CULTURE

Most research describing the construction of social problems focuses on the exaggerated attention in the news media.[10] This decision to focus on the news media as a primary definer makes sense considering the pervasiveness of news images, the success of important agents of social control in gaining access to news venues, and the public's uncritical acceptance of what the news media conveys. It is clear that the video-enhanced sound bites of television news, the analyses provided in newspapers and other print outlets, and the supporting stories and images provided on the Internet contribute significantly to the constructed realities about social problems. A limitation of focusing solely on news images, however, is that one fails to consider how fact-based accounts take on particular meanings only because of cultural myths. These myths certainly influence what crime incidents are presented as news, whether the events become celebrated, how events are framed, and how news coverage affects the public's consciousness.

There are many sources that contribute to the existence of news myths, but images produced for mass consumption are particularly important and can be considered part of popular culture. Films, television shows, music, and other less widely disseminated forms of entertainment, such as comics, jokes, video games, and toys, can contribute significantly to defining and solidifying the myths and frameworks that influence behavior and decision making. Indeed, popular culture images may be particularly significant because there is limited resistance to the way these outlets exaggerate society's fears. Stories are usually told in their most exaggerated form in order to attract an audience, but doing so confirms some of the most threatening extremes of reality. People who create fiction are not constrained by the need to present materials in a realistic manner, and thus truth, justice, and morality are generally presented in black-and-white terms. This creative freedom makes popular culture interesting to the mass audience, but it is also a particularly effective mechanism of social control and is worthy of study. People who create public culture purposefully and knowingly create or solidify stereotypes. The public cannot resist borrowing from the exaggerated realities presented in fictional accounts when viewing factual accounts of events. Similarly, as the Gritz-Rambo-militia connection demonstrates, news personnel will often refer to fictional accounts when creating news stories.

The lines between fact-based news accounts and the fiction of popular culture are therefore becoming increasingly blurry. News organizations, in an effort to maintain a profitable market share, have de-emphasized the presentation of hard and investigative news and increasingly adopted entertainment formats and storylines. The personal lives of celebrity figures have become top-priority news-agenda items, and general entertainment news is almost as important as news about political and world events. Some news organizations have attempted to capitalize on the popularity of celebrities by hiring a star as an anchor or reporter. Considering the images about crime presented in the news, one could argue that the sensational, "body-count" stories reflect an attempt to keep up with the blood-and-guts excesses of Hollywood crime movies. Ray Surette refers to the merger of news and entertainment formats as "infotainment," examples of which would be tabloid-style reality programs and the co-option of criminal justice trials for the benefit of the media.[11] Many entertainment sources borrow heavily from news headlines when creating stories, providing the public with the opportunity to revisit a storyline that was first presented as news and exploiting the most sensational aspects of the "facts" for mass appeal. Television crime shows, such as *Law and Order*, borrow directly from news headlines. The reciprocal relationship between popular culture and news images, and how these images influence the public, was also demonstrated in how popular-culture outlets were immediately influenced by the September 11 attacks. The release of several films involving terrorists was delayed, warning labels were added to videos of movies depicting scenarios similar to the attacks, and popular television shows, such as *The West Wing*, *NYPD Blue*, and *Third Watch*, did episodes related to the attacks.

Popular-culture sources have frequently used news coverage of crime as a primary storyline. Films like *Natural Born Killers* and *15 Minutes* provide direct commentary on the news media's role in creating crime, and consumers identify with the films' extreme violence and the criminal characters' craving for public attention because they are consistent with the sensationalizing of crime in the news media.

A few social-construction researchers have acknowledged the overlapping roles of the news media and popular culture in generating and sustaining cultural myths as well as in perpetuating society's fears and prejudices.[12] When a social problem is created or revisited following a celebrated event, the architects of social-problem construction tap into a pool of existing cultural myths in deciding what problems are worth emphasizing and how they should be presented. Once a social problem has dominated public concern for a period of time, various popular-culture outlets solidify the frames used to describe the issues connected with that problem. Since there are few constraints on how a popular medium presents an issue, the framing of the social problem—as well as the outsider that was created or resurfaced as a source of concern—is legitimized because the presentation occurs in the most extreme way possible.

Celebrated cases, and the social problems emanating from them, are quickly defined according to the constraints and myths of the culture.

News and popular-culture vultures capitalize on the opportunity to heighten the significance of such cases. The compelling images that became embedded in public culture after the Oklahoma City bombing have seeped into other forms of artistic expression, building on the compassion that was generated and further heightening the importance of the case. The image of the partially destroyed building, constantly broadcast on television news and pictured in newspapers across the country as a backdrop to the search for survivors, was also reproduced frequently in fictional accounts. For example, the opening scene from the film *X-Files*, based on the popular television series of the same name, has the main characters, Fox Mulder and Dana Scully, assigned to investigate terrorism. They are responding to a bomb threat with hundreds of other agents, and Mulder determines that the responding team is searching for the bomb in the wrong place. After discovering it in a vending machine in a nearby building, he makes an unsuccessful attempt to disarm it. When the agents realize the bomb is going to explode despite their efforts, they make a dramatic last-second escape. After the explosion, the screen shows the remains of the building as resembling the destroyed Murrah Building. Similarly, one of the most unforgettable photographs taken following the Oklahoma City bombing, described briefly in the opening pages of this book, is the picture of a rescue worker cradling one-year-old Baylee Almon in his arms. Amateur photographer Charles Porter captured this dramatic image; it was then distributed worldwide and became, according to Oklahoma governor Frank Keating, "a metaphor for what's happened here."[13] This image was so memorable that it was used immediately in other forms of expression such as editorial cartoons. (See Figure 3.) This image was reproduced in another editorial cartoon following the terrorist attacks on the World Trade Center and the Pentagon in September 2001. (See Figure 4.)

This chapter explores the important feedback relationship between news and popular-culture influence on public understanding of militias. Popular-culture imagery contributed to the framing of militias when attention to them first intensified, and popular-culture depictions of conspiracies and terrorists, particularly, resulted in militias being presented in certain ways. News coverage of militias following the bombing helped create a new demon that was useful to creators of popular culture, and television and film outlets perpetuated the dominant frames first presented to the public as news. Popular-culture images also impacted the lives and thinking of members of the targeted deviants: mili-

3. *Nick Anderson, American Innocence. © 1995 The Washington Post Writers Group. Reprinted with permission.*

tia members used fictional accounts to legitimize their ideology and deviant behavior, as well as to confirm their presence as outsiders.

CREATING CONSPIRACIES

The news media attributed a wide range of strange and elaborate conspiracies to the militia movement, including the government's involvement in preparing missile silos to house detained patriots, allowing United Nations military forces to take residence in national parks, and implanting microchips in people to track citizens or segregate patriots. Reporters also emphasized that some people affiliated with the movement subscribed to one of several paranoid conspiracies that pointed to an alternative truth about what happened in Oklahoma City. Norm Olson was one of the militia members who had virtually uninhibited access to the media and was usually described as a member of the Michigan Militia, even though he was relieved of his command and ostra-

4. *Gary Varvel, Fallen Heroes. By permission of Gary Varvel and Creators Syndicate, Inc.*

cized because of his conspiracy theory about the Oklahoma City bombing. Other militia members asked: Who was John Doe 2? What accounts for the presence of an extra leg found near the bomb site? Why weren't federal law-enforcement agents from Alcohol, Tobacco, and Firearms at work in the Murrah building on April 19? Why was more than one explosion recorded? Such conspiracy concerns crossed over into other media that influenced the social construction of militias, including films, television, and editorial cartoons. (See Figure 5.) I spoke with another celebrity figure of the movement who pushed the idea that multiple bombs caused the building to collapse and that the bombing occurred to demonize the militia movement. He discussed his efforts to educate the public about what really happened at Oklahoma City:

> When the bombs went off in Oklahoma, we contacted our attorney to have him get a court injunction to stop the demolition of what was left of the building. The harder we pushed, the faster it came down. And Mc-Veigh's attorney was at the head of the class to bring it down. And since it was brought down, we've been trying to promote public awareness of the three seismic printouts from two different sources from the Norman,

5. *Tom Toles, Theory #2743. TOLES © 1995 The Buffalo News. Reprinted with permission of UNIVERSAL PRESS SYNDICATE. All Rights Reserved.*

Oklahoma epicenter and the Omni-Plex Museum, which is about a fourth of the distance from where the bombs went off—and the media won't even talk about it. They used the federal government to cover it up. One was the bomb and the other was the airwave and the other was when the building hit the ground. How come that didn't show up when they destroyed the evidence? These three seismic printouts show three different activities. And what was the lamppost doing standing alongside of where the truck was? And how come the first pictures never showed a hole in the ground where that truck was sitting? And why was the bomb squad equipment there prior to the bombs going off?

When I asked him who he thought was involved in the conspiracy, he accused the judicial and political system:

The judicial system, we believe, did not do their job. They just did damage control. We're sick and tired of that. They've done damage control for Weaver; they've done damage control for Waco; they've done damage control for Gordon Kahl; they've done damage control for the Murrah Building; they've done damage control for Flight 800; they've done damage control for the Lockerbie flight; they've done damage control, damage control, damage control, and never the truth. And we're sick and tired of it as Americans. Who has something to gain from a terrorist activity? Certainly, not militias. We believe those buildings belong to the people; they're public buildings. And there's public servants working in that building, and without government, we'd have chaos. So why would we want to play into the hands of George Bush that made that statement 'out of chaos shall come the New World Order'? Why do we want either one? We need our infrastructure. We need our country. We need a government. We need things left in place. Now those that had something to gain are those that were trying to pass the antiterrorism bill, which was stalled out in the U.S. Senate. Well, two days after the bombs went off, the bill took off. I wonder who had something to gain?

The news emphasized the most extreme conspiratorial theories adhered to by militia members. The public is generally suspicious of the government, and the limited access to decision-making processes cultivates an atmosphere in which such conspiracy thinking can thrive. Richard Hofstadter's classic treatise describes this ingrained cultural suspicion as the "paranoid style," "because no other word adequately evokes the qualities of heated exaggeration, suspiciousness, and conspiratorial fantasy." He documents the significance of this "style" throughout history, arguing that it is important not because fringe elements of a society embrace it but because "more or less normal people" do. Hofstadter also concludes that such paranoid thinking is not constant but thrives during times of rapid social change, conflict, catastrophe, or fear of catastrophe. In 1992, Sanford Pinsker remarked that "conspiracy-spinning is a growth industry and this is a boom time," and Peter Knight stated, "that conspiracy theories are everywhere."[14] The 1990s were a fruitful time in which to explore conspiracies due to the social, political, and religious tensions resulting from the end of the cold war and the approaching millennium. The public, affected by this brewing tension, explored new fears and revisited old ones, and their paranoia gained momentum as various media suggested that there might be a hint of truth to some of the most outrageous conspiracies. News media capitalized on this tension, offering a wide range of ideas that influenced public and militia thinking. Three of the most celebrated news events of the 1990s inspired discussion of conspiracy. First, conspiracy theory was woven into the early presentations of the Branch Davidian siege in such a way as to influence significantly how militia members came to interpret this event. Second, when O. J. Simpson was on trial for the murder of Nicole Brown and Ronald Goldman, the defense team claimed that the Los Angeles Police Department had conspired to frame the football star. Third, when Bill Clinton was struggling to avoid impeachment because of the Monica Lewinsky scandal, Hillary Rodham Clinton appeared on national television and described a great right-wing conspiracy attempting to undermine the president.

Mass-market media also provided an outlet to explore conspiracies. Consider the impact that news coverage of George Bush's comments on September 11, 1990, describing an approaching "new world order," had on the militia movement and public leaders. Militia leaders often cite this speech as evidence of a plan to relinquish our national sovereignty, but militia groups were not alone in their concerns. Pat Robertson, televangelist, voice of the popular 700 Club, leading figure of the Christian Coalition, corporate mogul, and one-time presidential hopeful, published a mass-market paperback under the title *The New World Order*. This best-selling book, first published in 1991, combines the extremist, anti-Semitic, conspiracy thinking of the John Birch Society and the Liberty Lobby.[15] He argued that an international conspiracy controlled by a conglomeration of Jews and Freemasons was working to establish a New World Order by taking control of the economy and then using that power to globalize politics. This book was significant because it offered its supporting evidence as undisputed truth. Robertson was able to air these ideas broadly because he had a large, loyal audience and some political clout among ultra-conservatives.

As Robertson and other conservatives used their access to mainstream markets to disseminate conspiracy thinking about a New World Order in the early 1990s, Hollywood offered a steady supply of films and television shows to solidify the importance of conspiracy images. For example, one of America's great, recurring conspiracies concerns a search for the truth about the assassination of John F. Kennedy. Few people believe that the Warren Commission investigation of the shooting is a complete account of how the assassination happened, and as a result, hundreds of conspiracy theories have been injected into public culture via different media to shed light on—or provide the truth about—the assassination. Few contributions have been more popular or controversial than Oliver Stone's 1991 movie *JFK*. Stone was highly effective in persuading the audience of the truth of his conspiracy theory that Oswald was a patsy for high-ranking members of the military and intelligence communities, who planned the assassination because they were concerned about Kennedy's efforts to end the cold war. The film uses images from documentaries, existing footage, reenactments, and reconstructed documentary clips to present the story as fact rather than as another fictional account. Stone's film also stands out from the other films and books about the assassination because it reignited a broader public debate about unknown truths. Officials from the Warren Commission, other government officials who testified, and reporters who covered the investigation all publicly criticized the film for its distortion of the truth.[16] But such defensiveness and denials only helped fuel paranoia because covering up the truth is central to any conspiracy.

Other films intensified the interest in conspiracy theories and government cover-ups before and during the celebrated coverage of the militia movement. Films like *A Few Good Men*, *The Pelican Brief*, *Blue Sky*, *Outbreak*, *Chain Reaction*, *Eraser*, *Independence Day*, *The Long Kiss Goodnight*, *Conspiracy Theory*, *Men in Black*, *Shadow Conspiracy*, and *Wag the Dog* all dealt with conspiracies, focusing on sinister behind-the-scenes forces controlling public figures and public events or constructing lies to mislead the public. *Conspiracy Theory* represents the culmination of the decade's paranoia, and such thinking is the centerpiece of the plot. The movie also makes extensive use of the conspiracy frames that dominated news coverage of the militia movement. Mel Gibson is featured as a former government mind-controlled assassin, turned cab driver and conspiracy theorist, who stalks Julia Roberts in the hopes of a romantic relationship. Their relationship oddly evolves into friendship and then a more romantic partnership, paralleling an exploration of Gibson's vast range of paranoid beliefs. Among his concerns are theories that were aired in actual media coverage of the militia movement—the government's ability to control natural disasters, the United Nations army taking residence in the United States and planning a government takeover, and communications using barcodes on street signs. Gibson is also depicted as having preparedness paranoia, stockpiling food, rations, and other supplies and configuring his apartment to avoid capture when confronted by his pursuers.

Television programming provides another good indication of the ripeness of the cultural environment for the exploration of conspiracy thinking. The *X-Files* was a highly popular and successful television show that capitalized on the public's fascination with conspiracy theories. Premiering in September 1993, the weekly television series focused on special agents Fox Mulder and Dana Scully. The cases they investigate—storylines that borrow heavily from real conspiracies, myths, and the paranormal—cannot be solved by other FBI agents or law-enforcement officials, who are unable to see, comprehend, and connect the sinister forces working to conceal the truth. The show's episodic exploration of various myths and unexplained phenomena, like the Bermuda Triangle ("Triangle"), the Loch Ness monster ("Big Blue"), satanic ritual abuse ("Die Hand Die Verletzt"), psychic powers ("Pusher"), and international Jewish conspiracies ("Drive"), is secondary to an overall conspiracy explored, unraveled, and revealed over time (and in the feature film). This larger conspiracy involves UFOs, alien abductions, cloning, government cover-ups, and evil unseen forces controlling history. Most of the show's energy is directed at uncovering the multiple and seemingly never-ending layers of this complex conspiracy involving a secretive syndicate of political, corporate, and other leaders working in collusion with alien forces in order to colonize the world with aliens. Mulder is a true believer and explains almost everything by referring to some conspiracy. Scully is supposed to be the cynical scientist, assigned to the *X-Files* to debunk Mulder's far-out theories and provide evidence to support the elimination of the unit. Over time, however, Scully, like many viewers, no longer questions the existence of such conspiracies but believes the irrational and impossible to be factual.

The vast pool of conspiracy images found in news and popular coverage—of governmental cover-ups and evil forces as the unseen puppeteers of national decision makers—easily seeped into the public exploration of the ideas of militia leaders. The news media presented militias as creating these far-out conspiracies and referenced only the most extreme versions of such thinking. This coupling of militia members and conspiracy thinking contributed significantly to the isolation of militias by portraying their beliefs as irrational. Some members of militia groups embraced the role of outsider, interpreting it as an opportunity to be a hero. Many militia members saw themselves as having a deeper understanding of the behind-the-scenes evil at work, and their efforts to prepare for the coming end would be rewarded when they prevailed. Holding such beliefs was taxing because militia members could no longer hide. Their beliefs were being challenged by the media, friends and family, and some militia leaders who depicted militia members with conspiracy beliefs as lunatics. The mavericks sought comfort in the large body of extremist literature made available to them; it was evidence that they were insightful rather than irrational. McVeigh's blueprint for the Oklahoma City bombing can be found in William Pierce's racist novel, *The Turner Diaries*. In the novel, Earl Turner destroys FBI headquarters with a truck bomb, and McVeigh discussed how he identified with Turner's concerns about gun laws and individual rights.[17] Although most of the militia members interviewed did not agree with McVeigh's methods, they said they understood his anger, and several discussed how the *Turner Diaries* accurately represented the state of affairs in the United States. Not only did McVeigh and militia members find validation of their beliefs by identifying with historical figures, they also were inspired by such popular culture figures as Jesse James, Robin Hood, Luke Skywalker, Clint Eastwood's Harry Callahan (*Dirty Harry*), Mel Gibson's William Wallace (*Braveheart*), and David Duchovny's Fox Mulder (*X-Files*). One militia leader called *Braveheart* the "militia film. We all want to be William Wallace and fight the British. Here's Scotland wanting to not have this centralized government oppressing [them], so they have this guy William Wallace who rises up and leads them and tries to break away from England." Another militia member asked me if I ever saw the movie *Red Dawn*. I had. He then said, "Watch it again. Remember how they get into this country. Just like the Russians in Afghanistan. They used commercial airlines and dropped special force paratroopers from commercial airlines. This shit is probably going to happen in the next couple of years."

IMAGES OF TERRORISM

Arnold Schwarzenegger's long Hollywood résumé includes many films in which he stars as a crime-fighting action hero. *True Lies*, a film first shown in theaters in mid-1994, was one of his more anticipated and controversial films. Schwarzenegger's character (Harry) leads a double life: to his family, he is a computer salesman unable to connect with his wife or daughter; to the U.S. government, he is a highly talented special agent. His dual life ends when he discovers that his wife (Helen), played by Jamie Lee Curtis, is having an extramarital affair. He confronts her and her companion, and in the process she discovers her husband's other life. The rest of the film focuses on the husband and wife's pursuit of a gang of Arab terrorists called the "Crimson Jihad," who are planning to explode nuclear weapons in several American cities. Harry and his wife-sidekick emerge victorious in numerous action-packed confrontations with the Arab terrorists, at times pursuing them on horseback, by helicopter, and by Harrier jet. The hero overcomes the terrorist villains, saving his child from Arab kidnappers and millions of Floridians from a nuclear blast.

This movie, directed by James Cameron, was lauded by critics for its stunning special effects and breathtaking action scenes. But the film was also heavily criticized by scholars, activists, and reporters for its stereotypical and ruthless portrayal of Arabs. Jack Shaheen's outstanding scholarly work on media images of Arabs includes reviews of over 900 films. In his opinion, *True Lies* helped "institutionaliz[e] the Arab stereotype." "Make no mistake, Cameron's *True Lies* is a slick film perpetuating sick images of Palestinians as dirty, demonic, and despicable peoples. The reel portraits are so remote from reality as to give normal viewers the willies."[18] After viewing the film, Abdullah Quick, president of the Islamic Social Services and Resources Association in Toronto, wrote that "Arabs/Muslims have superseded Japanese, Germans, Russians, Spanish drug lords, Black gang-bangers and Native people as the enemies of America and the most menacing threat to the Western world."[19] Reporters were also troubled by the negative images of Arabs promoted in the film. Amy Swartz concluded in *The Washington Post* that the film "portrays Arabs and Muslims as crazy, all-purpose, anti-American, terrorist bad guys."[20]

This movie's depiction of Arabs as terrorist villains is not an isolated incident. Indeed, when Hollywood and television screenwriters, novelists, and other makers of popular culture need to conjure up a demon for a story, the Arab terrorist works well because he is a known commodity—an established stereotype immediately viewed by audiences as an evil target worthy of pursuit. The events of September 11, 2001, have only solidified the public's deepest fears. Shaheen's comprehensive review found that one of the commonest ways in which Arabs are depicted in films is as villains—often as terrorists or part of a terrorist network. Audiences are familiar with the stereotype and thus react "with a sense of solidarity . . . united by their shared distance from these peoples of ridicule." The most unfortunate aspect of this prejudicial representation of Arabs is the consistency with which this frame reoccurs in popular culture.[21]

It is easy to understand how the Arab enemy was created and why the public is so willing to accept this imagery uncritically: both news and popular culture fail to offer any contradictory, more representative, images of Arabs. Over the last thirty years, Hollywood has consistently presented the Arab terrorist as a source of evil in films such as *Black Sunday, Nighthawks, Delta Force, Iron Eagle I, Iron Eagle II, Delta Force Commando II, Navy Seals, Delta Force III: The Killing Game, Under Siege, True Lies, Executive Decision, G.I. Jane, The Siege,* and *Rules of Engagement.* Moreover, the strength of this stereotype is heightened by Hollywood's use of actual news events when depicting terrorist acts. It was impossible for an audience viewing *True Lies* not to recall the celebrated news coverage of the World Trade Center bombing in 1993. Airplane bombings and hijackings are covered extensively in the news, and there are entire Hollywood films focusing on Arab terrorists who have hijacked a plane (*Delta Force, Executive Decision*). *Delta Force,* for example, is partly based on the hijacking of TWA flight 847 in June 1985.[22]

Black Sunday, the first film to focus on Palestinian involvement in a terrorist attack on American soil, was about an attempted bombing at the Super Bowl.[23] The film conjured up memories of real terrorist actions at the world's most important sporting event—the Olympics. In 1972, the world was stunned when Israeli athletes were taken hostage and murdered at the Munich Olympics. In the 1977 film, one of the terrorists involved in the Super Bowl attack makes direct reference to this news event. When Ronald Reagan was president in the early 1980s, international terrorism was a top policy issue, fueled in part by a wave of celebrated events that received extensive coverage in the news. Federal policymakers went to considerable lengths to form policy to respond more effectively to terrorist attacks abroad—including expanding the role of the military. Thus it is not surprising that there was a series of films in the middle- to late 1980s in which military personnel or military units responded to terrorism, including a retired Air Force colonel (*Iron Eagle, Iron Eagle II*), an elite commando unit (the *Delta Force* trilogy), and navy seals (*Navy Seals*).

Immediately following the Oklahoma City bombing, many of the reporters and officials responsible for making sense of this tragedy stated that it was the work of "Middle Eastern Terrorists." This conclusion was consistent with ingrained expectations about who was probably responsible for such a horrible act, and the public accepted such speculation as fact because it was consistent with a shared understanding of the groups or peoples capable of committing such acts. (Some individuals retaliated by victimizing Arabs.) Although McVeigh's capture shifted public and media focus toward radical militias, the initial national dialogue about terrorist threats and Arabs as a threatening group had already seeped into the coverage of this new threat. Since McVeigh's attack was an act of terrorism and because he was linked to the militia movement, reporters borrowed the dominant terrorist imagery solidified in popular culture to characterize militia organizations.

Several aspects of the representation of terrorists in popular culture were useful to the representation of militia groups in the news, but we focus here on four issues. First, the terrorist in popular culture has to be presented as a significant threat, typically established in films by the heartless killing of innocent citizens, by the weapon or weapons used, and by the number of victims killed or targeted to be killed by terrorist groups. Bombs or explosive devices were used in films such as *Black Sunday*, *The Next Man*, *Wanted: Dead or Alive*, and *The Siege*; a nuclear bomb was the weapon of choice in *Back to the Future*, *G.I. Jane*, *Frantic*, *Delta Force Commando II*, *Delta Force III: The Killing Game*, and *True Lies*. Other films, such as *Wanted: Dead or Alive* and *Executive Decision*, depicted terrorists as threatening and likely to kill millions using biological weapons. It is interesting that, although the gun link was a particularly effective way to demonstrate that militias were threatening, reporters also frequently discussed the possibility that militias might be stockpiling explosives and bombing devices. (See Figure 6.) Militia members themselves also discussed the possibility of biological warfare. News media explored the possibility that "militia fanatics" might have access to biological weapons, viruses, or poisonous gases and deploy them to kill hundreds of thousands of citizens, and films emphasized the use of biological agents.

Second, the potential threat of the popular-culture terrorist organization is demonstrated by focusing on the violent actions of a small cell of individuals who receive assistance and aid from an elaborate, invisible chain of supporting groups and individuals. Good examples include the films *True Lies*, *The Siege*, and *Rules of Engagement*. The support system typically includes a large range of citizens willing to provide information, supplies, or protection for a terrorist cell. Media coverage of the militia movement also stressed the existence of an interconnected network of militia organizations. Reporters discussed how new technologies allowed militias to monitor activities, share information, and spread their ideology. The media provided extensive coverage of these links, claiming that militias were well connected in their region or were part of a national network of militia groups. Some militia groups were un-

6. *Mike Luckovich, We'll be safe here. By permission of Mike Luckovich and Creators Syndicate, Inc.*

derground or went underground after their invisibility was compromised. News reporters frequently emphasized the "leaderless resistance" structure, which took on heightened meaning in part because it confirmed the popular images of the secrecy and danger of terrorist cells.

Third, films consistently depict the terrorist as a fanatic—irrational, uncompromising, and willing to die for some greater cause. For most Arab terrorists in films, the cause is religion. In the opening scene of *Executive Decision*, for example, a fanatic walks into a crowded restaurant with the Koran in one hand and a bombing device in the other. He commits suicide and kills numerous others. The rest of the film focuses on a specially trained group of military commandos who daringly board a hijacked plane to disarm a biological weapon and kill a group of terrorists driven by religion. Throughout the film, the terrorists frequently refer to passages of the Koran and describe how its words justify their actions and prejudices. Other films with a particular emphasis on the religious fanaticism of terrorists include *Delta Force, Iron Eagle, Delta*

Force III, and *The Siege*. In the 1990s militia members were frequently portrayed as having irrational beliefs. They had deep and paranoid beliefs in national and international conspiracies, passionately hated the U.S. government and the United Nations, and were unrelenting in their convictions about government cover-up and its responsibility for the incidents at Waco and Ruby Ridge. They were depicted as blaming the government for everything. Finally, militia members were fanatics about their guns, unwilling to compromise what they believed was their constitutional right.

Fourth, films emphasized specific physical characteristics and dress in their depictions of Arab terrorists as the ultimate source of evil. For example, in *Wanted: Dead or Alive*, all the *Delta Force* films, *True Lies*, and *Rules of Engagement*, the terrorists are shown as dirty and slimy.[24] The standard uniform for the Arab terrorists in films is beige military-style dress, long unkempt beards, and headdresses. Dress was also important in the discussion of the militia threat. In particular, the dominant public image of militias was of their preference for military-style dress and camouflage. It was such a central point that television reporters ignored militia leaders or representatives who refused to represent themselves in such a fashion. Moreover, several celebrities of the militia movement gained prominence primarily because of their willingness to appear in public in camouflage. This style of dress carried a larger meaning—that militias were preparing to go to war.

MILITIAS IN POST–OKLAHOMA CITY POPULAR CULTURE

The creators of images of crime and justice in comics, television, film, and other popular-culture outlets seized upon the opportunity to exploit the fear and shared understandings that emerged from news coverage about militias in 1995. The fictional accounts of militia groups presented on television and film following the Oklahoma City bombing is emphasized here for several reasons. First, compared with other popular-culture outlets, film and television images are the most likely to influence public thinking about social problems because they are designed to reach the largest and most diverse audience. Second, the people responsible for producing these images have considerable creative license to represent characters in their most extreme fashion. Third, the images presented in television and film carry significant meanings about the nature of evil in society, and the characterization of the deviant targeted for pursuit in fiction is as important to an intriguing and meaningful moral tale as is the creation of the hero working in the interests of justice. Fourth, many scholars agree that the portrayal of crime and justice in television and movies is consistent with that used in other popular outlets.[25]

TELEVISION COP SHOWS AND THE MILITIA THREAT

Television provides unlimited opportunities to consider important ethical, legal, and moral issues tied to crime and deviance. Watching television has become a primary leisure activity, and the public relies on it for entertainment, information, and understanding. Most households possess multiple television sets, which are turned on for over eight hours a day.[26] The public also has a ravenous appetite for crime and justice themes, which are exploited by all types of programming, from cartoons to soap operas to made-for-television movies to prime-time shows. Since the earliest days of television, images of crime and deviance have accounted for between 20 and 40 percent of all programming. Such emphasis caused Ray Surette to conclude that "the popular mass entertainment media, first in the form of film and today led by television, have thus become a significant social factor, conveying thematic images and lessons about whom to emulate and fear in society, what the base causes of crime are, and how crime should be fought."[27]

The early stages of criminal justice, especially police activities, are emphasized on television. It is not necessary to prove guilt beyond a reasonable doubt in a criminal court; the hero's pursuit of a deviant is sufficient justification for the chase. These heroes tend to pursue extreme cases and extreme criminals unrepresentative of the day-to-day concerns of real law-enforcement officers. Television crime fighters have an incredible clearance rate for their cases under investigation, showing that they play an important role in responding to society's threat. The popularity of such programming provides their creators with the opportunity to reflect upon general trends and issues faced by law enforcement. When real-life police investigative priorities focus on a certain type of crime or specific class of deviants, popular-culture cops take action against them.

Television cops were among the first popular media characters to respond to the militia threat after the Oklahoma City bombing. Several heroes of popular crime programs—including *Law and Order*, NYPD

Blue, *Walker Texas Ranger*, and *X-Files*—pursued militias, in the process confirming their criminal status. Another example of a television show that presented militias was a short-run show about the work of a U.S. attorney in New York called *Michael Hayes*. This show, modeled in part on the career of New York mayor Rudy Giuliani, was one of very few popular television crime shows focusing solely on federal investigations and prosecutions. Since federal authorities had come to play a central role in investigating militias—a role that was examined in the news media and congressional hearings on terrorism, Ruby Ridge, and Waco in the mid-1990s—it was fitting that Hayes would tangle with a militia group. The pertinent episode aired on October 28, 1997, and explored many of the tensions between federal law-enforcement officers and militias caused by the different interpretations of what actually occurred at Ruby Ridge and Waco. Militias were depicted as extremely dangerous in both their actions and organizational structure. The investigation focused on the murder of an Alcohol, Tobacco, and Firearms agent who participated in the siege at Waco. The militia movement was depicted as a significant threat—a "nationwide epidemic"—and the murder investigation was representative of the type of domestic terrorism, hate crimes, and killings in which such groups would be expected to participate. The fictional militias were well coordinated and used the Internet to communicate and monitor law enforcement. Ruby Ridge, Waco, New World Order conspiracies, and the antigovernment ideology of militias were emphasized. The images in this show depicted militias in the most extreme manner possible—the standard way they were presented in television shows in the late 1990s.

Probably the best example of the feedback relationship between news and popular culture on television is the popular television drama *Law and Order*. This program routinely steals storylines from sensational news headlines, providing a behind-closed-doors, albeit fictional, viewpoint of the dilemmas involved in the processing of particular cases. One of this program's innovative features is that it provides a criminal justice system perspective generally lacking in television crime shows. Most fictional programs focus on cops or courts, providing only brief glimpses into those stages of the process not judged central to the plot, but *Law and Order* pays equal attention to the investigation and arrest stages of law enforcement processing and the pretrial and trial stages of court processing. This approach provides the viewer with rather different than usual understandings of the activities of law enforcement, prosecutors, defense attorneys, and judges. It is one of the few television shows that explores the supporting relationship between police and prosecution, the tensions that result because of conflicting goals, and the negotiated meanings that are inevitable when parties with different goals try to resolve cases.

Given the show's preference for providing fictional interpretations of well-known real cases, it was inevitable that the heroes of *Law and Order* would take on a militia group in the wake of the Oklahoma City bombing. David Wolf, the creator of the series, made his contribution to public debate about militias on November 5, 1997 ("Nullification"). The first half of this show focuses on the investigation of an armored car robbery that results in the murder of one security officer and serious injury to another. Although the three suspects are wearing body armor during the robbery attempt, one of them is killed and another wounded. It is no coincidence that these two suspects have eagle tattoos and the words "Fortune Favors the Brave" over their hearts. The two homicide detectives assigned to investigate the case begin by talking with the coroner when she has just completed her examination of the dead suspect. She describes many scars, probably twenty to thirty years old, caused by shrapnel—implying that he served in the Vietnam War. The investigation continues with a discussion with a ballistics expert, who explains that the guns used in the robbery were converted fully automatic weapons and that the ammunition was homemade. The discovery of a replica of their tattoos on the Internet directs the investigation to a group of approximately twenty suburbanites—carpenters, storeowners, and police officers—who have formed a militia called the "Sons of Liberty." The name of this militia is not completely fictional; the news media had provided considerable coverage of a militia lobby group with that name organized in several states, and there is an above-ground militia by the same name in Northern California. With insufficient evidence to charge the surviving suspect or find the third shooter, the detectives and a small army of law-enforcement officers in riot gear serve warrants on all members of the militia and in the process uncover a large cache of guns and ammunition matching what was used in the robbery-murder. The militia refuses to cooperate during interrogation, only reciting name and rank when questioned by detectives.

The militia chooses to be represented by one of its members, who criticizes the government during the trial, distorting the Constitution and the judicial process with archaic legal interpretations. At a bail hearing, where each member is detained on 1 million dollars bail, their "attorney" demands that the militia be tried as prisoners of war. When the judge states that they are being tried in a criminal court, the militia member refers to the U.S. flag and its gold fringe, claiming that it is a military flag and the court a military court. Although they lose their motion to be declared prisoners of war, the judge agrees that the militia members can represent themselves. The trial goes forward, but the proceedings are frequently interrupted by patriotic rhetoric shouted by members of the group. Except for the member who serves as their attorney, they are all escorted from the courtroom. The state attempts to put the defendants on trial for committing a serious crime, and the militia in turn tries to put the government on trial, using history and anecdotal examples to evoke concern about multinational corporations, the New World Order, and governmental excess. The show is somewhat sympathetic to the militia, as depicted by an acknowledgment of the legitimacy of some of the characters' claims and the jury's inability to reach a verdict.

It is clear that Wolf was influenced by the dominant frames of the celebrated coverage of militias when deciding what to emphasize in depicting his "Sons of Liberty." On several occasions the law-enforcement and prosecutorial teams charged with investigating the "Sons of Liberty" refer to them as angry, irrational, and violent terrorists. The group is made up of ordinary, suburban citizens livid with the government and government policy. Although there is no direct reference to the Oklahoma City case, other celebrated cases are discussed. Waco and Ruby Ridge are mentioned as an explanation for the anger of such groups. The show does not make direct reference to the Montana Freemen case, but certainly it was influenced by media coverage, and it emphasizes the convoluted legal theories and courtroom theatrics that were central to that case. The "Sons of Liberty" are depicted as a significant threat with a very large cache of guns—all fully automatic weapons. The technological links between groups across the United States are emphasized, and reference is made to a large, sympathetic public supporting this group. For example, the defendants receive millions of dollars from across the country in order to make the 20 million dollar bail set by the judge. Conspiracy rhetoric is also used. One of the detectives, asked why he is peering out of a window, says "I'm looking for black helicopters," and concerns about multinational corporations involved in a plot to eliminate the sovereignty of the United States and replace it with a New World Order are presented at several points.

The *X-Files*, which contributed significantly to the fund of conspiracy images in the air when the panic about militias was first ignited, wove fears about them indirectly into the overall conspiracy and directly into several episodes ("Unrequited," "Tunguska," and "Terma"). The focus of the news media on militia conspiracies, sinister forces, and government cover-up fits well with the show's search for hidden truths. For example, in "Tunguska" and "Terma," a militia group's plans to use a fertilizer bomb like the one detonated at Oklahoma City is combined with the show's broader search for signs of extraterrestrial life. The episode titled "Unrequited," first aired in February 1997, focuses on a radical right-wing militia group called the "Right Hand," which is suspected of murdering several high-ranking military officials. The leader of this militia points agents Scully and Mulder in the direction of Nathan Teager, a former Green Beret who spent over twenty years in a Vietnam POW camp. Teager has supposedly been liberated from the camp by the "Right Hand." When they arrive in the United States with him, government agents unsuccessfully try to detain him, and he disappears. Teager, who looks a lot like Timothy McVeigh, is able to avoid capture because he can hide outside a person's field of vision—a skill he has learned as a prisoner of war. It is revealed that his motivation for killing the military officials is that they were part of a secret commission that murdered South Vietnamese soldiers during the war.

Finally, in an episode aired in May 1998, the *X-Files* focused specifically on a militia's use of biological weapons. The episode ("Pine Bluff Variant") begins in a city park, where agents Scully and Mulder and a team of FBI operatives are closing in on Jacob Haley, a member of the New Spartans militia, who is wanted on domestic terrorism charges. It is suspected that Haley plans to exchange money for automatic weapons to be used in domestic terrorism activities as part of an attempt to overthrow the government. The team of agents watches some sort of exchange between Haley and an arms dealer, who then dies from a toxin that eats away his skin. The agents pursue Haley, but he escapes with Mulder's assistance. It is soon discovered that Mulder was invited to work with the New Spartans after hearing him speak at a UFO conference at which he espoused several government-conspiracy theories. When the group suspects Mulder of double-crossing them, one of its skinhead look-alikes interrogates him and breaks his finger. Haley, however, believes that Mulder is sincere in his efforts to assist the militia. The threat of this fatigue-wearing group is that it attempts to spread a biological pathogen. The man in the park in the opening scene dies from a genetically engineered bioweapon, as do fourteen innocent people in a movie theater. The militia group attempts to have a greater impact by spraying the biological weapon on a bank's money supply during a robbery. This tragedy is avoided because a CIA mole, who is actually the leader of a militia group, does not use the toxin on the money. When Mulder realizes he had been set up, and the biological toxin was actually engineered in the United States, he confronts one of the CIA agents:

CIA agent: What do you hope to accomplish, Agent Mulder, as a whistle-blower? To mobilize a civil rights action? To bring down the federal government? To do the very work that group you were a part of is so bent on doing? What do you want? Law against those men or laws protecting them?
Mulder: I want people to know the truth.
CIA agent: Well, sometimes our job is to protect those people from knowing it.

MILITIAS IN FILMS

The images of militias in crime-and-justice television, supplemented by an assortment of other entertainment images including made-for-television movies (*Nightmare in Big Sky Country, A.T.F., First Daughter*), have corroborated the depictions of militias in the news. The extreme presentation of militias has contributed significantly to the development of the public's shared understandings of militias. In thinking about the influence of public-culture images, let us remember that television is viewed in isolation and competes against the many distractions of household life. Television advertisements are structured to provide op-portunities to take care of some of these distractions, but telephone calls, doorbells, and disputes between children occur at random. Cable television provides a seemingly endless supply of channels for the casual viewer, and most households have two or three different television sets. Distractions and competing images minimize the influence of television messages. Big-screen films are distributed on a grander scale and ulti-mately "help to define what it means to be an American."[28] The people who create films have more flexibility to convey moral messages for many reasons, including the wider canvas, the uninterrupted pacing, and the length of time available to tell a story. Movie theaters bring together a random sample of the community who momentarily are iso-lated from the distractions of the world. The collective vicarious experience that occurs in movie theaters is in some ways comparable to yesterday's public celebrations of punishment, including town square hangings, lynchings, and corporal punishment. The viewing of such acts of torture brought people together in a clear statement of community solidarity that was confirmed by the discussions, gossip, and institutionalized myths following the acts. Similarly, the messages conveyed in films take on particularly important meanings because they are combined with experiential group reactions. The audience viewing a film can share a range of emotions with others in the community and may be reminded of the experience as they discuss the film with others, read reviews, and watch the film again when it is released for video and television.

The post–Oklahoma City focus on militias helped to create a deviant that the community was concerned about, so it was inevitable that films would put the dominant understandings of militias to work. The creation, production, and release of films occurs at a much slower pace than that of other popular-culture outlets, but several films still made direct or indirect contributions to public understanding of militias. The following discussion focuses on *Arlington Road* and *The Patriot* because they were the most popular of the films that directly used the militias and extremism as the central threat. There were other films that included militia images, including *Land of the Free*, the *Blues Brothers 2000*, and *Militia*. Films like the comedy *Blues Brothers 2000* presented militia images tangentially but stereotypically, as militias were among the organizations, individuals, and groups who pursued the Blue Brothers on their latest "mission from God." Like *Conspiracy Theory*, the film *Militia* is clear about its issue of concern. A BATF agent infiltrates a militia group plotting to assassinate the president using anthrax-impregnated missiles. It is a really poor film, ignored by the public, but it does illustrate an extreme stereotype of militias. The film opens with a Waco-like siege in which a fleet of BATF agents in black helicopters destroys one of the compounds of the "Brotherhood of Liberty" militia. Members of this militia and a hate-spewing shortwave radio talk-show host cite Ruby Ridge, Waco, and Oklahoma City as the rationale for their anger towards the government. The militia complains about the United States conspiring with the United Nations to institute a New World Order. Many of the members of the militia wear camouflage, are highly trained with weapons and explosives, and are part of a sophisticated organization with connections throughout the United States.

Arlington Road

Mark Pellington's *Arlington Road* provides a unique contribution to popular-culture imagery of militias and extremist activities. One of the film's main characters is Michael Faraday (Jeff Bridges), a history professor with an interest in domestic terrorism. Faraday is grieving over the death of his wife, an FBI agent killed in the line of duty, when he meets Oliver Lang (Tim Robbins) and his wife Cheryl (Joan Cusack)—neighbors from across the street. Faraday and the Langs become friends after he rushes their son Brady to the hospital when he is seriously injured in a firework accident. As the friendship progresses, however, Faraday becomes suspicious of the Langs when he discovers that Oliver has lied about his background and he sees Oliver attempting to hide some architectural drawings. Faraday pursues his suspicions and discovers that Lang is actually William Fenimore, who was convicted as a juvenile of attempting to blow up a federal building with a pipe bomb. Faraday also suspects that his neighbor played a role in the bombing of a federal building in Saint Louis that killed sixty people. The Langs murder Faraday's girlfriend and kidnap his son in an effort to deter him from continuing to pry into their affairs. Oliver tells Faraday that his son will not be harmed as long as he keeps quiet until after Oliver completes his mission. Faraday surreptitiously continues his investigation, suspecting that Lang is conspiring with others to bomb FBI headquarters. He follows a "Liberty" moving van, which he suspects is loaded with explosives, to the FBI building and is surprised when the security officers at the gate allow the van to enter the underground garage. Faraday breaks through security to stop the bombing and save his son. In a provocative plot twist, Faraday discovers that neither his son nor the bomb are in the moving van, but a bomb is in the trunk of his car. He realizes that he has been set up just before the bomb goes off and destroys the building.

Faraday uses the classroom and a course he is teaching on terrorism to work through his anger and grief over his wife's death. One of the most powerful scenes in the movie occurs when he lectures his class about the Saint Louis federal building bombing. Many of the facts and images, the motive for the bombing, the characteristics of the suspect, and the general conclusions about the responsible party—a lone wolf acting out his anger against the government—were lifted from the Oklahoma City case. Pellington uses this scene to remind the audience of their fear when the bombing occurred and their relief when McVeigh was arrested. Faraday confronts his students directly, exploring how they felt when they learned of the bombing then heard that the suspect was killed in the act. The class talks about their fears and how they felt safe because the terrorist was dead. Faraday emphasizes that the public needed someone to blame in order to feel safe: "Here was the man unlike the rest of us—we maimed him and he is no more."

Oklahoma City was not the only celebrated case that influenced the script of this film. Later, Pellington uses Faraday's terrorism class once again to show how his wife was murdered in a Ruby Ridge–like standoff. Faraday takes his class to Copper Creek, West Virginia, where the FBI surrounded a remote cabin in an effort to arrest a right-wing extremist suspected of stockpiling weapons. As shown in a flashback scene, the agents surround the house and, while contemplating what they should do, are discovered by the extremist's ten-year-old son. The agents do not identify themselves as federal authorities, and thus the son concludes that they are coming to steal his daddy's guns. He runs towards the house, warns the family, grabs his gun, and starts firing in the direction of the agents. The shootout between the family and the agents results in the death of the boy and his mother. Then, in what appears to be Pellington's revenge for the killing of Vicki Weaver and her son at Ruby Ridge, Faraday's wife is killed with a sawed-off shotgun by a young woman holding a baby. It is also clear that Faraday is angry with the FBI because of its unwillingness to take responsibility for what happened at Copper Creek. Pellington borrows from the Waco siege when Faraday describes the multiple errors made in the Copper Creek standoff. Faraday tells his students that the FBI had inadequate intelligence because the man suspected for stockpiling weapons was not even home when the FBI arrived, had planned to sell rather than use the weapons, and had instructed his family that somebody would come to try to steal their weapons so they needed to be prepared.

Arlington Road attempts to explore more broadly the reasons for extremists' discontent and avoids the stereotypical style of dress found in most television and film depictions of militias. Pellington and screenwriter Ehren Kruger decided to deviate from such imagery after Kruger "attended several militia meetings while researching the script." According to Ann Hornaday, Pellington "research[ed] militia movements so that *Arlington Road* would be 'ideologically sound,'" relying primarily on FBI antiterrorism reports and Joel Dyer's book *Harvest of Rage*. The influence of Dyer's book becomes clear when Lang confronts Faraday about his attempts to uncover the past. Lang tells Faraday that he grew up on a Kansas farm that went bankrupt when "some government bureaucrat stuck a pin in a map" and eliminated its water supply. The audience learns that Lang's father killed himself because he could not farm and pay his bills. Pellington admitted using an anecdote from Dyer's book to show the character's anger.[29] Moreover, the Langs are depicted as being part of a broad network of ordinary suburbanites working to overthrow the government while deflecting the blame onto lone-wolf terrorists. Pellington depicts Faraday and the bomber suspected in the Saint Louis case as patsies of this highly coordinated network.

Arlington Road ends but does not put the audience's fears to rest. Law enforcement is unable to control this elaborate network of terrorists, able to commit horrendous acts and divert the blame to specific individuals. Such a presentation forces the audience to reconsider the question of McVeigh's lone-wolf status.

The Patriot

There are certain characters, or actors who play those types of character, who are immediately identifiable to the movie audience. The audience knows what to expect from such characters as Rambo (*First Blood, Rambo II–III*); Harry Callahan (*Dirty Harry, The Enforcer, Magnum Force, The Dead Pool*), John McClane (*Die Hard I–III*), Riggs and Murtaugh (*Lethal Weapon I–IV*), and Alex Cross (*Kiss the Girls, Along Came a Spider*). These memorable characters approach justice in a similar manner. Similarly, the roles played by Steven Segal take on special meaning because, although he does not play the same character in name, the audience knows what to expect. Like Jackie Chan, Chuck Norris, and Jean Claude Van Damme, Segal conquers evil in breathtaking hand-to-hand combat. *The Patriot* provided a clear depiction of the outsider status of militias, reconfirmed the popular-culture images that helped to define militias in the period following the Oklahoma City bombing, and provided Segal with yet another opportunity to demonstrate his martial-arts prowess.

Steven Segal plays a compassionate but powerful hero who has to save a small Montana town from a radical militia group. Segal's character is Wesley McClaren, an ex-government immunologist who runs a ranch and uses alternative medicine to cure both humans and animals. His character evokes images of the cowboy hero of the Western film genre in that he is highly skilled with rope or gun, on horseback, and in hand-to-hand combat. He is also compassionate; a caring father raising a daughter on his own, he accepts blueberry pies and carpentry in exchange for medical services and saves a tiny horse that others would put down. McClaren is also a highly skilled warrior who takes action when a radical militia group uses a deadly biological agent in the town, killing many residents, federal law-enforcement officials, and military personnel.

This film presents militias in several ways that echo the dominant imagery presented in news and popular-culture outlets. First, militia groups are worthy of pursuit because they are a significant threat to society. Militia members are terrorists, driven by irrational ideology and willing to inflict unspeakable harm in an effort to further their cause. Biological toxins, guns, and explosives are the weapons of choice in their war against the government, a war in which they are not concerned about killing innocent victims. Militia groups can also be easily identified by their military style of organization, camouflage uniforms, and war training. In *Arlington Road*, extremists bomb federal buildings, attempt to kill as many people as possible, and remain at large. Militias in *The Patriot* and *Militia* prefer biological weapons. It is not clear how the militia groups in *The Patriot* gets access to a deadly biological weapon called NAM-37, but they are willing to use the weapon to kill as many people as possible, believing they possess an antitoxin that will prevent them from being affected. The militia surrenders to law enforcement near the beginning of the movie, and its leader is taken into custody, providing an opportunity to spread the virus. As the people of Ennis, Montana, flock to the hospital because of unidentified illnesses, the militia group learns that their antitoxin is ineffective because the biological agent in it has mutated. The militia, thinking that the government team that arrives has a cure, breaks its leader out of jail and takes control of the town by murdering numerous federal agents who are on duty at the jail and military personnel protecting the antitoxin. Once the militia takes control of the hospital and the town, it realizes the government is using the same ineffective antitoxin. McClaren is temporarily detained by the militia group, but he escapes to concoct a cure in a secret government facility.

Second, the threat supposedly presented by militias is supported by the irrationality of their beliefs. Popular-culture militias believe strongly in conspiracy theories and spew antigovernment rhetoric or excerpt history to illustrate their patriotism. Bar codes, mind control, Y2K, and the AIDS epidemic are all among the concerns of *The Patriot*'s Fifth Montana Militia. Biological weapons are often their weapon of choice because they evoke the most fear and concern and because they depict the length to which such groups are willing to go on behalf of their beliefs. The Fifth Montana Militia, for example, are willing to kill millions of innocent people in order to further their cause. This camouflage-clad group quotes Jefferson and Franklin Roosevelt and uses other historical quotes to highlight its seriousness of purpose. It argues that government officials are tyrants, federal law-enforcement officers are storm troopers, and courts have no constitutional authority.

Third, similar to how *Arlington Road* drew on specific celebrated cases, *The Patriot*'s presentation of militias borrows directly from the news media's focus on the Militia of Montana and its celebrated coverage of the Montana Freemen case. The Militia of Montana is one of the best-known organizations of the militia movement and some writers have even called it the "Mother of all Militias."[30] Although it is primarily a profit-oriented clearinghouse for extremist and militia literature, John Trochmann's celebrity status and his accessibility to reporters helped solidify an association between a rural Montana lifestyle and militias. The public believes that rural America generally, and Montana specifically, are great havens of extremist activities. (See Figure 7.)

The Freemen case is indirectly referenced in *The Patriot*. The Fifth Montana Militia is introduced to the audience as being involved in a prolonged standoff with federal agencies after taking refuge at a ranch in a remote location. During the standoff, and later when the leader is arrested and appears before a judge in court, the militia members recall historic events and figures to support their beliefs and cite the Constitution as the only legal authority. The leader of the militia represents himself at the bail hearing but refuses to recognize the legal authority of the court.

Fourth, popular culture usually explores the possibility that there is some justification for the militia's anger and concern. In the *Law and Order* episode discussed earlier, the jury cannot reach a verdict because some the militia's beliefs strike home. The *X-Files* agents are never able to uncover the whole truth. In *Arlington Road*, Faraday is upset because the FBI will not admit the mistakes they made that resulted in his wife's death. In *The Patriot*, McClaren also is concerned about government activity. He has quit his government job because of the government's role in stockpiling and using deadly biological weapons. The government contributes to the deaths of the people of Ennis because it cannot control the militia or the biological agent, and government agencies are consistently depicted as withholding information or covering up their mistakes. The government asks for McClaren's help but does not explain

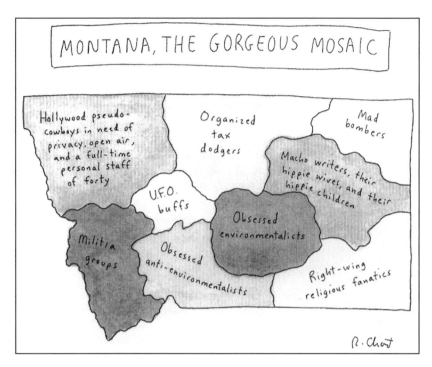

7. Roz Chast, Montana, The Gorgeous Mosaic. © The New Yorker Collection 1996 Roz Chast from cartoonbank.com. All Rights Reserved.

why they need him. Later, McClaren identifies the biological agent as government created. In order to create an antitoxin, Segal has to go to a laboratory controlled by the government. The difference between McClaren and the militia members is that he does not commit crimes because of his concerns. Although many characters have legitimate questions about the government, their anger is usually very different from the militia's irrational and uncompromising beliefs, usually depicted as having been created by the standoffs at Ruby Ridge and Waco.

Conclusion

After militia groups were spuriously linked to McVeigh, reporters portrayed militias using images of conspiracy and terrorism. The celebrated nature of the bombing triggered enormous interest and momentum that resulted in the depiction of militias in a way that produced a shared understanding of what militias supposedly stood for and the extent to which they were threatening to the public. The news media played a critical role in the construction of militia images, providing unprecedented coverage and using specific frames sponsored by particular institutions and agencies. This focused attention resulted in the development of a commonsense understanding that militias were a legitimate threat—monsters worth fearing. Popular-culture outlets helped solidify this view of militias by regurgitating the most extreme of the distorted images presented in the news. The cross-pollination and consistency of representation that occurred in both fact-based and fictional outlets solidified the public's view that militias must reside on the outer boundaries of mainstream society.

Constructing Good Demons

I first heard about the events of September 11, 2001, during my morning commute to Indiana University. I had not bothered to turn on a television that morning and was about fifteen minutes into a twenty-minute commute when I turned on the radio. The disc jockey was struggling to find words to describe what he was watching on television: smoke was billowing from the Twin Towers of the World Trade Center. Information was scarce, but he knew that two different airplanes striking a great symbol of America's economic prosperity was more than coincidental. He tried to be as objective as possible and reserve judgment until more facts were in, but it was obvious he had concluded that what had occurred was an act of terrorism. He was right.

I parked my car and rushed to the seminar classroom where I was supposed to teach that morning to tell my students to go home. Nobody was there, so I went to the closest room with a television set and found my students watching the events unfold with other students, staff, and faculty members, all trying to find out whether what they had heard was really true. "Did the building fall?" one of the students asked after the south tower collapsed. She refused to believe what she saw and was hoping that somebody would tell her that it was just an illusion, but several people nodded their heads. Everyone was mesmerized by the images on the television, trying to comprehend what was occurring but overwhelmed. When the north tower collapsed, people started to leave because the emotional atmosphere was too intense. Nobody could handle the fear, anger, shock, disbelief, and sadness that we were experiencing. We needed to find something more familiar.

"America will never be the same." Many people have said something like this, and I heard it as I left the classroom that morning. It is still too early to know how different the United States will be; the nerve that the event exposed is still raw and our fears continue to simmer. Yet, as in the aftermath of the Oklahoma City bombing, it is clear that social-control priorities are changing, social structures are transforming, foreign and domestic policies are evolving, public perceptions are shifting, and new frameworks for thinking about social problems are being constructed and old ones are being repackaged. It is also important to recognize that new community boundaries are being constructed and manipulated. It is going to take a long time to fully grasp the impact that September 11 will have on society. I can conclude, however, after observing how perceptions and social structures changed following the Oklahoma City bombing, that in order to fully understand the impact of these terrorist attacks on public culture, one has to closely examine the role of the media. Specifically, it will be important to examine the amount and type of coverage given, the claims-makers used and their motivations for participating in the construction process, the framing of terrorism and why certain frames are selected and others ignored, what ceremonies are instituted to give legitimacy to new boundaries, and how the event and the response to it is recreated and defined in various cultural forums.

The events of September 11 have helped to relegate fears about homegrown terrorism to the nether regions of public concern, but it was inevitable that the news media would compare the World Trade Center and Pentagon attacks to the destruction caused by McVeigh at Oklahoma City. Direct comparisons were made in several ways. First, the Oklahoma City bombing gave reporters and the public a baseline comparison to assess the impact of the more recent attacks. The public was reminded of the number killed and injured when the Murrah building was destroyed, and it was clear that the casualties from the attacks of September 11 would be significantly greater. Second, reporters compared the hatred, motivation, and backgrounds of McVeigh and Osama bin Laden. Indeed, bin Laden became, as McVeigh had once been, society's top public enemy. McVeigh was the terrorist bred from within who hated the federal government, and bin Laden was the foreign terrorist who hated the powerful influence that the United States has on the Middle East. McVeigh became the public face of the domestic terrorist threat; bin Laden was the best representative of the foreign terrorist threat. In the aftermath of their evil deeds, all other social problems became temporarily invisible. Dan Herbeck and Lou Michel, the reporters from the *Buffalo News* who wrote *American Terrorist*, even discussed how McVeigh might have reacted to the bombings if he were still alive. They also reminded readers that when McVeigh was imprisoned at the supermax prison in Colorado, he shared a cellblock—nicknamed "Bomber Row"—with Ted Kaczynski, Ramzi Yousef, and Eyad Ismoil. Yousef and Ismoil were convicted of the 1993 World Trade Center bombing and are connected to Al Qaeda.[1] Third, although the acts of September 11 were not like any terrorist act that has been seen before, the perpetrators were very well known. The public was reminded that Arab terrorists were initially suspected of committing the Oklahoma City bombing because they were known to use truck "bombs." Reporters immediately tapped into these same broader cultural understanding of terrorism after the attacks on the World Trade Center and the Pentagon. Osama bin Laden was well known and coverage of his evil deeds helped solidify the public's understanding of the Arab terrorist as did media coverage of McVeigh and the militia movement. Fourth, many Oklahoma City bombing images were revisited after the attacks. For example, as was noted in Chapter 7, perhaps the most powerful, enduring image of the Oklahoma City bombing—the rescue worker cradling Baylee Almon in his arms—was repackaged by a cartoonist who depicted Uncle Sam carrying a fireman away from the rubble of the World Trade Center. Other images of the destroyed Murrah building were brought back into public culture as rescue workers, law-enforcement officers, fire fighters, and other disaster-related personnel went about the painstaking search for survivors and bodies in New York City, and the media provided frequent progress reports of the efforts to clean up the rubble. Reporters speculated that the clean-up crews, as well as reporters who covered the attacks, would suffer psychological distress similar to what occurred after Oklahoma City. Finally, reporters discussed the changes in society's social-control apparatus that were implemented following the Oklahoma City bombing and described how additional measures were still necessary because of the destruction caused by bin Laden.

The terrorist attacks of September 11 also provided an opportunity for reporters to revisit the militia movement and draw parallels between militia groups and the Al Qaeda terrorist network. The public's understanding of the militia movement had been firmly established, and thus the images used to demonize this movement were useful for describing the more recent terrorist attacks. In particular, the possibility that a militia group might use biological weapons, a scenario frequently used by reporters to illustrate militia danger in 1995 and 1996, was fearfully revisited as anthrax spread through the U.S. mail. The media first assumed that the same terrorist network that attacked the World Trade Center and the Pentagon was spreading it, but it was difficult to prove this link. As reporters concluded that the Al Qaeda terrorist organization was probably not responsible for the anthrax attacks, they searched for other potential culprits including domestic terrorists such as militia groups. Reporters argued that militia groups could have been responsible for the attack, reminding readers of several cases in which a militia member or other domestic terrorist was arrested with some biological agent, such as anthrax, ricin, or Yersinia pestis (the bacteria that causes bubonic plague).[2]

Several other parallels can be drawn between the representations of militias and Al Qaeda in the media. Images of Middle Easterners training at terrorist camps in the deserts of Afghanistan and efforts to destroy such camps were frequently presented in the news. Many images of bin Laden were available, but one that was presented frequently found him sitting in the desert on his heels, firing an automatic weapon at some unknown target. His facial expression clearly indicates that he enjoys firing the weapon. Militia members were often shown wearing their camouflage and war paints, shooting their guns at targets in the woods. Both groups were depicted as preparing for war against America. Federal and local governments implemented the war in Afghanistan and other policy responses not only to bring bin Laden and the terrorists to justice but also to disrupt what was apparently a worldwide threat and prevent such an attack from happening again. Just as the terrorism legislation passed after the Oklahoma City bombing was considered justified in part because the militia movement was depicted as having a presence in all states and supporters from all walks of life, the response to September 11 was justified by the presence of this international terrorist network. Reporters asked how extensive the threat was in America and abroad: Were other terrorist cells waiting to be activated in America and where would they strike next? The Golden Gate Bridge? A sporting event? Another airplane? Would such cells strike at American interests abroad? Such speculation about a looming and inevitable post–September 11 strike was frequently presented in the news media. The militia threat, discussed in more detail below, was depicted by referencing the Oklahoma City bombing and by discussing the few militia members who were carrying out various criminal activities, stockpiling weapons and bombing materials, and planning to use biological weapons. It was obvious that the Al Qaeda terrorist network was a significant threat because of its involvement in many tragic incidents, but it was possible that the network was planning bigger and more sinister plots, including using biological weapons on a massive scale, deploying nuclear weapons, and ordering more suicide attacks. Finally, in parallel to the comparisons made between McVeigh and bin Laden, reporters compared the underlying concerns of militias to those of the Al Qaeda terrorists. The reporters described how the militia movement was a connected network of American groups that hated the federal government and were organized to undermine it. The new threat was a network of foreign individuals and groups that hated America and everything American. The terrorists' motivation was not to move the country back to a more constitutional form of government but to destroy Western influence.

The public was intensely fearful after the attacks on the World Trade Center and the Pentagon, and the spread of anthrax only intensified that fear. There followed a public spending spree on preparedness materials and self-protection measures, such as gas masks, generators, food and water supplies, firearms, and survival manuals. The militia groups who had been preaching preparedness since their first contacts with the media used the public concern as an opportunity to gloat as well as share their expertise about items worth storing. Other reporters discussed how militia members were offering their services to law-enforcement and government officials, willing to put their differences aside in order to work together in response to this foreign threat. Militia members volunteered to ride on airplanes with their guns to protect the public. But reporters emphasized that these groups were still considered dangerous and that government officials were not interested in receiving their assistance. The attacks on the World Trade Center and the Pentagon led to celebrations of America and what it means to be American, and militia members embraced the patriotism that swept the country.

Reporters also considered whether the terrorist attacks of September 11 would revive militias, discussing how key crisis events, like Ruby Ridge, Waco, and the Oklahoma City bombing, had contributed to the movement's growth in the early to mid-1990s. They assumed that the terrorist attacks would relight the militia flame and reenergize the fear that had motivated people to participate earlier. Celebrity militia figures also tried to seize the opportunity to reinvigorate their stagnated movement. John Trochmann, still willing to talk to the media, reported that the Militia of Montana could not keep preparedness materials on the shelves. Sticking with the theme of militia movement as "neighborhood watch" that he had emphasized at the 1995 Senate hearings, he discussed how doctors, lawyers, politicians, and bankers were buying what his movement had available. It was also publicized that Norm Olson sent word to President Bush that he and his militia were ready to serve in the war on terrorism as "the eyes and the ears and the feet of America's security," again promoting the argument that militias were only a "protective" not "aggressive" force. Other leaders simply made themselves available by convening meetings and posting announcements in areas where the public was likely to go to search for preparedness materials. All these leaders were using the terrorist acts of September 11 and the need for preparedness as a hook, hoping to reel in citizens to share some of their broader concerns. This strategy was similar to how gun control, the Brady Bill, and the semiautomatic weapons ban was used in the early 1990s to attract people to the movement. Militia leaders reported that there seemed to be a renewed interest in their work and attendance at their public meetings was increasing.[3]

THE REMNANTS OF THE MILITIA MOVEMENT

The militia movement had not completely disappeared from the public's radar screen after the militia panic ended in 1997. A steady supply of images reminded the public about the nature and extent of the militia threat. For example, as was demonstrated in Chapter 7, some popular-culture outlets, especially films, operate on a delayed production timeline compared with the immediacy of news accounts. The panic about the militia movement after Oklahoma City provided an obvious target for popular-culture law enforcers, but creating, financing, casting, and producing films is a long, arduous process. Most of the films that included militia or militia-like villains came out after the news media had lost interest in the militia movement. The entertainment industry thus helped to sustain public concern about the movement because the dominant stereotypes that had been produced in the news were exaggerated in films.

The news media did not completely abandon coverage of the militia movement after 1997 and prior to the World Trade Center and Pentagon attacks. The coverage was not nearly as intense as that observed in the second half of 1995 and in 1996, but local and regional stories were written about the criminal activities of some militia members, and national coverage of Oklahoma City–related events provided reporters with additional opportunities to discuss the militia movement. It was not necessary for reporters to provide investigative exposés of the militia movement, as they had when these groups were first discovered, just to provide continuing coverage of crime incidents involving militia members. This reduced coverage, however, presented militias in a familiar way: they were terrorists alienated from society, plotting to overthrow the government. Several national news stories were published in December 1999 that raised concerns about militia plans for Y2K. One of them involved the San Joaquin County militia and their plans to blow up large liquid propane tanks in Sacramento County, California. This militia group had hoped that their crimes would lead citizens to participate in an armed overthrow of the government. The coverage emphasized that the individuals arrested in this case were well connected with other paramilitary groups, believed that the new millennium would bring anarchy, and adhered to a variety of conspiracy theories, including that anyone using a supermarket discount card would have their name entered into a satanic database.[4]

Most of the militia incidents covered after 1997 were not of national interest but were presented as regional or local stories. For example, local Dallas media provided extensive coverage of an incident involving a man arrested for possessing explosive materials and weapons. Deanna Boyd, a reporter from the *Fort Worth Star-Telegram*, reported that, on the day McVeigh was put to death, police seized "alarming right-wing literature," "bombing-making chemicals and militia-type equipment, including a M-16 rifle, a disassembled M-16, about half a dozen other assault rifles, a handgun, and 9,000 rounds of ammunition." Another regional incident that received coverage was the conviction of a Wyoming man for manufacturing pipe bombs. Like McVeigh, he had been influenced by the *Turner Diaries* and was constructing the bombs in order to further the interests of a "clandestine supermilitia." *The Saint Petersburg Times* reported the involvement of the Saint Petersberg militia and its leader in a plot to bomb power lines in the hope of inciting civil war. Donald Beauregard, an active militia leader since the mid-1990s, was sentenced to five years in federal prison for his role in this crime, having been convicted using the "tough laws against terrorism—and recent case law stemming from the Oklahoma City bombing case." The *Peoria Journal Star*, the *Burlington Hawkeye*, the *Register-Mail*, and the *Daily Review Atlas* extensively covered the court proceedings of a Western Illinois militia leader who was arrested for intimidation, threatening public officials, and unlawfully using a weapon, but the case did not receive broader national attention.[5]

Reporters also revisited the link between militias, McVeigh, and Oklahoma City. It was clear that the association between McVeigh and militias had never really been extinguished in the public's mind, and there were several ways in which the news media had helped to sustain that association. As was demonstrated above, McVeigh was mentioned in a large percentage of the stories about the militia movement in the immediate aftermath of the bombing, and this strategy continued throughout the 1990s. Once McVeigh was convicted, media interest in him decreased significantly because he had been put away and received what the media thought he deserved, but their interest was renewed when the government executed him on June 11, 2001.

THE EXECUTION OF MCVEIGH

Timothy McVeigh's execution in June 2001 was an extremely important news event.[6] The most obvious reason for the extensive coverage was that his death would help bring closure to a celebrated event. The state's ultimate punishment was being administered to one of its great villains, and it was important to provide play-by-play coverage leading up to and through the execution. The public could follow the legal maneuvering to prevent the execution, the discussions about the possibility of showing the execution to the public, and after such a request was denied, the accommodations made so that family members of the victims murdered in the bombing could watch the execution if they wanted to do so. McVeigh also attempted to use the media to define his own legacy, granting numerous interviews and telling "his story" to two reporters who released a book near his execution date. Although McVeigh could have delayed the execution for several years by exhausting all avenues of appeal, he decided to waive these rights in order to become the first federal prisoner executed in nearly thirty years. Even when it was discovered that the Federal Bureau of Investigation had withheld over 3,000 pages of documents from his attorneys during his trial, causing both public and political outrage, McVeigh allowed this revelation to stall the execution of his death sentence only temporarily.

Most major news outlets, including representatives from almost every continent, were present in Terre Haute, Indiana, to cover the execution.

The number of media representatives outnumbered the citizens, protestors, and law-enforcement officials present, reaffirming the consensus that the media has come to be the representative of public interest. Reporters provided details about the events leading up to the execution, including whom McVeigh met in the days before, what he ate, how he slept, and how the execution was carried out. The witnesses who attended the execution gave firsthand accounts of McVeigh's final moments, discussing his demeanor, facial expressions, and attitude. The media reported that his final message to the public was the poem "Invictus" by William Ernest Henley, a message of strength and power when faced with adversity. The media reported that McVeigh was to be cremated, and his ashes would be spread at some location unknown but rumored to be Oklahoma City (his attorneys denied this claim). Of course, many news stories summarized the events leading up to execution, including what drove McVeigh to commit the crime, the bombing and its effect on survivors and the public, the political and social response to the case, the trials of both McVeigh and Nichols, and reactions to the punishment. Reporters also used the coverage of the event to consider McVeigh's influence on the militia movement.

One of the major questions asked by reporters was whether antigovernment enthusiasts would anoint McVeigh as a martyr. Many articles attempted to answer this question, and most reporters concluded that he would not achieve this status. Many of the militia members I interviewed hated McVeigh. They were angry because he had brought massive attention to the movement and caused it to be demonized. Although they admitted understanding the nature of his hatred, they strongly disagreed with his methods and shared the general public's belief that he was a villain. Some newspaper reporters described how high-profile figures, like John Trochmann and Norm Olson, did not believe he would become a martyr but thought he was an Oswald-like stooge—used by the government or part of a government conspiracy to destroy the militia movement. A militia member I interviewed shared the belief that McVeigh was another Oswald: "It is just like the Kennedy assassination. There was a patsy—Lee Harvey Oswald. Kennedy was killed by the military industrial complex, the CIA, and the FBI because he was going to take and have all U.S. troops out of Vietnam by 1964. That's why they killed him in November of 1963. Have you ever watched the movie *JFK* with Kevin Costner? That's exactly what happened."

The news media also used McVeigh's execution to report on the status of the militia movement. Reporters concluded that the size of the movement had declined significantly since 1995, attributing the change to the demonization of militias through their link to McVeigh. Joe Roy from the Southern Poverty Law Center said that there were over 1,000 militia groups when the bombing occurred, but by 2001 the number had dwindled to under 200.[7] Other reporters described the declines in militia membership. The *New York Times* reported that Norm Olson was disbanding his militia because membership had decreased. Another reporter concluded that "when McVeigh died, . . . so did the movement to which he was connected." Another called the militia movement "the 169th victim of the Oklahoma City bombing." Some called the bombing the worst thing that ever happened to the movement, reporting that the movement was in steep decline, "running out of steam," had "disintegrated into chaos," was "fading away" or "kaput."[8]

The Great Militia Scare

After Timothy McVeigh bombed the Murrah building in Oklahoma City, the media pelted the public with information about this event and related policy issues. Militia groups were at the center of one such policy issue as they became the public face of an as yet undefined domestic terrorism threat. The extensive publicity they received when the social problems marketplace opened its doors made it seem as though militias were everywhere. National media organizations presented overview pieces describing the militia movement with sweeping generalizations and using specific frameworks to highlight militia concerns, strategies, influences, and ideologies. The media also highlighted certain individuals, events, and activities. Regional media organizations focused on conducting statewide profiles or analyses of local groups, yet they presented militias in a similar manner.

Both national and local media provided several types of evidence to support the conclusion that militias were a significant threat. First, national estimates of the size of the movement were usually provided by a watchdog agency, like the Southern Poverty Law Center, whose figures showed that the threat was large and increasing. Second, criminal activities, including many incidents that would usually have been ignored if militias were not under scrutiny, were used as examples to confirm the threat, depicting militia members as terrorists planning to target innocent civilians. Groups like the Washington State Militia, West Virginia Mountaineer militia, Freemen, and Viper Militia, as well as other regional cases, provided a steady supply of events that reporters emphasized when highlighting the militia threat. Third, key social-control institutions started to monitor these groups more closely, and such increased scrutiny alone enhanced the credibility of the militia threat. Policymakers conducted hearings and passed legislation, and law-enforcement officials funneled resources to conduct investigations of these groups—all confirming that a response was necessary. When a problem is defined as being worthy of scrutiny, law-enforcement agencies will respond and ultimately uncover some type of criminal activity, the results of their investigations often providing the justification for continued or expanded support. News media cover successful investigations, legitimizing their pursuit.

Popular-culture outlets also play an important role in this process because they tap directly into the public's fears, manufacturing and then feeding extreme stereotypical images to the public. Militias were convenient targets of the entertainment industry for three reasons. First, popular culture not only creates and contributes to the public's understanding of crime and justice but also reacts to it. The emphasis on militias in the news provided images and ideas that were seen and then used by the creators of popular culture. Second, entertainment sources could easily present this new threat visually because they only had to reengineer what was shown and told about militias in the news. Often when groups are demonized in the news, the public can only formulate an image in its mind based on media reports because photographs and video are difficult to obtain; popular culture then helps bring clarity to these formulated images and validates the stereotypes existing in the public's mind. Militias were unique among demonized groups in that they, and many of their celebrity leaders, provided reporters with copious photo opportunities to supplement textual depictions. Indeed, television news was significantly interested in militias only because they could show groups using guns, wearing camouflage, and conducting training exercises and military drills. Thus, the existing images of militias were consistent with the fears being created in textual depictions, and popular-culture outlets simply expanded and confirmed the threat as it was presented in the news. Third, the militia movement was a good entertainment source because these groups manifested cultural concerns about deviance and demons. Militia groups fit nicely into existing understandings of terrorism, conspiracy thinking, and extremism. Entertainment media described militias in a way that heightened these understandings.

A central question that should be addressed when considering the media's role in the social construction of social problems is whether the depiction of a threat is consistent with the actual threat. It is often assumed that an empirical appraisal after a moral panic has taken place will reveal that the threat was exaggerated, and that the media play a critical role in creating an unbalanced response because they are not concerned with an accurate empirical account of a problem but rather respond primarily to the immediate pressure to satisfy the insatiable appetite of public curiosity. The media could have closely examined official statistics, such as police reports or sentencing data, to determine the number of militia members involved in certain types of offenses, but the collection and analysis of such data are prohibitively expensive, especially for media organizations. The time and effort required to collect such data are also inconsistent with the immediate need to capitalize on the public's interest in a topic. Statistics, however, have a strong aura, and they help to justify devoting a large amount of space to a topic, so the media welcomed figures from an apparently credible source, the Southern Poverty Law Center.

Numerical estimates of militia membership grew briskly in the months following the Oklahoma City bombing, and that growth was strongly correlated with media attention on militias. It is difficult to know whether this growth was caused merely by law enforcement, watchdog groups, and media paying closer attention to militia groups, whether more groups were organizing (perhaps because of the publicity), or whether the growth was simply an exaggeration created to support the interests of certain claims-makers. I asked the interviewees to assess the accuracy of the figures provided by the Southern Poverty Law Center because the media cited their data frequently when describing the militia threat. Reporters who had limited interest in the subject matter and covered militias because they were instructed to do so were generally satisfied with the accuracy of the figures and usually included them in their story. Other reporters were more skeptical simply because they had a long-term interest in the subject and had conflicting information. One reporter said:

> Like everybody else, when I started to cover militias, I relied on them [SPLC] a lot, and now I seldom do. Far too many reporters and researchers rely on the SPLC for too much of their information. That information may or may not be accurate. I happen to think that a good part of it is not accurate. Bad information may be gathered with the best of intentions

and motives. I happen to think a lot of the intentions and motives are questionable.

Several militia interviewees also reacted to the figures cited in the media. Some were surprised how widespread the movement was, and they used the information to attempt to establish communication with groups that they had not known existed. For many, the figures gave them confidence and a sense of pride because others were working for the same goals using the same means. Other militia interviewees, however, believed that the national figures were exaggerated in order to demonize militias, and many of the groups included did not consider themselves part of the militia movement or did not even exist. The following lengthy tirade is illustrative:

> Liberals often run down Joe McCarthy and his tactics, and indeed I'm no defender of Joe McCarthy. But Joe McCarthy doesn't hold a candle to the SPLC, the Center for Democratic Renewal, and the Clinton Administration. Joe McCarthy never listed the names. He waived around a list and said 'I have this list of names,' but you know when they finally said, 'Well look, Joe, put up or shut up,' he couldn't do it. Morris [Dees] goes around and says 'I have this list of names,' and when he goes to visit a state for a speaking engagement, local papers dutifully print the list. But such lists always include names that shouldn't be on it. Like Palladin Arms in Boulder, Colorado, listed as a member of the 'Patriot' community and anti-Semitic. A local reporter went out to the guy who owned Palladin Arms, whose last name is Glass, and the guy happens to be Jewish and he says 'How can I be anti-Semitic for crying out loud—I'm Jewish!' Well, when challenged on it, Morris said, 'Well, any gun dealer is a part of the militia support network.' Now, ain't that lovely? I mean, they make statements like this, and the press does not call them on it. And to this day, despite all of the rumblings, no one has ever taken the time, although we've certainly tried to get reporters to do it.

Documenting the actual size of the militia movement is really an impossible empirical inquiry because of the changing affiliations of people in the movement, the lack of clear definition regarding what should be included in any count, the secretive nature of some militias, and the lack of any official mechanism to record such data. The interview and observation data I collected provide a somewhat different but still limited perspective on this issue. I did find people involved in the militia movement who fit the dominant frames being emphasized in the news, but how threatening such groups were varied considerably. News organizations simply ignored that variation. For example, the militia interviewees were consistently angry about the direction in which the United States was moving on social and political issues. They were of course angry about gun control and government regulation of guns, but the strong feeling on this issue was simply an outlet for their anger about broader issues. Certainly, there were militia members who acted, or were planning to act, violently because of this anger. Anger drove others to participate in the movement, which provided a safe environment for venting their frustrations and sharing their interests. Other militia members attempted to influence legislators directly through legitimate political means. Militia members ran for political office, others attended local policymaking meetings, and others used informational resources, such as newsletters, letters to the editor, and the World Wide Web, to share their ideas.

I interviewed people involved in the militia movement who hated not only the current practices of the government, but also specific groups of people, primarily Jews. It is hard to uncover such prejudice in an interview, but it was certainly behind many of their broader conspiracy concerns. Many interviewees had extensive libraries of hate literature and used it as supporting documentation for their concerns. (As we have noted, these materials, which are rarely bought by the casual consumer, sold well at militia events.) Other interviewees, however, said they despised the racists in the movement, would directly confront racism when given the opportunity, and organized protests when the Klan held a rally. Other militia leaders simply stated that the majority of people actively involved in the militia movement were not racist. Militias were certainly not consistent on this issue, so many people driven by prejudice preferred to be affiliated with other types of extremist groups.

I do not know how many people I interviewed were terrorists. Some celebrity figures went into long diatribes, including general threats and plans to respond with unprecedented force if political change did not occur. My sense was that it was an act. They were skilled in the art of propaganda and attempted to provide what they thought I wanted to hear. I kept waiting for a violent revolution but was not surprised when it never occurred or when such celebrity figures disappeared from the limelight. I think there has been enough evidence in media accounts and law-enforcement testimony to support the conclusion that some people in the militia movement are dangerous, but I also believe that the proportion of militia members who are plotting major crimes is very small.

The news media are not generally concerned with capturing such variations, preferring to emphasize extreme, unrepresentative cases. This is one of the major reasons why celebrated cases are such powerful boundary-defining events. One consequence of representing a deviant group only in this manner is that the public comes to believe that the extreme case represents an entire movement. The size of the movement was significant because the numbers, real or imagined, were large and growing, and the media depicted militias as if all groups were dangerous. Media coverage of militias provided politicians the opportunity to discuss domestic-terrorism issues and explore the existence of other types of extremist groups. The media focused on Christian Identity beliefs, the paper-terrorism strategies of Sovereign Citizens, and the history of violence used by other groups, such as the Posse Comitatus and the Aryan Nations, to fund the activities of their organizations and accomplish their goals. Militia activity was strongly associated with the ideas and strategies of these other groups because news and entertainment organizations made little effort to distinguish between groups. More importantly, the focused coverage on extremism melded militias together with these other groups in the public's mind, and militias became the group that encapsulated public concern about domestic terrorism. The representation of militias, framed for the public by its most extreme cases, therefore helped to create strong public fears that legitimized a strong social-control response but was far out of proportion to the danger of these groups.

Another consequence of the celebrated media coverage was that it significantly shaped the militia movement itself. In the early 1990s, prior to the Oklahoma City bombing, the militia movement had gained momentum because of what occurred at Ruby Ridge and Waco. Leaders of various types of extremist groups attempted to capitalize on these events, using them as evidence of the larger concerns conservatives had about what they perceived to be an increasingly hateful and intrusive federal government. Some people were in agreement with what such leaders were preaching because they were past the point of being frustrated and felt that they did not have an outlet for their concerns.

The militia movement changed in four dramatic ways after the media linked McVeigh to militias. First, the media provided the movement with their public identity by framing them in specific ways. The militia movement was publicly invisible before the bombing; afterwards the public came to understand the movement in the media's terms. Second, the media used celebrity figures to define the goals, strategies, and ideology of the movement. When the media are interested in a movement, they look for spokespersons. Some of the figures who became the celebrities of the militia movement were reluctant, but others embraced the publicity and learned how to accommodate the media's preferences. The number of citations of the media's anointed celebrities in news stories was somewhat diminished by the decentralized structure of the militia movement, and reporters searched for local militia figures. But the influence of these celebrity figures was significant because they provided frames consistent with media preferences, and, in turn, they influenced how reporters interacted with all members of the militia movement and what it was about these interactions that the news emphasized.

Third, membership changed dramatically after the bombing. Some people were attracted to the media's spotlight but left when the media were no longer interested. For example, one leader of a countywide militia discussed how his membership changed in the immediate aftermath of the bombing:

> If we've got bad elements in the militia today, which I'm sure we do just like any other group, it is because of the image the government and the media have given the American people about the militia. There are people out there who call themselves militia who have never read a copy of the Constitution or the Declaration of Independence. They just want to be viewed as badasses. We started getting that element. You know, you've got guys that are not interested in the issues, that are just interested in telling somebody, 'Hey, I'm in the militia now, don't mess with me.' Believe it or not, there are people out there who truly want to be feared. They truly want to be feared, so they go out and they say I'm in the militia and they hope that somebody will fear them. I don't want to be feared; I wanted to be liked.

Some of the people who left did so because they were not fully committed to the movement and could not take the pressure that was being exerted by family members, friends, and others because they belonged to "terrorist groups." "There were a lot of groups who lost people, like half of their membership, because these people only wanted to be weekend warriors. When the heat got too much for them, and they started getting called 'terrorist' and 'murderer' and 'baby killer,' and you may not truly believe in what you're doing, you're going to run," said the same militia leader mentioned above. Others left because they feared that the publicity would result in increased attention from law enforcement.

Fourth, the media coverage of the militia movement following the bombing ultimately contributed to its demise. It never was able to recover from being linked to McVeigh. Many militia members were as angry with McVeigh as they were with the media for contributing to the demonization of the movement. McVeigh hoped to be a martyr; instead militia members despised him because of the negative publicity he brought to the movement. Militias, and celebrity figures of the movement, attempted to have a presence at several high-profile standoffs similar to Ruby Ridge and Waco in the late 1990s and early 2000s in order to renew interest in the movement. For example, Reverend Greg Dixon and parishioners of the Indianapolis Baptist Temple held a three-month vigil, preventing law-enforcement authorities from seizing their church. A federal judge ruled that the church could be seized because it refused to withhold federal income and Social Security taxes from employee paychecks.[9] Militia groups were initially interested in the standoff but disappeared when Dixon stated that he did not want their help and did not want violence to be used. Militia groups and celebrated leaders also resurfaced in Idaho during the McGuckin family standoff, a case in which JoAnn McGuckin's children squared off with law enforcement after she was arrested on child-neglect charges. Offered assistance by militia groups, the mother made it clear that "she want[ed] no part of a movement that produced the likes of Timothy McVeigh."[10] There were other factors that contributed to the movement's demise, including the fading of memories of Ruby Ridge and Waco, the passing of time without predicted occurrences like United Nations troops coming out of the nation's parks or a violent New Year's Eve for 1999, the disappearance of gun control from the national policy agenda, and the arrests and prison terms of many militia leaders. The media's contribution through their demonization of militias was perhaps the most significant because it created the expectation of a great menace that never manifested itself.

The creation of "evil" plays an enormously important role in shaping the "collective conscience" of the public and ultimately legitimizes the activities and policies of social-control institutions. The demonization of militias is a good example of the role that the media play in demarcating the outermost boundaries of society's behavioral preferences and helping to define society's winners and losers. The media's coverage of deviance, and the ceremonies ignited in response to crime, help to create, reinforce, and justify the casting out of certain groups of people. The public is both appalled and intrigued by deviant groups and individuals, as well as by the heroes who pursue them, and craves information about them when a celebrated case occurs. Yet one of the consequences of the mechanical and ceremonial processes discussed above is the systematic withholding from the public of certain types of knowledge. The public is not completely informed about social problems, and, more importantly, the public's limited access to information encourages individuals to fill the gaps with myths and rumors. Celebrated events create an almost insatiable appetite for news, but some angles of a story are simply inconsistent with news expectations about the processing of events, other information is simply ignored, and stories are framed in specific ways. The public is curious about what is said but also about what is unsaid, and so we are susceptible to rumors, exaggerations, half-truths, and lies. Even militia leaders attempted to take advantage of this by offering alternative explanations. The media and other social-control organizations could offer more information, and more diverse types of information, but doing so would seriously undermine the most effective social-control management tool at their disposal—the creation of society's demons.

The public has been manipulated by policymakers into believing that the nature and causes of crime should be of less concern than the people who break the law. This is a significant and important paradigmatic shift. Society's top social-control powerbrokers and rule-enforcers have taken the responsibility for managing behaviors that fall outside the normative expectations they themselves have created. Yet they have neither the means nor the understanding to manage crime problems. Instead, they manage how the public defines a crime problem and accepts how best to respond to it. Effort is focused on defining the problem in a way that isolates decision makers from concern. It is not surprising, then, that the response to deviance and crime does not focus on ameliorating the structural determinants of crime or questioning the effectiveness of specific types of punitive policy, but rather on purging wrongdoers from society. In order to win a war on crime, it is necessary only to create opportunities for symbolic victories.

Certain individuals can reach the status of monster, but defining a group as evil is a much more effective opportunity for a victory. Public fear of individual monsters subsides once they are caught or purged from society—unless they are representative of a threatening group. The group is used to illustrate what constitutes unacceptable behavior, and all individuals who are part of a group are considered equally evil and dangerous. Once a group's evil has been established, "all mention of the representatives of this group revolves around their central, and exclusively negative, features."[11] Such demonization is certainly tied to the hate crimes committed against innocent Arabs following the September 11 attacks. It also provides the necessary justification for casting a wide social-control net. Then these newly created outlaws can be legitimately pursued or cast out—actions that ultimately maintain the strength and influence of powerbrokers. Without such deviants, the moral fabric of society, its social-control capacities, and its hierarchy of power would dissolve. It is therefore imperative that deviants are created with regularity, efforts are made to respond to them, and they are symbolically purged from society. Since society's punishment apparatus is invisible, the media provide the battlefield on which this symbolic war is fought. The media play a role in defining a group as threatening, reporting that policies, programs, and institutions have been put in place to respond, and then deciding when we can declare the symbolic victory.

The celebrated case often enables certain claims-makers to compete in the highly competitive social-problems marketplace, which was described in Chapter 3 as functioning in public culture like a carousel. A long line of social-problems waits around the carousel, and soon one may be able to take a ride because of a number of factors, including the media's coverage of a celebrated case. Although other forces can initiate significant public concern about a social problem, the media's coverage of a celebrated case is emphasized here because it set off a chain reaction of events in response to the militia movement. The carousel metaphor has several important features. First, it is a restricted ride, open only to problems that fit well into the structures of how policy issues are debated in society. The limits on the marketplace, and the opportunities that come from ownership of a social problem, affect which problems are promoted for consideration and remain issues of concern. Many of the seriously considered problems share several characteristics not necessarily related to the reality of the problems, but consistent with the policy needs and preferences of people in power. Second, a limited number of seats can be occupied. Described as the "carrying capacity" of the social-problems marketplace, this restriction exaggerates the competition to promote and gain ownership of the problems being considered.[12] Third, the length of the ride depends on the nature of the problem and its power to invoke public legitimizing ceremonies. Some social problems can occupy a portion of policymakers' time for decades, while others are given scant attention.

Celebrated criminal cases are obviously rare compared with the thousands of crimes that occur daily—which is perhaps why such cases are so often ignored when scholars attempt to explain criminal justice decision making. The news media process only a small percentage of the very large pool of incidents as news, and their production routines create an unrepresentative and biased view of the nature of crime and justice in society. Most crimes are indeed unremarkable, and so the public views what the media identify as newsworthy with indifference. But celebrated cases are different: they command the space, time, and resources of multiple media outlets and are constructed using familiar processes. The public's logic adapts, accepting that these sensational events, and the policy and social issues that can be attached to them, are important because the media have defined them as priority items. It is clear that only a few, rare events are transformed into celebrated cases and only a select pool of issues can cross the threshold of the social-problems marketplace. Because of inherent organizational constraints tied to news construction, other news events compete against the celebrated cases and related issues. Other events are unable to achieve celebrity status because of inherent cultural resistance that impedes development of significant public concern. The perpetrator may be an inadequate evil presence, unable to be made over as a monster that can evoke the requisite fear to move a community to concern, or the victim may not be deserving of enough compassion to justify a societal reaction. If a problem produces conflict among claims-makers, construction of a celebrated case is likely to be slowed down. Some celebrated events do create good and newsworthy demons that can be exploited for a large array of benefits. If the ideological battlefield is clearly mapped out, because a group fits well into our understanding of what is threatening, then it is likely that great changes will occur. Individuals involved in the group are moved into action, and public concern about their activities enhances their commitment to their ideology. Media organizations process the demon according to their preferred formats, and policymakers and bureaucrats put forward a response consistent with their priorities. Resources are expended to address a social problem, but then public perceptions of the threat grow exponentially, justifying requests for additional resources.

Militias were a group that achieved "monster" status in the 1990s, but it is likely that they would have remained invisible had it not been for

McVeigh's terrorism. This celebrated case provided an opportunity to win a symbolic victory in the war on crime and reconfigure society's social-control priorities by creating a new and powerful demon—the militia movement. There are several overlapping reasons why militias made such a worthwhile target. First, the public had no experience with militias prior to their being linked to McVeigh. Reporters had a blank canvas on which to depict this unknown presence of evil existing in the community, and they were excited about this opportunity because it allowed them to step outside their daily news-construction routines to explore something new. Second, militias were an extremely interesting topic. They were photogenic, running around in the woods in camouflage in preparation for a New World Order. They liked to talk about their freedoms, especially their constitutional right to bear arms, and some militia members were arrested for stockpiling weapons, which contributed to their threatening aura. Reporters thought that it was comical but newsworthy that militia members talked about black helicopters, microchips, invading foreign troops, mind control, weather control, and other conspiracies, and these beliefs helped justify the representation of militia members as alienated from society. Third, militias were represented by publicity-seeking celebrities. Some of the members who advocated the most extreme viewpoints were also among the movement's most articulate speakers. These celebrity figures knew how to manufacture publicity, and their influence on the construction of the movement was tied to the expectations they created among reporters. Reporters preferred using material from people like Gritz, J. J. Johnson, McLamb, Olson, and Trochmann, or relied on the local leaders who were most similar to these celebrated figures. Dissident voices of the militia movement attempted to challenge these images but were not very successful. Fourth, each of the previous factors is linked directly to the fact that militia behavior fit well into existing societal frames. News coverage of militias drew directly on pre-existing conceptions of extremism, terrorism, conspiracy thinking, opposition to gun control, and hate, which helped to define militias and in the process solidified those conceptions. Finally, the militia movement was very useful to key insider claims-makers. Clinton's presidency was in disarray in 1995, and it is very likely he would have lost in 1996 had it not been for his demonization of the militia movement and his establishment of himself as a leader in the fight against domestic terrorism. Several other politicians, as well as federal law-enforcement officials, also took full advantage of the demonization of the militia movement by exploiting their access to the news media and holding a series of congressional hearings to legitimize their position as an important opposition voice. Extremist watchdogs, and especially Morris Dees and the Southern Poverty Law Center, used the militia panic to push their antihate agendas.

THE MASS MEDIA AND SOCIAL CONTROL

The media are fundamental to society's social-control apparatus, binding diverse ideologies together in a way that creates, maintains, and legitimizes community boundaries by engineering specific understandings of priority issues such as crime and criminal justice. The information the media collect and present as fact, and also the information that they exclude, is of great ideological significance because the information is critical to the creation and maintenance of the frames we use to structure our understandings of the world. Consumers of mass-mediated images are not passively obedient, and they do not pay attention only to issues that the media determine to be significant. Yet the public does learn about social problems through media depictions, comparing them with their preconceived understandings of social issues. If people have little prior experience with an issue, the media's influence is likely to be strong. Thus the public is methodological in its attempt to match the media's representations of events with any preconceived understandings, and its views are constantly evolving. Although militias were a new problem that the public was eager to learn about, previous understandings of other issues and the most appropriate solutions helped to pave the way for specific understandings to take priority and increased the likelihood that the public would accept the images the media provided.

The limits on the social-problems marketplace and the opportunities that come from ownership of a social problem affect the problems that are promoted for consideration and remain issues of significant concern. Many of the problems that are seriously considered share several characteristics not necessarily related to the reality of the problem. When a group or person is demonized to the point of being defined as a significant threat, then the construction of the related problem is likely to trigger the involvement of insider claims-makers. Insiders, such as political and criminal-justice officials, have virtually uninhibited access to the news media and work to manufacture images consistent with their priorities. Such access provides these officials with the opportunity to gain ownership of an issue and use their position and access to institutions to maximize their own interests in the claims that are given serious public attention. Public thinking about an issue is therefore likely to reflect the preferences of these insider claims-makers. Although public debate does occur, engaging many parties with differing viewpoints, the individuals involved in these battles do not question the legitimacy of the process but rather struggle over the semantics of the issue of concern. There is a governor inherent in the public discussion of social problems because the traditional ceremonies, such as political hearings, are always invoked in response to high-priority problems, and the way that social problems are responded to in society inherently legitimizes this process. High-profile problems are often examined in special political hearings where the nature of the problem is defined and the parameters of an appropriate response are formulated. Hearings about terrorism and the militia movement provided a controlled public forum that magnified the threat, defined the response, and helped produce support; the priorities of political insiders were emphasized in media coverage of the hearings. Guilty verdicts from criminal trials, especially when the case is celebrated, have a similar effect. Such legitimizing ceremonies help confirm the representation of an issue in the news. The structure of society ensures that most social problems that are given serious consideration will eventually be controlled by standard agencies and the institutionalized responses promoted by those agencies. This process places the definition of the problem, the response, and solution in easily understood language, and the end result is that the way in which problems are debated in society is likely to reaffirm the preferences of these institutions.

Insider claims-makers bring confirmatory power to the construction of crime events because they represent powerful institutions. These insiders are conveniently available, and most have a working understanding of the goals and priorities of news organizations. For example, these insiders played a highly important role in defining the nature of the militia threat, understanding the sources of the militia's anger, and recommending the best practices for responding to these groups. The current research has demonstrated that politicians, law-enforcement officials, and other social-control representatives were cited frequently in stories about the militia movement. The Oklahoma City bombing was such a destabilizing event that representatives of society's primary social-control institutions found an opportunity to use their position at the top of the power hierarchy to broker a response and reassure the public that those who were involved were different from the rest of society. Similarly, organizations whose mission is to eradicate hate from society were asked whether they considered militia groups to be a priority threat. These organizations provided data showing that the threat was large and increasing, and also shared their expertise to describe how militias were similar to other, better-known extremists. These experts raised concerns about the ideology and methods of the militia movement, and instructed the media to look more closely at the plethora of other potential domestic terrorist threats.

Ironically, such claims-makers attempted to capitalize on media publicity of celebrated cases to reaffirm their position as "experts" on the militia and play a role in shaping how this problem was constructed for public consumption. However, the involvement of insider claims-makers and experts, and the heightened coverage and demonization of the militia movement in the media, strengthened the commitment of many militia members to their cause. Militia members are critical of anything said by federal law-enforcement officials, political leaders, and watchdog organizations, and their presence as key figures defining the movement in the media provided documented proof that there was a broader conspiracy to demonize the militia movement. As high-profile cases were used by key claims-makers to reaffirm their positions of leadership and recommend the appropriate responses to this social problem, media reliance on these sources ensured that militia members would become even more firmly entrenched in their beliefs and distance themselves further from the mainstream. An unintended consequence was that insider involvement isolated militias even further from the public, drove the individuals or organizations considering an offensive strike against the New World Order even deeper underground, and motivated some people to commit crimes.

It may seem surprising that militia leaders and members had significant access to the media, but my analysis also indicates that these sources were used by the media primarily to solidify the dominant frameworks being provided by mainstream sources. Although these groups were "new," at least in the sense that reporters had not previously been asked to investigate them, reporters were not completely handicapped in deciding what should be emphasized and how militias should be represented. Media organizations are frequently asked to define new social problems and process celebrated events—many of which are crime-related and linked to criminal-justice policy issues. Thus routines are institutionalized that provide direction on how to pursue a new threat. These routines—which steer reporters toward using established frameworks—influence who should be consulted, what questions should be asked, and how the event should be presented to the public. They provide convenient ways to define and organize social problems, and they reflect the broader concerns and priorities of a society. Thus, evaluating which frames are selected and which are ignored is essential to understanding our culture and its priorities, as well as how news media and popular culture have a significant influence in the creation of these frames. According to the media, militias were irrational terrorists—a dangerous, growing outsider threat that needed eradicating. Although militia groups may have had some legitimate concerns worth debating, because they were framed as a threat their position was both weakened and ignored.

We should not be surprised now that militias, once considered a significant social problem, have for the most part disappeared from public scrutiny. The news media helps to bind the masses together in a highly symbolic way, feeding off and contributing to the social-control processes of a society. The media ultimately play a central role in defining what is normal, what is deviant, and what problems need to be eradicated in society. It was clear that the public never really got past the initial coupling of the militia movement with Timothy McVeigh. The media stopped emphasizing a direct link between the two, but they could never present militias without invoking him in some fashion—often using pictures of McVeigh in camouflage as well as emphasizing his anger about Waco and his passion for guns. McVeigh was a terrorist who committed a horrible act. Domestic terrorism jumped to the forefront of the policy-making line because of this act, and militia groups were a convenient target for continuing to explore and promote this issue. Although public concern about the militia movement has now disappeared, the social construction of militias following the Oklahoma City bombing has had a lasting effect on public understandings of terrorism and extremism. Moreover, many of these understandings have been revisited as society has begun to process the terrorist acts of September 11.

APPENDIX

FILMS CITED IN CHAPTER 7 WITH RELEASE DATES

Along Came a Spider (2001)
Arlington Road (1999)
A.T.F. (1999)
Back to the Future (1985)
Black Sunday (1977)
Blue Sky (1994)
Blues Brothers 2000 (1998)
Braveheart (1995)
Chain Reaction (1996)
Conspiracy Theory (1997)
The Dead Pool (1988)
Delta Force (1986)
Delta Force Commando II (1990)
Delta Force III: The Killing Game (1991)
Die Hard I (1988)
Die Hard II (1990)
Die Hard III (1995)
Dirty Harry (1971)
The Enforcer (1976)
Eraser (1996)
Executive Decision (1996)
A Few Good Men (1992)
15 Minutes (2001)
First Blood (1982)
First Daughter (1999)
Frantic (1988)
G.I. Jane (1997)
Independence Day (1996)
Iron Eagle I (1986)
Iron Eagle II (1988)
Kiss the Girls (1997)
Land of the Free (1997)
Lethal Weapon I (1987)
Lethal Weapon II (1989)

Lethal Weapon III (1992)
Lethal Weapon IV (1998)
The Long Kiss Goodnight (1996)
Magnum Force (1973)
Men in Black (1997)
Militia (2000)
Natural Born Killers (1994)
Navy Seals (1990)
The Next Man (1976)
Nighthawks (1981)
Nightmare in Big Sky Country (1998)
Outbreak (1994)
The Patriot (2000)
The Pelican Brief (1993)
Rambo II (1985)
Rambo III (1988)
Red Dawn (1984)
Rules of Engagement (2000)
Shadow Conspiracy (1997)
The Siege (1998)
True Lies (1994)
Under Siege (1992)
Wag the Dog (1997)
Wanted: Dead or Alive (1987)
The X-Files (1998)

NOTES

CHAPTER 1: CONSTRUCTING COMMUNITY BOUNDARIES

1. Martha T. Moore, "Tot's Image Stabs at Hearts Again: Cartoon Protesting McVeigh's Penalty Opens Old Wounds," *USA Today*, 20 June 1997, 3A.
2. See U.S. Senate Committee on the Judiciary, *The Militia Movement in the United States*, 104th Cong., 1st sess., 15 June 1995; Mark Hamm, *Apocalypse in Oklahoma: Waco and Ruby Ridge Revenged* (Boston: Northeastern University Press, 1997); Jonathan S. Landay, "Clinton's Antiterrorism Chief Marshals His Troops," *Christian Science Monitor*, 1 July 1998, 4.
3. Sue Anne Pressley, "Bomb Kills Dozens in Oklahoma Federal Building," *Washington Post*, 20 April 1995, A1.
4. See Hamm, *Apocalypse in Oklahoma*; Lou Michel and Dan Herbeck, *American Terrorist: Timothy McVeigh & the Oklahoma City Bombing* (New York: Regan Books, 2001).
5. Philip Jenkins, *Using Murder: The Social Construction of Serial Murder* (Hawthorne, N.Y.: Aldine De Gruyter, 1994).
6. Most of the interviews were taped and transcribed, allowing me to provide the interviewee's exact words. The interviews were edited only for clarity and brevity, and to preserve confidentiality. An attempt was made not to compromise the perspective being provided by the interviewee. I presented my academic credentials and human subjects paperwork when soliciting involvement. Some of my first contacts were by e-mail, some by telephone, and others were made in person. Sixty percent of the people contacted by e-mail agreed to be interviewed, and every subject contacted by telephone agreed. Most of the telephone contacts were made after a militia member suggested another person to interview, allowing me to use his name as an introduction. I also had good success arranging interviews when attending gun shows, preparedness expositions, and gun shoots. I was surprised how willing militia members were to talk to me, but in part they were motivated by the nature of the study. They had strong opinions about the news media and about what they perceived as a demonization of the movement.

    Questions of representativeness are much more difficult to answer. I was, however, aware of the bias that would result if I only talked to people involved in above-ground militias, and I made an effort to interview a range of militia members. Attending various events helped broaden my exposure to the diverse range of people involved in the movement. The interviews conducted at these events were helpful, as were my observations and brief interactions.

7. Emile Durkheim, *The Division of Labor in Society* (Glencoe, Ill.: Free Press, 1960), 102.

8. James T. Duke, *Issues in Sociological Theory: Another Look at the "Old Masters"* (New York: University Press of America, 1983), 32.

9. Emile Durkheim, *The Rules of Sociological Method* (New York: Free Press, 1966), 66–71.

10. Kai T. Erikson, *Wayward Puritans: A Study in the Sociology of Deviance* (Needham Heights, Mass.: Simon & Schuster, 1966), 10, 69.

11. Nicholas N. Kittrie, *The War Against Authority: From the Crisis of Legitimacy to a New Social Contract* (Baltimore: Johns Hopkins University Press, 1995), 20.

12. Durkheim, *Division of Labor*, 108.

13. Erikson, *Wayward Puritans*, 12.

14. Gus Schattenberg, "Social Control Functions of Mass Media Depicts of Crime," *Sociological Inquiry* 51, no. 1 (1981): 72, 76.

15. David S. DeMatteo, "Welcome to Anytown, U.S.A.—Home of Beautiful Scenery (and a Convicted Sex Offender): Sex Offender Registration and Notification Laws in E.B. v. Verniero," *Villanova Law Review* 43 (1998): 581.

16. Stephen Hilgartner and Charles L. Bosk, "The Rise and Fall of Social Problems: A Public Arenas Model," *American Journal of Sociology* 94, no. 1 (1988): 59–60.

17. For background reading on moral panics, see: Stanley Cohen, *Folk Devils and Moral Panic* (London: MacGibbon and Kee, 1972); Jenkins, *Using Murder*; Philip Jenkins, *Moral Panic: Changing Concepts of the Child Molester in Modern America* (New Haven, Conn.: Yale University Press, 1998); Philip Jenkins, *Synthetic Panics: The Symbolic Politics of Designer Drugs* (New York: New York University Press, 1999); Kenneth Thompson, *Moral Panics* (London: Routledge, 1998); Erich Goode and Ben-Yehuda Nachman, *Moral Panics: The Social Construction of Deviance* (Cambridge, Mass.: Blackwell, 1994).

18. Steven M. Chermak and Alexander Weiss, "The Effects of the Media on Federal Criminal Justice Policy," *Criminal Justice Policy Review* 8, no. 4 (1997): 323–341; Robert J. Spitzer, *The Politics of Gun Control* (Chatham, N.J.: Chatham House, 1995).

19. Cohen, *Folk Devils*, 9.

20. See note 17 above.

21. Thompson, *Moral Panics*.

CHAPTER 2: RUBY RIDGE AND WACO REVISITED

1. Joel Best, *Threatened Children: Rhetoric and Concern about Child Victims* (Chicago: University of Chicago Press, 1990).

2. Police Against the New World Order, *Operation Vampire Killer 2000: American*

Police/Military Action Plan for Stopping World Government Rule (Phoenix, Ariz.: Police Against the New World Order, 1992).

3. Preparedness Shows, "Preparedness Expo '97: Peace of Mind in our Changing World" (Salt Lake City, Utah: Preparedness Shows, 1997), 3.

4. Mark Pitcavage, "Camouflage and Conspiracy: The Militia Movement From Ruby Ridge to Y2K," *American Behavioral Scientist* 44, no. 6 (2001): 960.

5. Chip Berlet and Matthew N. Lyons, *Right-Wing Populism in America: Too Close for Comfort* (New York: Guilford Press, 2000); John George and Laird Wilcox, *American Extremists: Militias, Supremacists, Klansmen, Communists and Others* (Amherst, N.Y.: Prometheus Books, 1996); Pitcavage, "Camouflage and Conspiracy"; Brent Smith, *Terrorism in America: Pipe Bombs and Pipe Dreams* (Albany, N.Y.: State University of New York Press, 1994).

6. See James William Gibson, *Warrior Dreams: Paramilitary Culture in Post Vietnam America* (New York: Hill and Wang, 1994).

7. Berlet and Lyons, *Right-Wing Populism*; Pitcavage, "Camouflage and Conspiracy."

8. Berlet and Lyons, *Right-Wing Populism*; David A. Neiwert, *In God's Country: The Patriot Movement and the Pacific Northwest* (Pullman, Wash.: Washington State University Press, 1999); Pitcavage, "Camouflage and Conspiracy"; Smith, *Terrorism in America*.

9. Pitcavage, "Camouflage and Conspiracy," 959; Neiwert, *In God's Country*; Berlet and Lyons, *Right-Wing Populism*.

10. This summary of the Gordon Kahl case is based on the following sources: Berlet and Lyons, *Right-Wing Populism*; Neiwert, *In God's Country*; Smith, *Terrorism in America*.

11. Neiwert, *In God's Country*, 237.

12. Smith, *Terrorism in America*, 58.

13. Joel Dyer, *Harvest of Rage: Why Oklahoma City is Only the Beginning* (Boulder, Colo.: Westview Press, 1998), 16.

14. Joshua D. Freilich, "Mobilizing Militias: Examining State Level Correlates of Militia Organizations and Activities" (Ph.D. diss., University at Albany, 2000).

15. George Bush, "Gulf Crisis An Opportunity For A 'New World Order,'" *Congressional Quarterly Weekly Report*, 15 September 1990, 2953–2956.

16. The summary of the Ruby Ridge incident is based on the following sources: David Johnston with Stephen Labaton, "F.B.I. Shaken by Inquiry into Idaho Siege," *New York Times*, 25 November 1993, A1; Neiwert, *In God's Country*; U.S. Department of Justice, *Report Regarding Internal Investigation of Shootings at Ruby Ridge, Idaho During Arrest of Randy Weaver* (Washington, D.C., 1999), retrieved June 2001 from: http://www.byington.org/Carl/ruby/ruby1.htm.

17. Department of Justice, *Ruby Ridge Report*.

18. Ibid.

19. Marc Cooper, "Montana's Mother of All Militias," *Nation* 260, no. 20 (1995): 714–720; Morris Dees and James Corcoran, *Gathering Storm: America's Militia Threat* (New York: HarperCollins, 1996); Dyer, *Harvest of Rage*; Neiwert, *In God's Country*; Leonard Zeskind, "Armed and Dangerous," *Rolling Stone*, 2 November 1995, 54–64.

20. James Bovard, "Why Congress Must Investigate Killings at Waco and Ruby Ridge," *Human Events* 51, no. 18 (1995): 5–7; Department of Justice, *Ruby Ridge Report.*

21. The summary of the Waco incident is based on the following sources: James Bowman, "Waco: The Rules of Reporting," *Skeptic* 7, no. 4 (1999): 8–10; Dees and Corcoran, *Gathering Storm*; Hamm, *Apocalypse in Oklahoma*; David Leppard, *Fire and Blood: The True Story of David Koresh and the Waco Siege* (London: Fourth Estate Limited, 1993); Clifford Linedecker, *Massacre at Waco: The Shocking True Story of Cult Leader David Koresh and the Branch Davidians* (London: Virgin, 1993); Dick J. Reavis, *The Ashes of Waco: An Investigation* (New York: Simon & Schuster, 1995); James D. Tabor, "The Waco Tragedy: An Autobiographical Account of One Attempt to Avert Disaster," in *From the Ashes: Making Sense of Waco*, ed. James R. Lewis (Lanham, Md.: Rowman & Littlefield, 1994), 13–21.

22. Tabor, "The Waco Tragedy," 15.

23. Reavis, *The Ashes of Waco*, 33–38.

24. Ibid.

25. Ibid.

26. Ibid.

27. Ibid, 142.

28. Lee Hancock, "Former Waco Prosecutor Indicted," *The Dallas Morning News*, 9 November 2000.

29. Bowman, "The Rules of Reporting;" Mark Sauer and Jim Okerblom, "Patriotism or Paranoia? Videos, Radio, Internet All Used to Spread Fears of the Far Right that Government Poses Danger," *The San Diego Union-Tribune*, 4 May 1995, E1.

30. Hamm, *Apocalypse in Oklahoma.*

CHAPTER 3: THE RISE AND FALL OF MILITIAS

1. Jack L. Walker, "Setting the Agenda in the U.S. Senate: A Theory of Problem Selection," *British Journal of Political Science* 7 (1977): 423–445; Frank R. Baumgartner and Bryan D. Jones, *Agendas and Instability in American Politics* (Chicago: University of Chicago Press, 1993).

2. Best, *Threatened Children*, 15.

3. Ibid.; Hilgartner and Bosk, "The Rise and Fall of Social Problems."

4. Stuart A. Scheingold, "Politics, Public Policy, and Street Crime," *Annals of the American Academy of Political and Social Science* 539 (May 1995): 166, 156.

5. These counts include two types of article. First, they include articles in which the majority of the text focuses on militia activities: articles describing a group, general information about the movement and certain individuals involved, and stories about crimes committed by militia members. Second, the counts include articles in which militias were not the primary focus of a story. For example, stories about other extremist groups, other incidents like Waco or Ruby Ridge,

domestic terrorist concerns, and gun control would often briefly mention militia concerns. Most of the articles included in these counts were in the first category of stories. Moreover, it is this first category of stories that is used in Chapters 4 and 5 when examining the sources cited in news stories and how militias were presented in them.

6. Although television news was not included in the analysis, other researchers have found an identical pattern of coverage when examining national television coverage of militias using the Vanderbilt Television News Archives; see Marie Curkan-Flanagan, "The Contemporary Militia: Network News Framing of a Social Movement" (Ph.D. diss., University of Tennessee-Knoxville, 2000).

7. Stephen Kroninger, "The Far Right is Upon Us," *Progressive* 59, no. 6 (1995): 8.

8. The Phineas Priesthood is considered among the most threatening of the groups tied to the Patriot Movement. Relying primarily on the Old Testament as its guiding doctrine, the Priesthood believes it is enforcing God's laws when murdering interracial couples, bombing abortion clinics and civil rights leaders, burning churches, and robbing banks. It is also among the most secretive and mysterious of groups, which has prevented law enforcement from truly knowing the extent to which it has been involved in illegal activities; see Neiwert, *In God's Country*.

9. Sam Walker, "'Militias' Forming Across US to Protest Gun Control Laws. Well-Armed Extremist Groups Refuse to Give Up Their Assault Weapons," *The Christian Science Monitor*, 17 October 1994, 1; Keith Schneider, "Fearing a Conspiracy, Some Heed a Call to Arms," *New York Times*, 14 November 1994, A1.

10. Chermak and Weiss, "The Effects of the Media;" Spitzer, *The Politics of Gun Control*.

11. Don Brown, "Oklahoma City, April 19, 1995," *Public Management* 77, no. 12 (1995): 6–10.

12. Gaye Tuchman, *Making News: A Study in the Construction of Reality* (New York: Free Press, 1978).

13. Ron Martz, "Suspect Held: FBI Sketch Leads to Man with Crewcut," *The Atlanta Journal and Constitution*, 21 April 1995, 1A.

14. Stephen Lang and Mitchell L. Bracey, "Squaring the One Percent: Biker Style and the Selling of Cultural Resistance," in *Cultural Criminology*, ed. Jeff Ferrell and Clinton R. Sanders (Boston: Northeastern University Press, 1995), 235–276.

CHAPTER 4: VOICES OF GOOD AND EVIL

1. The summary of the Viper case is based on the following sources: Alan W. Bock, "Raiding the Vipers' Nest," *Reason* 28, no. 7 (1996): 30–35; James Brooke, "Agents Seize Arsenal of Rifles and Bomb-Making Material in Arizona Military Inquiry," *The New York Times*, 3 July 1996, 18; Patricia King and Randy Collier, "'Vipers' in the 'Burbs," *Newsweek*, 15 July 1996, 20–23; Brad Knickerbocker, "'Viper' Arrests Mark Victory in Domestic Terrorism War," *Christian Science Monitor*, 3 July 1996, 3; Louis Sahagun, "Case Closed, Informant Abandoned:

Drew Nolan Helped Behead the Viper Militia for the ATF," *Los Angeles Times*, 29 November 1997, 1; Diane Wagner, "What Drives Viper Case, Politics or Real Threat? U.S. Finding Smoking Guns, but No Plot," *The Arizona Republic*, 12 July 1996, 1.

2. Wagner, "What Drives Viper Case," 1.
3. King and Collier, " 'Vipers' in the 'Burbs," 20.
4. Knickerbocker, " 'Viper' Arrests Mark Victory," 3.
5. Bock, "Raiding the Vipers' Nest," 30–35.
6. Ibid.; Brooke, "Agents Seize Arsenal," 18.
7. Neiwert, *In God's Country*.
8. The following material provides a good introduction to the relationship between reporters and sources: Steven M. Chermak, *Victims in the News: Crime and the American News Media* (Boulder, Colo.: Westview Press, 1995); Steven M. Chermak, "The Presentation of Drugs in the News Media: News Sources Involved in the Construction of Social Problems," *Justice Quarterly* 14, no. 4 (1997): 687–718; Steven Chibnall, *Law and Order News* (London: Tavistock, 1977); Richard V. Ericson, Patricia M. Baranek, and Janet B. L. Chan, *Negotiating Control: A Study of News Sources* (Toronto: University of Toronto Press, 1989); Mark Fishman, *Manufacturing the News* (Austin: University of Texas Press, 1980).
9. Joseph R. Gusfield, *The Culture of Public Problems: Drinking-Driving and the Symbolic Order* (Chicago: University of Chicago Press, 1981), 5, 15, 22.
10. Howard Kurtz, *Spin Cycle: Inside the Clinton Propaganda Machine* (New York: Free Press, 1998).
11. John Hohenberg, *Reelecting Bill Clinton: Why America Chose a "New" Democrat* (Syracuse, N.Y.: Syracuse University Press, 1997), 273–274.
12. Elizabeth Drew, *Showdown: The Struggle Between the Gingrich Congress and the Clinton White House* (New York: Simon & Schuster, 1996), 196.
13. Todd S. Purdum, "Terror in Oklahoma: The President; Clinton Assails The Preachings of the 'Militias,'" *New York Times*, 6 May 1995, 1A.
14. Wagner, "What Drives Viper Case," 1.
15. Stephen Labaton, "Wide Net Case in U.S. Inquiry on Gathering," *New York Times*, 31 August 1995; John Kelly, "Militia Exposed Racist Agents: Alabama 'Minutemen' Blew Whistle on ATF's 'Good Ol' Boys' Event," *Toledo Blade*, 28 February 1997.
16. Don Plummer and Doug Payne, "Targeting Terrorism: Alabama Militia Members Tied to Georgia Group. One of Three Questioned about Olympic Park Bombing Had Testified on Behalf of Macon-Area Pair Facing Bomb Charges," *The Atlanta Journal and Constitution*, 30 July 1996.
17. John M. Swomley, "Armed and Dangerous: The Threat of the 'Patriot Militias,'" *Humanist* 55, no. 6 (1995): 11.
18. See http://www.militiawatchdog.org.
19. Ken Silverstein, "The Church of Morris Dees: How the Southern Poverty Law Center Profits From Intolerance," *Harper's*, November 2000, 54; Andrea Stone, "Morris Dees: At Center of the Racial Storm," *USA Today*, 3 August 1996, 7A.
20. Dees and Corcoran, *Gathering Storm*; Kenneth S. Stern, *A Force Upon the Plain:*

The American Militia Movement and the Politics of Hate (New York: Simon & Schuster, 1996).

21. Stone, "Morris Dees."

22. Dees and Corcoran, *Gathering Storm*, 199.

23. Rick Steelhammer, "FBI Thwarts Plot," *Charleston Gazette*, 12 October 1996.

24. I used two strategies to determine the national figures of the militia movement. First, the interview data were an excellent resource. The interviews with national and local reporters, for example, provided information on the staple sources used to represent the movement. I also asked militia leaders to comment on who has been asked to represent the movement nationally. I was surprised to see how closely they followed such coverage and how consistent the reporters and militia members were in identifying the celebrity figures of the movement. Second, I used other documents to highlight top figures of the movement: political documents, source material from watchdog organizations, and articles published in national publications. It is important to note that some of these individuals and their affiliations have changed, and others are no longer active in the militia movement. I was concerned, however, with assessing their status when quoted as a source. There are certainly other individuals who might be considered local or regional celebrities, but the interest here is in identifying the national figures of the movement.

25. Joel Best, *Images of Issues: Typifying Contemporary Social Problems* 2d ed., (Hawthorne, N.Y.: Aldine De Gruyter, 1995); Todd Gitlin, *The Whole World is Watching* (Berkeley: University of California Press, 1980).

26. Gitlin, *The Whole World is Watching*, 3.

27. Olson claimed that the CIA and the U.S. government were responsible for the nerve-gas attack that took place in a Tokyo subway. Six people were killed in that attack. He also believed that the Japanese bombed the Murrah building and that the U.S. government allowed it to happen.

28. Art Pine, "Army Takes Action to Defend Its Image; Military: Oklahoma City Bombing Suspects' Service History is a Sore Point. Officers Begin to Engage in Damage Control," *Los Angeles Times*, 21 May 1995, A10.

29. Kim Masters, "Recoil from the NRA's Two Top Guns: New Direction Worries Old Members," *Washington Post*, 29 April 1995, D1.

CHAPTER 5: TERRORISTS AND OUTSIDERS

1. Katherine Beckett and Theodore Sasson, *The Politics of Injustice: Crime and Punishment in America* (Thousand Oaks, Calif.: Pine Forge Press, 2000); Chermak, *Victims in the News*; Ericson, Baranek, and Chan, *Negotiating Control*.

2. Gitlin, *The Whole World is Watching*.

3. Valerie Jenness, *Making it Work: The Prostitute's Rights Movement in Perspective* (Hawthorne, N.Y.: Aldine de Gruyter, 1993), 120.

4. The following sources provide a good introduction to the frames used to construct reality and frame analysis: Katherine Beckett, "Setting the Public

Agenda: 'Street Crime' and Drug Use in American Politics," *Social Problems* 41, no. 3 (1994): 425–447; Beckett and Sasson, *The Politics of Injustice*; Amy Binder, "Constructing Racial Rhetoric: Media Depictions of Harm in Heavy Metal and Rap Music," *American Sociological Review* 58 (1993): 753–767; Murray J. Edelman, *Constructing the Political Spectacle* (Chicago: University of Chicago Press, 1988); Robert M. Entman, "Framing U.S. Coverage of International News: Contrasts in Narratives of the KAL and Iran Air Incidents," *Journal of Communication* 41 (1991): 6–27; Robert M. Entman, "Framing: Toward Clarification of a Fractured Paradigm," *Journal of Communication* 43 (1993): 51–58; William A. Gamson and Andre Modigliani, "The Changing Culture of Affirmative Action," *Research in Political Sociology* 3 (1987): 137–177; William A. Gamson and Andre Modigliani, "Media Discourse and Public Opinion on Nuclear Power: A Constructionist Approach," *American Journal of Sociology* 95, no. 1 (1989): 1–37; Gitlin, *The Whole World is Watching*; Erving Goffman, *Frame Analysis* (Cambridge, Mass.: Harvard University Press, 1974); Michael Parenti, *Inventing Reality: The Politics of News Media* (New York: St. Martin's Press, 1993); David A. Snow et al., "Frame Alignment Processes, Micromobilization, and Movement Participation," *American Sociological Review* 51 (1986): 464–481.

5. Goffman, *Frame Analysis*, 21; Gitlin, *The Whole World is Watching*, 7. See Binder, "Constructing Racial Rhetoric"; Gamson and Modigliani, "The Changing Culture"; Gamson and Modigliani, "Media Discourse."

6. Entman, "Framing Toward Clarification," 52; Parenti, *Inventing Reality*; Beckett and Sasson, *The Politics of Injustice*.

7. William S. Lofquist, "Constructing 'Crime': Media Coverage of Individual and Organizational Wrongdoing," *Justice Quarterly* 14, no. 2 (1997): 243–263.

8. Joel Best, "'Road Warriors' on 'Hair-Trigger Highways,'" *Sociological Inquiry* 61, no. 3 (1991): 327–345; Joel Best, *Troubling Children: Studies of Children and Social Problems* (Hawthorne, N.Y.: Aldine de Gruyter, 1994); Binder, "Racial Rhetoric"; Entman, "Framing Toward Clarification"; Gitlin, *The Whole World is Watching*; Gamson and Modigliani, "The Changing Culture"; Gamson and Modigliani, "Media Discourse"; William J. Swart, "The League of Nations and the Irish Question: Master Frames, Cycles of Protest, and 'Master Frame Alignment,'" *Sociological Quarterly* 36, no. 3 (1995): 465–482; Rhys H. Williams, "Constructing the Public Good: Social Movements and Cultural Resources," *Social Problems* 42, no. 1 (1995): 124–144.

9. Binder, "Racial Rhetoric," 755; Beckett, "Setting the Public Agenda," 444; Swart, "The League of Nations," 469; Best, *Troubling Children*, 9.

10. Bethami A. Dobkin, *Tales of Terror: Television News and the Construction of the Terrorist Threat* (New York: Praeger, 1992).

11. The following source material was used for this section: Anti-Defamation League, "Paranoia as Patriotism: Linda Thompson," (1995), retrieved from http://pub/orgs/American/adl/paranoia-as-patriotism/linda-thompson; Jason Vest, "The Spooky World of Linda Thompson: Her Videos Inflame the Militias. Is She the Radical Right or Radically Wrong?" *Washington Post*, 11 May 1995; Jason Vest, "Leader of the Fringe," *Progressive* 59, no. 6 (1995): 28–30;

Maryanne Vollers, "The White Woman From Hell," *Esquire* 124, no. 1 (July 1995): 50–52.

12. I retrieved the fax she sent titled "Waco: Time for the Militia," from: http://www.outpost-of-freedom.com/Warms.htm.

13. Vest, "The Spooky World," 1.

14. Linda Thompson, "Waco: Another Perspective," (Indianapolis, Ind.: American Justice Federation, 1993).

15. The following sources discuss the manipulation of statistics: Best, *Threatened Children*, 64; Joel Best and Tracy Memoree Thibodeau, "Measuring the Scope of Social Problems: Apparent Inconsistencies Across Estimates of Family Abductions," *Justice Quarterly* 14, no. 4 (1997): 719–737; Dobkin, *Tales of Terror*, 89; Neil Gilbert, "Advocacy Research and Social Policy," in *Crime and Justice: A Review of Research*, ed. Michael Tonry (Chicago: University of Chicago Press, 1997), 101–148; James B. Jacobs and Jessica S. Henry, "The Social Construction of a Hate Crime Epidemic," *Journal of Criminal Law and Criminology* 86, no. 2 (1996): 366–391; James B. Jacobs and Kimberly A. Potter, "Hate Crimes: A Critical Perspective," in *Crime and Justice: A Review of Research*, ed. Michael Tonry (Chicago: University of Chicago Press, 1997), 1–50.

16. Tom Kenworthy and George Lardner, "The Militias: Guns and Bitter; Federal Push to Rein in Arms Sparked Fire of Resentment," *Washington Post*, 4 May 1995, A23; Serge F. Kovaleski, "Oklahoma Bombing Conspiracy Theories Ripple Across the Nation," *Washington Post*, 9 July 1995.

17. Dees and Corcoran, *Gathering Storm*, 6.

18. Thomas G. Watts, "Number of Militia Units in U.S. Still Increasing, Monitors Report," *The Dallas Morning News*, 15 December 1996; Southern Poverty Law Center, "The Intelligence Project," (2001), retrieved from: http://www.splcenter.org/intelligenceproject/ip-index.html.

19. MaryAnn Struman, "He's 'Mark from Michigan:' Janitor, Far-Right's Point Man," *Detroit News*, 20 August 1995.

20. This summary of the Joe Holland case is based on the following sources: Maureen Hayden, "Militia Leader Confesses to Targeting Montana Officials," *Scripps Howard News Service*, 11 December 1995; Neiwert, *In God's Country*; Mark Pitcavage, "'Patriot' Profiles #1: Joe Holland, Calvin Greenup, and the Anti-Tax Militia" (1996), retrieved July 1, 2001 from the Militia Watchdog Web site: http://www.militia-watchdog.org/holland.htm

21. Fox Butterfield, "Period of Confusion Expected After Ruling on Brady Law," *New York Times*, 28 June 1997; Shawn E. Tuma, "Preserving Liberty: United States v. Printz and the Vigilant Defense of Federalism," *Regent University Law Review* 10 (1998): 193.

22. Hayden, "Militia Leader Confesses."

23. Police Against the New World Order, *Operation Vampire Killer*.

24. Cooper, "Montana's Mother of All Militias"; Clair Johnson, "Bo Gritz: Hero to Some but a Bigot to Others," *Billings (Montana) Gazette*, 1 May 1996; Neiwert, *In God's Country*.

25. Dyer, *Harvest of Rage*, 76–77.

26. Dale Russakoff, "Grass-Roots Rage: Below the Surface: Alienation Simmers in Corner of Mid-America," *Washington Post*, 5 May 1995, A1.

CHAPTER 6: CONFIRMING THE THREAT

1. Kenworthy and Lardner, "The Militias: Guns and Bitter."
2. Katherine Bell, *Ritual Theory, Ritual Practice* (New York: Oxford University Press, 1992), 213; Daniel Dayan and Elihu Katz, "Articulating Consensus: The Ritual and Rhetoric of Media Events," in *Durkheimian Sociology: Cultural Studies*, ed. Jeffrey C. Alexander (New York: Cambridge University Press, 1988), 165; Hans-Peter Muller, "Social Structure and Civil Religion: Legitimation Crisis in a Later Durkheimian Perspective," in *Durkheimian Sociology: Cultural Studies*, ed. Jeffrey C. Alexander (New York: Cambridge University Press, 1988), 131.
3. See Gary Goodpaster, "On the Theory of American Adversary Criminal Trial," *The Journal of Criminal Law and Criminology* 78, no. 1 (1987): 118–154.
4. U.S. Senate Committee on the Judiciary, *Terrorism in the United States: The Nature and Extent of the Threat and Possible Legislative Responses*, 104th Cong., 1st sess., 27 April and 24 May 1995; U.S. Senate Committee on the Judiciary, *The Militia Movement in the United* States, 104th Cong., 1st sess., 15 June 1995; U.S. House Committee on the Judiciary, *Nature and Threat of Violent Anti-Government Groups in America*, 104th Cong., 1st sess., 2 November 1995; Bryan Sierra, "Democrats Open Militia Hearings," *United Press International*, 11 July 1995.
5. John W. Kingdon, *Agendas, Alternatives, and Public Policies* (Boston: Little, Brown, 1984); see also, Chermak and Weiss, "The Effects of the Media."
6. Senate Committee, *Terrorism in the United States*, 1–2, 2.
7. Ibid., 115.
8. See Penny Bender, "Senators Vow to Move Quickly with Anti-Terrorism Legislation," *Gannett News Service*, 27 April 1995; Francis X. Clines, "Terror in Oklahoma," *The New York Times*, 28 April 1995, A25; Heather Dewar and Robert A. Rankin, "Attack May Open Militias to U.S. Surveillance: Bombing Could Be 'Criminal Intent' Needed Under Rights Law," *Knight-Ridder News Service*, 24 April 1995.
9. This hearing was first scheduled for May 25, but was postponed.
10. Senate Committee, *The Militia Movement*, 1, 66.
11. Jeff Barker, "Militias Misunderstood, Senate Told; Strange Claims Belie 'Mainstream' Defense," *The Arizona Republic*, 16 June 1995, A1; James Risen, "Militia Leaders Bring Their Fiery Talk to Capitol Hill Hearing: They Claim Mainstream Roots But Voice Fringe Hostilities to Senators," *Los Angeles Times*, 16 June 1995, A1.
12. Senate Committee, *The Militia Movement*, 2–5, 44–45.
13. Daniel Levitas, "Senate's Hearings on Militia Groups Could Foster Hate," *Roll Call*, 15 June 1995.
14. Sierra, "Democrats Open Militia Hearings."
15. Senate Committee, *The Militia Movement*, 102, 110, 107.

16. Dennis B. Roddy, "Did Militia Man Conceal True Colors in Senate?" *Pittsburgh Post-Gazette*, 18 June 1995, A1.

17. Senate Committee, *The Militia Movement*, 94–95.

18. John Mintz, "Militias Meet the Senate with Conspiracies to Share: Leaders Sound Off on Oklahoma, Citizen Anger," *Washington Post*, 16 June 1995, A1.

19. Senate Committee, *The Militia Movement*, 100.

20. Senate Committee, *Terrorism in the United States*, 10–11; John F. Harris, "Clinton Attacks GOP for Rejecting NRA-Opposed Provision," *Washington Post*, 10 August 1995, A14.

21. House Committee, *Nature and Threat*, 2, 12–13, 4.

22. Ibid., 39.

23. The analysis of the Lampley case is based on the following articles retrieved in July 2001 from Dow Jones & Co. database (Dow Jones Interactive) at: http://www.djinteractive.com/sources: *ABC News*, "Increased Risk? Mounting Numbers of Domestic Incidents Raise Concern," 1 October 1999; *Agence France-Presse*, "Three Arrested in Oklahoma for Alleged Bomb Making," 13 November 1995; *Associated Press*, "3 Charged with Plotting Bombings," 1995; *Dallas Morning News*, "3 Face Court Today in Alleged Bomb Plot Oklahoma Leader of Separatists Baffled by Suspected Conspiracy against Group," 13 November 1995; Doug Ferguson, "3 Charged with Plotting Bombings," *The Columbian*, 14 November 1995; Doug Ferguson, "Four Accused of Plotting to Blow Up Buildings," *Associated Press*, 13 November 1995; Jerry Fink, "Four Indicted by Grand Jury in Alleged Bombing Conspiracy," *Tulsa World*, 6 December 1995, N8; Jerry Fink, "Bomb Suspects' Hearing Changed," *Tulsa World*, 21 November 1995, N12; David Foster, "Early Detection of American Terrorism a Daunting Task," *The State Journal-Register*, 7 April 1996; David Foster, "Beyond Militias: Extremism's Many Faces Vex Anti-Terrorism Efforts," *The Associated Press*, 6 April 1996; Kelly Kurt, "Informant's Credibility Questioned in Bomb Plot Case," *The Associated Press Political Service*, 4 April 1996; *National Public Radio*, "Bombing Conspiracy Charges Against Four in Oklahoma" [broadcast, 14 November 1995]; Scott Parks, "Outposts of Race-based Theology: Authorities say 'Christian Identity' Message Binds Many White Separatists Across the Nation," *The Dallas Morning News*, 5 August 1995, 1G; Bill Swindell, "Suspects Ordered Held: Pair Denied Bail in Bomb Conspiracy Charges," *Tulsa World*, 30 November 1995; Bill Swindell, "Threats Linked to Suspect in Conspiracy," *Tulsa World*, 29 November 1995; Bill Swindell, "Militia Coordinator on Federal Payroll," *Tulsa World*, 7 April 1996; Bill Swindell, "Church Infiltrated, FBI Informant Says," *Tulsa World*, 5 April 1996; Bill Swindell, "Jury Picked for Trial," *Tulsa World*, 2 April 1996; Bill Swindell, "3 Planned for Bomb, U.S. Says," *Tulsa World*, 3 April 1996; "Bomb Charges Provide Eerie Echo," *The Globe and Mail*, 15 November 1995; "Court Date Set in Alleged Plot," *Tulsa World*, 13 November 1995. Other sources include: Tom Morganthau, "A Shadow Over the Olympics; the Feds get Ready for Threats Large and Small," *Newsweek*, 6 May 1996, 34; Robby Trammell, "Informant Proud of Role in Arrests of Bomb-Plot Suspects," *The Daily Oklahoman*, 15 November 1995, 1.

24. Trammell, "Informant Proud," 1.
25. "Court Date Set," *Tulsa World*.
26. Morganthau, "A Shadow," 34.
27. Ferguson, "Four Accused"; Swindell, "Militia Coordinator."
28. Larry Crow pleaded guilty and received six months in a halfway house and probation. He also testified against the other defendants.
29. Trammell, "Informant Proud," 1.
30. Swindell, "Suspect Ordered Held."
31. "Bomb Charges," *The Globe and Mail*.
32. Swindell, "Church Infiltrated."
33. Swindell, "3 Planned for Bomb."
34. M. L. Stein, "Less of a Circus," *Editor & Publisher* 130, no. 23 (1997): 12–14.
35. The trial testimony provided in this section was downloaded from: *United States of America v. Timothy McVeigh*, United States District Court, District of Colorado, Criminal Action No. 96-CR-68, retrieved October 1, 2001 from: http://www.oklahoman.com/opub/bombing/btranscripts.
36. Robert J. Cottrol, "Perceptions and Decision Making: Racial Perspectives: Through a Glass Diversely: The O. J. Simpson Trial as Racial Rorschach Test," *Colorado Law Review* 67 (1996): 909.
37. Bruce Brown, "Jury Still Out on McVeigh Trial," *Quill* 85, no. 1 (1997): 12–14; John A. Walton, "From O. J. to Tim McVeigh and Beyond: The Supreme Court's Totality of Circumstances Test as Ringmaster in the Expanding Media Circus," *Denver University Law Review* 75 (1998): 549; Lois Romano and Tom Kenworthy, "McVeigh Guilty on All 11 Counts," *Washington Post*, 3 June 1997, A1.
38. Jillian Lloyd, "Judge Keeps McVeigh Trial Under His Tight Rein," *Christian Science Monitor*, 13 May 1997, 1; Stein, "Less of a Circus," 12; Editorial, *Denver Post*, 3 June 1997, 8.
39. Karen Roebuck and Ted Gest, "A Tearful Start to McVeigh's Trial," *U.S. News and World Report*, 5 May 1997, 30.
40. *United States v. Timothy McVeigh*.
41. Ibid.
42. Ibid.
43. Romano and Kenworthy, "McVeigh Guilty."
44. Editorial, "Getting McVeigh," *Nation* 264, no. 24 (1997): 3; Warren Richey and Jillian Lloyd, "McVeigh Verdict: Chill to Terrorists," *Christian Science Monitor*, 4 June 1997, 1.
45. *United States v. Timothy McVeigh*.
46. Ibid.
47. Peter Annin and Tom Morganthau, "The Verdict: Death," *Newsweek*, 23 June 1997, 40–43; Thomas Kenworthy and Lisa Romano, "McVeigh Condemned to Die," *Washington Post*, 14 June 1997, A1.
48. *United States v. Timothy McVeigh*.
49. Stephen Jones and Holly Hillerman, "McVeigh, McJustice, McMedia," *The University of Chicago Legal Forum* (1998): 53.
50. *United States v. Timothy McVeigh*.

1. The following sources were used for background information about Bo Gritz: Valerie Alvord, "Mistrust of Government Ripples Across the Nation," *The San Diego Union-Tribune*, 1 May 1995, A1; Neil A. Hamilton, *Militias in America: A Reference Handbook* (Santa Barbara, Calif.: ABC-Clio, Inc., 1996); David M. Herszenhorn, "Militia Leader Acquitted of Plotting to Kidnap Boy," *New York Times*, 9 March 2000, B12; Clair Johnson, "Bo Gritz: Hero to Some but a Bigot to Others," *Billings (Montana) Gazette*, 1 May 1996; Neiwert, *In God's Country*; Preparedness Shows, "Preparedness Expo;" Martin Walker, "Is America Insane?: The Nation is Falling Apart, A Foreign Observer Says," *Vancouver Sun*, 29 April 1995, B1.

2. The films cited in Chapter 7 and their release dates are provided in the appendix.

3. Carol Fry and Christopher Kemp, "Rambo Agonistes," *Literature-Film Quarterly* 24 (1996): 367–75, 368; Gibson, *Warrior Dreams*; Gaylyn Studler and David Desser, "Never Having to Say You're Sorry: Rambo's Rewriting of the Vietnam War," in *From Hanoi to Hollywood*, ed. Linda Dittmar and Gene Michaud (London: Rutgers University Press, 1990), 101–112; Frank Sweeney, " 'What Mean Expendable?': Myth, Ideology, and Meaning in *First Blood* and *Rambo*," *Journal of American Culture* 22 (3): 67.

4. Sweeney, " 'What Mean Expendable?,' " 63.

5. Gibson, *Warrior Dreams*; Sweeney, " 'What Mean Expendable?' "

6. Mitchell Fink, "The Insider," *People*, 14 July 1997, 41.

7. Johnson, "Bo Gritz."

8. *United States v. Timothy McVeigh*.

9. Aline McKenzie, "Guilt by Misidentification: State-Sanctioned Defense Forces Say their Reputation Tainted by Private Militias' Anti-Government Bent," *The Dallas Morning News*, 26 May 1995, A1; Rob Eure, "Green, Armed and Angry," *The Oregonian*, 13 November 1995, B1; Scott Parks and Victoria Loe, "McVeigh Fits Pattern of Notorious Killers, Expert Says. Ex-Agent Sees a 'Dangerous' Profile Emerge in Bomb Suspect's History," *The Dallas Morning News*, 9 July 1995, 1A; Judy Thomas, "Militias Distribute Plans for 'War' Against U.S. Government: 'Rules of Engagement' include Attacks Against Law," *The Kansas City Star*, 13 April 1996, A18.

10. Jenkins, *Using Murder*.

11. Ray Surette, *Media, Crime, and Criminal Justice: Images and Realities* (Belmont, Calif.: West/Wadsworth, 1998).

12. Joel Best and Philip Jenkins have furnished numerous model studies.

13. "Tiny Symbol of Life and Death," *People*, 8 May 1995, 56.

14. Richard Hofstadter, *The Paranoid Style in American Politics and Other Essays* (New York: Alfred A. Knopf, 1965), 3, 39; Sanford Pinsker, "America's Conspiratorial Imagination," *Virginia Quarterly Review*, 68, no. 4 (1992): 605; Peter Knight, *Conspiracy Culture: From Kennedy to the X-Files* (New York: Routledge, 2000), 1.

15. Berlet and Lyons, *Right Wing Populism*.

16. William D. Romanowski, "Oliver Stone's JFK," *Journal of Popular Film & Television*, 21, no. 2 (1993): 63–72.

17. Michel and Herbeck, *American Terrorist*, 39.

18. Jack G. Shaheen, *Reel Bad Arabs: How Hollywood Vilifies a People* (New York: Olive Branch Press, 2001), 500.

19. Abdullah Quick, "The False Reality of True Lies," *The Toronto Star*, 3 September 1994, G10.

20. Russell Baker, "All in What Family?," quoted in Shaheen, *Reel Bad Arabs*, 503; Don Bustany and Salam Al-Marayati, "Hasta la Vista Fairness," quoted in Shaheen, *Reel Bad Arabs*, 503; Amy E. Swartz, "Satire, Stereotype, Schwarzeneggar," *The Washington Post*, 22 July 1994, A23.

21. Shaheen, *Reel Bad Arabs*, 15.

22. Ibid.

23. Ibid.

24. Ibid.

25. Surette, *Media, Crime, and Criminal Justice*.

26. David Croteau and William Hoynes, *Media Society: Industries, Images, and Audiences* (Thousand Oaks, Calif.: Pine Forge Press, 2000); Robert Elias, *The Politics of Victimization: Victims, Victimology, and Human Rights* (New York: Oxford University Press, 1986).

27. Surette, *Media, Crime, and Criminal Justice*, 37.

28. Wes Shipley and Gray Cavender, "Murder and Mayhem at the Movies," *Journal of Criminal Justice and Popular Culture* 9, no. 1 (2001): 2.

29. Ann Hornaday, "Paranoia—or Are They Out There?" *The Baltimore Sun*, 11 July 1999, 5F.

30. Cooper, "Montana's Mother of All Militias."

CHAPTER 8: CONSTRUCTING GOOD DEMONS

1. Dan Herbeck and Lou Michel, "Inside the Terrorist's Mind," *Buffalo News*, 7 October 2001, H1.

2. Jo Thomas, "A Nation Challenged: Hate Groups; U.S. Groups Have Some Times to Germ Warfare," *The New York Times*, 2 November 2001, B8.

3. Craig Welch, "Militia Groups See a Revival," *The Seattle Times*, 16 October 2001, A1; Ellen Barry, "America Prepares Domestic Impact. Taking Arms; Militias Turn Fight Away From the US, as its Enemies," *The Boston Globe*, 22 September 2001, A3.

4. Lance Williams, "Militia Planned Propane Tank Attack Near Sacramento," *Pittsburgh Post-Gazette*, 29 December 1999, A11.

5. Deanna Boyd, "Bomb-Making Materials, Assault Weapons Seized: Anti-Government Literature Also Found in Motel Room, Storage Unit," *Fort Worth Star-Telegram*, 14 June 2001, 4; Karen Abbott, "Bomb Maker Sentenced to 35 Months in Prison," *Rocky Mountain News*, 20 April 2001, 14A; Larry Dougherty, "Militia Leader Draws Prison Term," *St. Petersburg Times*, 29 July 2000, 1B; Jodi Pospeschil, "Militia Chief's Trial Remains in Galesburg," *Peoria Journal Star*,

20 October 2000, retrieved December 7, 2001 from: http://www.rickross.com/reference/militia/militia34.html.

6. The following source materials were used for this section: *Associated Press*, "Some Say McVeigh Wants to Become a Martyr For Anti-Government Causes," *St. Louis Post-Dispatch*, 25 December 2000; Chris Burritt, "In Militia Country, McVeigh No Martyr," *The Atlanta Journal and Constitution*, 10 June 2001, 12A; Nancy Gibbs, "Botching the Big Case," *Time*, 21 May 2001, 30–36; Susan Greene, "Militias Shedding No Tears for McVeigh," *Denver Post*, 6 July 2001, A2; Carl Hiassen, "Militia Nuts Have a Martyr in McVeigh," *The Tampa Tribune*, 16 June 1997; Toni Locy, "Anti-Government Forces Still Struggle to Recover from Oklahoma City Fallout," *USA Today*, 9 May 2001, 9A; Bryan Robinson, "No Militia Patsy: Militias Will Not Consider McVeigh a Martyr," *ABC News*, 12 June 2001, retrieved from: http://www.rickross.com/reference/militia/militia45.html; Karen Sandstrom, "The Story Behind McVeigh's Favorite Verse," *The Plain Dealer*, 13 June 2001, 1E.

7. Robinson, "No Militia Patsy."

8. Keith Bradsher, "Citing Declining Membership, A Leader Disbands His Militia," *New York Times*, 30 April 2001, A17; Nicholas K. Geranios, "Militias See Treatment of Idaho Family as Example of Intrusive Government," *Associated Press*, 17 June 2001, retrieved December 7, 2001 from: http://www.rickross.com/reference/militia/militia47.html; Greene, "Militias Shedding No Tears"; Helen Kennedy, "A Movement That's in Retreat," *New York Daily News*, 8 May 2001, 8A; Brad Knickerbocker, "A McVeigh Legacy: Militias Wane," *The Christian Science Monitor*, 11 June 2001, 1; Robert L. Jackson, "Militia Movement 'a Shadow' of Its Past," *Los Angeles Times*, 6 May 2001, 20; Robinson, "No Militia Patsy"; Mark Shaffer, "McVeigh Factor Destroys Militias," *The Arizona Republic*, 6 May 2001, retrieved December 7, 2001 from: http://www.rickross.com/reference/militia/militia42.html.

9. *Associated Press*, "U.S. Marshals Seize Indianapolis Church that Had Accumulated $6 Million Tax Debt," *St. Louis Post-Dispatch*, 14 February 2001.

10. Geranios, "Militias See Treatment."

11. Goode and Ben-Yehuda, *Moral Panics*, 29.

12. Best, *Threatened Children*.

REFERENCES

Baumgartner, Frank R., and Bryan D. Jones. *Agendas and Instability in American Politics*. Chicago: University of Chicago Press, 1993.

Beckett, Katherine. "Setting the Public Agenda: 'Street Crime' and Drug Use in American Politics." *Social Problems* 41, no. 3 (1994): 425–447.

Beckett, Katherine, and Theodore Sasson. *The Politics of Injustice: Crime and Punishment in America*. Thousand Oaks, Calif.: Pine Forge Press, 2000.

Bell, Katherine. *Ritual Theory, Ritual Practice*. New York: Oxford University Press, 1992.

Berlet, Chip, and Matthew N. Lyons. *Right-Wing Populism in America: Too Close for Comfort*. New York: Guilford Press, 2000.

Best, Joel. *Images of Issues: Typifying Contemporary Social Problems*. 2d ed. Hawthorne, N.Y.: Aldine De Gruyter, 1995.

———. "'Road Warriors' on 'Hair-Trigger Highways.'" *Sociological Inquiry* 61, no. 3 (1991): 327–345.

———. *Threatened Children: Rhetoric and Concern about Child Victims*. Chicago: University of Chicago Press, 1990.

———. *Troubling Children: Studies of Children and Social Problems*. Hawthorne, N.Y.: Aldine de Gruyter, 1994.

Best, Joel, and Tracy Memoree Thibodeau. "Measuring the Scope of Social Problems: Apparent Inconsistencies Across Estimates of Family Abductions." *Justice Quarterly* 14, no. 4 (1997): 719–737.

Binder, Amy. "Constructing Racial Rhetoric: Media Depictions of Harm in Heavy Metal and Rap Music." *American Sociological Review* 58 (1993): 753–767.

Bock, Alan W. "Raiding the Vipers' Nest." *Reason* 28, no. 7 (1996): 30–35.

Bovard, James. "Why Congress Must Investigate Killings at Waco and Ruby Ridge." *Human Events* 51, no. 18 (1995): 5–7.

Bowman, James. "Waco: The Rules of Reporting." *Skeptic* 7, no. 4 (1999): 8–10.

Brown, Bruce. "Jury Still Out on McVeigh Trial." *Quill* 85, no. 1 (1997): 12–14.

Brown, Don. "Oklahoma City, April 19, 1995." *Public Management* 77, no. 12 (1995): 6–10.

Cavendar, Gray, Linda Bond-Maupin, and Nancy C. Jurik. "The Construction of Gender in Reality Crime TV." *Gender and Society* 13, no. 5 (1999): 643–663.

Chermak, Steven M. "Image Control: How Police Affect the Presentation of Crime News." *American Journal of Police* 14, no. 2 (1995): 21–43.

————. "The Presentation of Drugs in the News Media: News Sources Involved in the Construction of Social Problems." *Justice Quarterly* 14, no. 4 (1997): 687–718.

————. *Victims in the News: Crime and the American News Media.* Boulder, Colo.: Westview Press, 1995.

Chermak, Steven M., and Alexander Weiss. "The Effects of the Media on Federal Criminal Justice Policy." *Criminal Justice Policy Review* 8, no. 4 (1997): 323–341.

Chibnall, Steven. *Law and Order News.* London: Tavistock, 1977.

Cohen, Stanley. *Folk Devils and Moral Panic.* London: MacGibbon and Kee, 1972.

Cooper, Marc. "Montana's Mother of All Militias." *Nation* 260, no. 20 (1995): 714–720.

Cottrol, Robert J. "Perceptions and Decision Making: Racial Perspectives: Through a Glass Diversely: The O. J. Simpson Trial as Racial Rorschach Test." *Colorado Law Review* 67 (1996): 909.

Croteau, David, and William Hoynes. *Media Society: Industries, Images, and Audiences.* Thousand Oaks, Calif.: Pine Forge Press, 2000.

Curkan-Flanagan, Marie. "The Contemporary Militia: Network News Framing of a Social Movement." Ph.D. diss., University of Tennessee-Knoxville, 2000.

Dayan, Daniel, and Elihu Katz. "Articulating Consensus: The Ritual and Rhetoric of Media Events." In *Durkheimian Sociology: Cultural Studies,* edited by Jeffrey Alexander, 161–186. New York: Cambridge University Press, 1988.

Dees, Morris, and James Corcoran. *Gathering Storm: America's Militia Threat.* New York: HarperCollins, 1996.

DeMatteo, David S. "Welcome to Anytown, U.S.A.—Home of Beautiful Scenery (and a Convicted Sex Offender): Sex Offender Registration and Notification Laws in E.B. v. Verniero." *Villanova Law Review* 43 (1998): 581.

Dobkin, Bethami A. *Tales of Terror: Television News and the Construction of the Terrorist Threat.* New York: Praeger, 1992.

Drew, Elizabeth. *Showdown: The Struggle Between the Gingrich Congress and the Clinton White House.* New York: Simon & Schuster, 1996.

Duke, James T. *Issues in Sociological Theory: Another Look at the "Old Masters."* New York: University Press of America, 1983.

Durkheim, Emile. *The Division of Labor in Society.* Glencoe, Ill.: Free Press, 1960.

————. *The Rules of Sociological Method.* New York: Free Press, 1966.

Dyer, Joel. *Harvest of Rage: Why Oklahoma City is Only the Beginning.* Boulder, Colo.: Westview Press, 1998.

Edelman, Murray J. *Constructing the Political Spectacle.* Chicago: University of Chicago Press, 1988.

Editorial. "Getting McVeigh." *Nation* 264, no. 24 (1997): 3.

Entman, Robert. "Framing: Toward Clarification of a Fractured Paradigm." *Journal of Communication* 43 (1993): 51–58.

————. "Framing U.S. Coverage of International News: Contrasts in Narratives of the KAL and Iran Air Incidents." *Journal of Communication* 41 (1991): 6–27.

————. "Modern Racism and the Images of Blacks in Local Television News." *Critical Studies in Mass Communication* 7 (1990): 332–345.

Ericson, Richard V., Patricia M. Baranek, and Janet B. L. Chan. *Negotiating Control: A Study of News Sources.* Toronto: University of Toronto Press, 1989.

————. *Representing Order: Crime, Law, and Justice in the News Media*. Toronto: University of Toronto Press, 1991.

Erikson, Kai T. *Wayward Puritans: A Study in the Sociology of Deviance*. Needham Heights, Mass.: Simon & Schuster, 1966.

Fair, Jo Ellen, and Roberta J. Astroff. "Constructing Race and Violence: U.S. News Coverage and the Signifying Practices of Apartheid." *Journal of Communication* 41, no. 4 (1991): 58–74.

Fishman, Mark. *Manufacturing the News*. Austin: University of Texas Press, 1980.

Freilich, Joshua D. "Mobilizing Militias: Examining State Level Correlates of Militia Organizations and Activities." Ph.D. diss., University at Albany, 2000.

Fry, Carol, and Christopher Kemp. "Rambo Agonistes." *Literature-Film Quarterly* 24 (1996): 367–75.

Gamson, William A., and Andre Modigliani. "The Changing Culture of Affirmative Action." *Research in Political Sociology* 3 (1987): 137–177.

————. "Media Discourse and Public Opinion on Nuclear Power: A Constructionist Approach." *American Journal of Sociology* 95, no. 1 (1989): 1–37.

Gans, Herbert J. *Deciding What's News: A Study of CBS Evening News, Newsweek and Time*. New York: Pantheon Books, 1979.

Geertz, Clifford. *The Interpretation of Cultures*. New York: Basic Books, 1973.

George, John, and Laird Wilcox. *American Extremists: Militias, Supremacists, Klansmen, Communists and Others*. Amherst, N.Y.: Prometheus Books, 1996.

Gibson, James William. *Warrior Dreams: Paramilitary Culture in Post Vietnam America*. New York: Hill and Wang, 1994.

Gilbert, Neil. "Advocacy Research and Social Policy." In *Crime and Justice: A Review of Research*, edited by Michael Tonry, 101–148. Chicago: University of Chicago Press, 1997.

Gitlin, Todd. *The Whole World is Watching*. Berkeley: University of California Press, 1980.

Goffman, Erving. *Frame Analysis*. Cambridge, Mass.: Harvard University Press, 1974.

Goode, Erich, and Ben-Yehuda Nachman. *Moral Panics: The Social Construction of Deviance*. Cambridge, Mass.: Blackwell, 1994.

Goodpaster, Gary. "On the Theory of American Adversary Criminal Trial." *The Journal of Criminal Law and Criminology* 78, no. 1 (1987): 118–154.

Gusfield, Joseph R. *The Culture of Public Problems: Drinking-Driving and the Symbolic Order*. Chicago: University of Chicago Press, 1981.

Hamilton, Neil A. *Militias in America: A Reference Handbook*. Santa Barbara, Calif.: ABC-Clio, Inc., 1996.

Hamm, Mark. *Apocalypse in Oklahoma: Waco and Ruby Ridge Revenged*. Boston: Northeastern University Press, 1997.

Hilgartner, Stephen, and Charles L. Bosk. "The Rise and Fall of Social Problems: A Public Arenas Model." *American Journal of Sociology* 94, no. 1 (1988): 53–78.

Hofstadter, Richard. *The Paranoid Style in American Politics and Other Essays*. New York: Alfred A. Knopf, 1965.

Hohenberg, John. *Reelecting Bill Clinton: Why America Chose a "New" Democrat*. Syracuse, N.Y.: Syracuse University Press, 1997.

Hughes, Everett C. "Dilemmas and Contradictions of Status." *American Journal of Sociology* 50 (1945): 353–359.

Jacobs, James B., and Jessica S. Henry. "The Social Construction of a Hate Crime Epidemic." *Journal of Criminal Law and Criminology* 86, no. 2 (1996): 366–391.

Jacobs, James B., and Kimberly A. Potter. "Hate Crimes: A Critical Perspective." In *Crime and Justice: A Review of Research*, edited by Michael Tonry, 1–50. Chicago: University of Chicago Press, 1997.

Jenkins, Philip. *Moral Panic: Changing Concepts of the Child Molester in Modern America*. New Haven, Conn.: Yale University Press, 1998.

———. *Synthetic Panics: The Symbolic Politics of Designer Drugs*. New York: New York University Press, 1999.

———. *Using Murder: The Social Construction of Serial Murder*. Hawthorne, N.Y.: Aldine De Gruyter, 1994.

Jenness, Valerie. *Making it Work: The Prostitute's Rights Movement in Perspective*. Hawthorne, N.Y.: Aldine de Gruyter, 1993.

Jones, Stephen, and Holly Hillerman. "McVeigh, McJustice, McMedia." *The University of Chicago Legal Forum* (1998): 53.

Kingdon, John W. *Agendas, Alternatives, and Public Policies*. Boston: Little, Brown, 1984.

Kittrie, Nicholas N. *The War Against Authority: From the Crisis of Legitimacy to a New Social Contract*. Baltimore: Johns Hopkins University Press, 1995.

Knight, Peter. *Conspiracy Culture: From Kennedy to the X-Files*. New York: Routledge, 2000.

Kroninger, Stephen. "The Far Right is Upon Us." *Progressive* 59, no. 6 (1995): 8–11.

Kurtz, Howard. *Spin Cycle: Inside the Clinton Propaganda Machine*. New York: Free Press, 1998.

Lang, Stephen, and Mitchell L. Bracey. "Squaring the One Percent: Biker Style and the Selling of Cultural Resistance." In *Cultural Criminology*, edited by Jeff Ferrell and Clinton R. Sanders, 235–276. Boston: Northeastern University Press, 1995.

Leppard, David. *Fire and Blood: The True Story of David Koresh and the Waco Siege*. London: Fourth Estate Limited, 1993.

Linedecker, Clifford. *Massacre at Waco: The Shocking True Story of Cult Leader David Koresh and the Branch Davidians*. London: Virgin, 1993.

Linenthal, Edward T. *The Unfinished Bombing: Oklahoma City in American Memory*. New York: Oxford University Press, 2001.

Lofquist, William S. "Constructing 'Crime': Media Coverage of Individual and Organizational Wrongdoing." *Justice Quarterly* 14, no. 2 (1997): 243–263.

Michel, Lou, and Dan Herbeck. *American Terrorist: Timothy McVeigh & the Oklahoma City Bombing*. New York: Regan Books, 2001.

Muller, Hans-Peter. "Social Structure and Civil Religion: Legitimation Crisis in a Later Durkheimian Perspective." In *Durkheimian Sociology: Cultural Studies*, edited by Jeffrey C. Alexander, 129–213. New York: Cambridge University Press, 1988.

Neiwert, David A. *In God's Country: The Patriot Movement and the Pacific Northwest*. Pullman, Wash.: Washington State University Press, 1999.

Parenti, Michael. *Inventing Reality: The Politics of News Media.* New York: St. Martin's Press, 1993.

Pinsker, Sanford. "America's Conspiratorial Imagination." *Virginia Quarterly Review,* 68, no. 4 (1992): 605–626.

Pitcavage, Mark. "Camouflage and Conspiracy: The Militia Movement From Ruby Ridge to Y2K." *American Behavioral Scientist* 44, no. 6 (2001): 957–981.

Reavis, Dick J. *The Ashes of Waco: An Investigation.* New York: Simon & Schuster, 1995.

Romanowski, William D. "Oliver Stone's JFK." *Journal of Popular Film & Television,* 21, no. 2 (1993): 63–72.

Sargent, Lyman Tower. *Extremism in America: A Reader.* New York: New York University Press, 1995.

Schattenberg, Gus. "Social Control Functions of Mass Media Depicts of Crime." *Sociological Inquiry* 51, no. 1 (1981): 71–77.

Scheingold, Stuart A. "Politics, Public Policy, and Street Crime." *Annals of the American Academy of Political and Social Science* 539 (May 1995): 155–168.

Schlesinger, Philip, and H. Tumber. *Reporting Crime: The Media Politics of Criminal Justice.* Oxford: Clarendon Press, 1994.

Shaheen, Jack G. *Reel Bad Arabs: How Hollywood Vilifies a People.* New York: Olive Branch Press, 2001.

Shipley, Wes, and Gray Cavender. "Murder and Mayhem at the Movies." *Journal of Criminal Justice and Popular Culture* 9, no. 1 (2001): 1–14.

Sigal, Leon V. *Reporters and Officials.* Lexington, Mass.: D. C. Heath, 1973.

Smith, Brent. *Terrorism in America: Pipe Bombs and Pipe Dreams.* Albany, N.Y.: State University of New York, 1994.

Snow, David A., and Robert D. Benford. "Ideology, Frame Resonance and Participant Mobilization." *International Social Movement Research* 1 (1998): 197–217.

Snow, David A., E. Burke Rochford, Steven K. Worden, and Robert D. Benford. "Frame Alignment Processes, Micromobilization, and Movement Participation." *American Sociological Review* 51 (1986): 464–481.

Snow, Robert L. *The Militia Threat: Terrorists Among Us.* New York: Plenum Trade, 1999.

Spitzer, Robert J. *The Politics of Gun Control.* Chatham, N.J.: Chatham House, 1995.

Stern, Kenneth S. *A Force Upon the Plain: The American Militia Movement and the Politics of Hate.* New York: Simon & Schuster, 1996.

Studler, Gaylyn, and David Desser. "Never Having to Say You're Sorry: Rambo's Rewriting of the Vietnam War." In *From Hanoi to Hollywood,* edited by Linda Dittmar and Gene Michaud. London: Rutgers University Press, 1990, 101–112.

Surette, Ray. *Media, Crime, and Criminal Justice: Images and Realities.* Belmont, Calif.: West/Wadsworth, 1998.

Swart, William J. "The League of Nations and the Irish Question: Master Frames, Cycles of Protest, and 'Master Frame Alignment.'" *Sociological Quarterly* 36, no. 3 (1995): 465–482.

Sweeney, Frank. "'What Mean Expendable?': Myth, Ideology, and Meaning in *First Blood* and *Rambo.*" *Journal of American Culture* 22 (3): 63–70.

Swomley, John M. "Armed and Dangerous: The Threat of the 'Patriot Militias.'" *Humanist* 55, no. 6 (1995): 8–12.

Tabor, James D. "The Waco Tragedy: An Autobiographical Account of One Attempt to Avert Disaster." In *From the Ashes: Making Sense of Waco*, edited by James R. Lewis, 13–21. Lanham, Md.: Rowman & Littlefield, 1994.

Thompson, Kenneth. *Moral Panics*. London: Routledge, 1998.

Tuchman, Gaye. *Making News: A Study in the Construction of Reality*. New York: Free Press, 1978.

Tuma, Shawn E. "Preserving Liberty: United States v. Printz and the Vigilant Defense of Federalism." *Regent University Law Review* 10 (1998): 193.

U.S. Department of Justice. *Report Regarding Internal Investigation of Shootings at Ruby Ridge, Idaho During Arrest of Randy Weaver*, 1999. Retrieved in June 2001 from: http://www.byington.org/Carl/ruby/ruby1.htm.

U.S. House Committee on the Judiciary. *Nature and Threat of Violent Anti-Government Groups in America*. 104th Cong., 1st sess., 2 November 1995.

U.S. Senate Committee on the Judiciary. *The Militia Movement in the United States*. 104th Cong., 1st sess., 15 June 1995.

———. *Terrorism in the United States: The Nature and Extent of the Threat and Possible Legislative Responses*." 104th Cong., 1st sess., 27 April and 24 May 1995.

Walker, Jack L. "Setting the Agenda in the U.S. Senate: A Theory of Problem Selection." *British Journal of Political Science* 7 (1977): 423–445.

Walton, John A. "From O. J. to Tim McVeigh and Beyond: The Supreme Court's Totality of Circumstances Test as Ringmaster in the Expanding Media Circus." *Denver University Law Review* 75 (1998): 549.

Williams, Rhys H. "Constructing the Public Good: Social Movements and Cultural Resources." *Social Problems* 42, no. 1 (1995): 124–144.

Zeskind, Leonard. "Armed and Dangerous." *Rolling Stone*, 2 November 1995, 54–64.

INDEX

Tables are indicated by an italicized t following the page number. Page numbers for illustrations are italicized.

books, on militia movement, 95
Boyd, Deanna, 217
Brady Bill, 170, 216
Branch Davidians (*see also* Waco incident): conspiracy theory, 188; gun dealing, 41; McVeigh's revenge of, x; Oklahoma City bombing connection, 4; standoff television coverage of, 36, 42
Bridges, Jeff, 204
Brown, Don, 64
Brown, Nicole, 188
Buchanan, Pat, 34
Bundy, Ted, 6
Bureau of Alcohol, Tobacco, and Firearms. *See* BATF (Bureau of Alcohol, Tobacco, and Firearms)
Bush, George H. W., 34, 86, 187
Bush, George W., 216
Butler, Richard, 37, 40

cable news networks, 86
Call Off Your Old Tired Ethics (COYOTE), 110
Cameron, James, 192
camouflage tradition, 122, 129, 159, 214
cartoons. *See* editorial cartoons
celebrated cases: affecting construction of social problems, 74–78; as boundary-defining events, 225; carousel metaphor, 229–30; group solidarity encouraged by, 149; initial focus of coverage, 65–66; inquiries into, 45–46; McVeigh trial, 166–74; and moral panics, 15–20; Oklahoma City bombing as, 64–67; packaging of, 109; and popular culture, 182–83; reporter reaction to, 109; ritual ceremonies in response to, 148–50; social-control institutions as claims-makers, 84–85; in social-problems marketplace, 53–54, 62, 230; susceptible to rumors, 228; as windows of opportunity for policymakers, 153
celebrity figures: as claims-makers, 81–82, 97–102; disappearance from limelight, 224; identifying national militia figures, 245 n. 24; Linda Thompson, 120–22; in policy and incident stories, 84*t*; publicity embraced by, 226; representation in militia stories, 83*t*; representation of frames by, 118*t*, 131; and September 11 attacks, 215–16; testimony in congressional hearings, 157–58

Centennial Park bombing, 88, 89
Center for Democratic Renewal, 59
Center for Strategic and International Studies, 154
Central Intelligence Agency: distrust of, 159; Gritz on, 175
chemical markers, 160
Christian Identity: and Aryan Nations, 37; Elohim City, 163; Gritz ties to, 136; influence on militias, 24; Kahl as follower, 30; and media, 60, 225; racist views of, 138
Christian Patriot Association, 27
Christian Science Monitor, 60
Christianity, 137–38
CIA: distrust of, 159; Gritz on, 175
civil libertarians, 160
claims-makers: capitalizing on celebrated cases, 74–78; categories of, 81–82; celebrity figures as, 81–82, 97–102; dissenters as, 105–8; examples as, 102–5; experts as, 91–97; individuals as, 96–97; media use of, 78–81; militia movement useful to, 231–32; in policy and incident stories, 84*t*; representation in militia stories, 82–84; social-control institutions as, 84–91; in social-problems marketplace, 52–55, 110; statistics used by, 124
Clinton, Bill: celebrity figure's criticism of, 101; commenting on specific cases, 80; counterterrorism proposals of, 152, 153, 154; hated by militias, 87–88; Lampley letter to, 165; in Lewinsky scandal, 188; Linda Thompson on, 122; manipulation of media, 14, 86–88, 152; at Pan Am Flight 103 memorial, 162; presidency in disarray, 231; reactions to Oklahoma City bombing, 4, 86–88, 170; Ruby Ridge and Waco fallout, 62
Clinton, Hillary Rodham, 188
closed-cell militias, 58
Cohen, Stanley, 18–19
collective conscience, 8–9, 227
Committee of the States, 29
common-law devotees, 24
community boundaries: after September 11 attacks, 212; defining, 8–10, 79–81; militia and, 116; reconfiguration of, 71; shaped by celebrated cases, 149
community voices: and deviant voices, 81–82; in policy and incident stories, 84*t*; representation in militia stories, 83*t*

computers, militia use of, 144

congressional hearings: about, 151–52; "Militia Movement in the United States, The," 155–60; "Nature and Threat of Violent Anti-Government Groups in America," 160–62; "Terrorism in the United States," 152–55

Conspiracy frame, 115*t*, 116–17, 131–33

conspiracy theory: Branch Davidians, 188; creation as growth industry, 187; in entertainment media, 189–91; government involvement, 184, 187; Kennedy assassination, 188–89, 219; and media, 188; militias coupled with, 190–91; Oklahoma City bombing, 104, 116–17, 158, 159, 184–87; of Olson, 184–85; and public culture, 187–91; in television drama, 200–202

Conspiracy Theory (film), 189, 203

Constitution of the United States: Bill of Rights, 147; Second Amendment, 43, 165

Constitutional Covenant Communities, 176

constitutionalists, 114

Cooper, William, 98*t*, 100

Corcoran, James, 95, 125

Costner, Kevin, 219

counterterrorism measures, 152–53

Covenant, Sword, and the Arm of the Lord (CSA), 29, 30

(COYOTE) Call Off Your Old Tired Ethics, 110

crime: competition with other social problems, 53; managing public definition of, 228; media coverage of, 14, 117–18; media emphasis on violence, 12–13; as normal aspect of social life, 9; in Puritan community, 9; and social solidarity, 8; television images of, 197

crime-control strategies, 53–54

crime-fighting institutions, as claims-makers, 78

criminal justice system (*see also* trials): crisis-management decision making, 53; death penalty cases, 171–73; and gun violence, 18; judicial objectivity, 168–69; jury as community conscience, 172, 173; in *Law and Order* (television show), 198–200; limited capacity of, 52; media emphasis on output data, 45; pace of justice, 151; processing of McVeigh and

Nichols, 72; public insight into, 11, 12; shaping of responses to problems, 52; television portrayals of, 197, 198–200; television reality programs about, 12–13; trial as only public direct role, 149–50

criminal trials. *See* trials

Crow, Larry Wayne, 162, 164

CSA (Covenant, Sword, and the Arm of the Lord), 29, 30

cultural myths, 181, 182

Curtis, Jamie Lee, 191

Cusack, Joan, 204

Dahmer, Jeffrey, 6

Danforth, John, 46

Dayan, Daniel, 148

death penalty, 171–73

Dees, Morris: antihate agenda of, 232; criticism of, 94, 136, 139, 223; *Gathering Storm*, 95, 125; testimony in congressional hearings, 153–54

Degan, William, 39

Delta Force (film series), 193, 194, 195

democratic process, frustration with, 31–34

demonization: commitment strengthened inside militia by, 234; consensus on threats, 147–48; fear as factor in, 117; of groups *vs.* individuals, 228–29; of guns, 134; of militias, 183, 227–28; triggering involvement of claims-makers, 232–33; of Viper Militia, 75–78

Denver Post, 169

designation ceremonies, 150–52

deviant voices: access during moral panics, 80–81; altering media landscape, 110; and community, 81–82; consequences of representing, 225; No Threat frame promoted by, 138; in policy and incident stories, 84*t*; public appalled and intrigued by, 228; publicity access of, 97; representation in militia stories, 83*t*

dissenters: as claims-makers, 82, 105–8; No Threat frame promoted by, 138–39; in policy and incident stories, 84*t*; representation in militia stories, 83*t*; representation of frames by, 118*t*

Division of Labor in Society, The (Durkheim), 8, 10–11

Dixon, Greg, 227

Freemen, 114, 208, 220–21
Freemen standoff, 88, 90–91
Freilich, Joshua, 31
Fry, Carol, 178

Gacy, John Wayne, 6
Gadsden Minutemen, 89, 98*t*
Gale, William Potter, 29
Garrett, Helena, 170
Gathering Storm (Dees and Corcoran), 95, 125
George, John, 161
Georgia State Defense Force, 179
Gibson, Mel, 189
Gitlin, Todd, 99–100, 110, 111
Giuliani, Rudy, 198
globalism, 34
Glover, Brad, 72
Goffman, Erving, 111
Goldman, Ronald, 188
good demons, 54
Good Morning America, 158
Good Ol' Boys Roundup case, 89, 98*t*, 136
Gorbachev, Mikhail, 177
Gorelick, Jamie, 153
government. *See* federal government
"Grass Roots Rage" (Russakoff), 141
Great Militia Scare, 220–22
Greenpeace, 59
Greenup, Cal, 128–29
Gritz, Bo: about, 175–77; as celebrity figure, 98*t*, 100, 102; as decorated Vietnam War veteran, 107, 175; racist ties of, 136, 176–77; as Rambo template, 179; reporters' preference for, 231; in Ruby Ridge negotiations, 39, 175–76, 179
Ground Zero, ix
Growing Movement frame. *See* Threat-Growing Movement frame
gun control: assault weapons debate, 62; legislation as militia concern, 32, 60, 133–35; sympathy for militia position, 89; used to attract people to militia movement, 216; waiting periods debate, 62
gun offenses, 43
gun owners, fears of, 76–77
Gun Owners of America, 40
Gun Policy frame, 115*t*, 117, 133–35
gun shops, 49
gun shows, and militia recruitment, 49
gun violence, 18, 133

guns: dealing in, 41; seizures of, 156, 162, 217
Gusfield, Joseph, 85

Harris, Eric, 16
Harris, Kevin, 38–39
Hartzler, Joseph, 169–70
Harvest of Rage (Dyer), 30–31, 205–6
Hatch, Orrin, 153
Haydeen, Maureen, 128
Hayes, Michael (fictional character), 198
hearings. *See* congressional hearings
Henley, William Ernest, 219
Henry, Patrick, 120
Herbeck, Dan, 119, 213
Hofstadter, Richard, 187
Hohenberg, John, 86
Holland, Joe, 128–29
Homan, Robert, 28
Horiuchi, Lon, 39
Hornaday, Ann, 205
House hearings. *See* congressional hearings
hybrid model militias, 70

Idaho, extremist groups in, 37–38
incident stories, 83–84
Independence Institute, 161
Indiana North American Volunteer Militia, 128–29
Indianapolis Baptist Temple, 227
individuals: as claims-makers, 81, 96–97; in policy and incident stories, 84*t*; representation in militia stories, 83*t*; representation of frames by, 118*t*, 128
informants, 38, 164, 166
information: limitations of social-problems marketplace, 51–55; media control of, 6
"infotainment," 182
Internal Revenue Service, in Populist Party platform, 175
international boundary changes, 34
International Monetary Fund, 105
Internet (*see also* World Wide Web): extremist literature, 26; and media competition, 86
interview techniques, 239–40 n.6
Islamic fundamentalists, 5
Ismoil, Eyad, 213
issue framing. *See* frames

Jack the Ripper, 6
Jenkins, Brian, 153–54
Jenness, Valerie, 110
JFK (film), 189, 219
John Birch Society, 24, 114, 188
Johnson, James "J. J.", 98*t*, 100, 156, 158
Johnston, Bill, 46
Jones, Stephen, 170, 172–73
journalist, as militia experts, 91
judicial objectivity, 168–69
juries, as community conscience, 172, 173

Kaczynski, Ted, 213
Kahl, Gordon, 29–30, 40, 187
Kanka, Megan, 15–16
Katz, Elihu, 148
Keating, Frank, 183
Kemp, Christopher, 178
Kemp, Jeff, 98*t*
Kennedy, Bobby, 18
Kennedy, John F., 18, 188–89, 219
Kenworthy, Tom, 125, 144
King, Martin Luther, Jr., 18, 89
King, Rodney, 62, 168
Kittrie, Nicholas, 10
Klanwatch Intelligence Project, 125–26
Klebold, Dylan, 16
Knight, Peter, 187
Knob Creek Machine Gun Shoot, 143–46
Koernke, Mark, 98*t*, 100, 106, 128
Koppel, Ted, 78
Koresh, David, x, 30, 40–44
Kovaleski, Serge, 125
Kroninger, Stephen, 59
Kruger, Ehren, 205
Ku Klux Klan, 28, 114, 135, 175, 224
Kupperman, Robert, 153–54
Kurtz, Howard, 86

Lampley, Cecilia, 162–64, 166, 168
Lampley, Willie Ray, 150, 162–66, 168
Lang, Cheryl (fictional character), 204
Lang, Oliver (fictional character), 204–6
Langton, Jeffrey, 129
Lardner, George, 125, 144
law-and-order agendas, 54
law-and-order frames, 112
Law and Order (television show), 182, 197–98, 198–200, 208
law-enforcement agencies: as cited sources, 85–86, 88–91; extremists monitored by, 163; Good Ol' Boy Roundup,

89, 98*t*, 136; justification for support, 221; militia anger diffused through media, 89–90; reliance on expert organizations, 126–27
leaderless resistance, 25, 51, 163
Lecter, Hannibal "The Cannibal" (fictional character), 6
Leech, Daniel, 141
Legitimate Concern frame, 115*t*, 117, 140–42
Levin, Carl, 156
Lewinsky, Monica, 188
LexisNexis, 55–56
Libertarianism, 24
Liberty Lobby, 188
Lieberman, Michael, 161
literature: books on militia movement, 95; extremist literature, 25–28, 137; militia literature, 49–50, 133
local militias, as news sources, 102–5
Lofquist, William, 112
Looker, Floyd, 96
Los Angeles Times, 108
Lyons, Kirk, 40

McCarthy, Joseph, 223
McClaren, Wesley (fictional character), 206–9
McCollum, Bill, 161
McGuckin, JoAnn, 227
Machine Gun Shoot, 143–46
McKenzie, Aline, 179
McLamb, Jack: about, 26; as celebrity figure, 98*t*, 100, 102; newsletters of, 26, 27; *Operation Vampire Killer*, 26, 133; reporters' preference for, 231; in Ruby Ridge negotiations, 176
McVeigh, Timothy: as "American Terrorist," 119; bin Laden compared to, 212–13; capture shifting attention from Arabs, 193–94; Clinton on, 87; comparisons to September 11 attacks, 212, 213; and conspiracy theory, 104, 116–17; diminished media interest in, 218; Elohim City link, 163; execution of, 7, 218–20; Lampleys linked to, 163; Linda Thompson's influence on, 121; linkage to militias, 56–57, 63, 97, 119–20, 155, 209, 218, 225–27, 230–31, 235; media portrayal of, 122; and Michigan Militia, 61, 67–68; military service of, 107, 108; motivation of, x, 5–6, 48, 170, 180; movie allusions

to, 201, 204–5, 206; Oklahoma City bombing, 3; Rambo comparisons, 179, 180; reporting on hateful views of, 103; scrutiny of, 134; similar figures, 217; trial of, 72, 166–74; and *Turner Diaries*, 191; waiver of appeal rights, 218

Magisono, Gus (informant pseudonym), 38

maintenance ceremonies, 174

"Mark from Michigan." *See* Koernke, Mark

marshalls. *See* U.S. Marshalls Service

martyrs, 30, 40, 219

Martz, Ron, 66

Masters, Kim, 108

Matsch, Richard, 168–69, 173

Matthews, Robert, 30, 40

Meadville, Pennsylvania, 141

media (*see also* militia media coverage; news; newspapers; television): claims-makers used by, 78–81; community boundaries defined by, 79–81; and conspiracy theory, 188; crime coverage by, 14; in demonization process, 5, 229–32; efficiency in decision-making process, 79; emphasis on violence, 12–13; environment of, 86, 112–13; exaggeration of social problems, 180–81; framing issues (*See* frames); impact of coverage on implicated targets, 76; information control by, 6; McVeigh execution coverage, 218–20; McVeigh lawyers' accusations against, 172–73; news selection process, 14; Nichols trial coverage, 174; and Oklahoma City bombing, 63–68, 166–67, 170–71, 172–74; on output data of criminal justice system, 45; politician manipulation of coverage, 86–88; public consciousness shaped by, 10–15; public understanding of militias, 6–7, 119; sensationalism in, 14–15; shared moral sentiments constructed by, 11–12; Simpson trial coverage, 168; and social control, 14, 150–51, 232–35; social problems role of, 71; societal hierarchies determined by, 13–14; statistics on militias, 124–27, 127–28; Viper Militia case, 75–78; Waco incident coverage, 36, 42

Michael Hayes (television show), 198

Michel, Lou, 119, 213

Michigan Militia, 61, 66, 67–68, 98*t*, 100

Middle Eastern terrorists, 4, 5, 66, 193, 214 (*see also* Arab terrorists)

military: admiration for, 57; disavowal of militia ties, 107–8; image overlaps with militias, 123

Militia (film), 203

militia literature, 49–50, 133

militia media coverage: from 1990–1998, 55–57; after 1997, 216–18; after Oklahoma City, 67–68, 220–21; contributing to demise of militia movement, 227; diminishing interest, 71–73; eras of, 57; impact of, 68–70; McVeigh trial as endpoint, 173; militia movement shaped by, 225–27; before Oklahoma City, 60; televisions news, 234 n. 6; types of articles, 242–43 n. 5

"Militia Movement in the United States, The" (congressional hearing), 155–60

Militia of Montana, 27, 98*t*, 100, 135, 208

Militia Watchdog Web site, 93, 244 n. 18

militias: Al Qaeda parallels, 213–15; antigovernment portrayal of, 130–31; books on, 95; celebrity figures as claims-makers, 97–99, 98*t*; Clinton hatred in, 87–88; closed-cell organizations, 58; concerns of, 31–37; conspiracy theory coupled with, 190–91; in current study, x, 6–8; decline of, 216–18, 227, 235; defensive nature of, 139; disunity of, 24–25; extremist groups overlap, 24–26; federal government infiltration of, 77; fictional accounts of, 196–97; in films, 202–9; framed by most extreme cases, 225; Great Militia Scare, 220–22; growth of, 58–60, 61–63, 102; hearings in wake of Oklahoma City bombing, 4, 72; ideologies of, 23–27; image overlaps with military, 123; influence of legislators, 224; issues angered by, 224; linkage to McVeigh, 6, 56–57, 63, 97, 119–20, 155, 209, 218, 225–27, 230–31, 235; local militias as news sources, 102–5; McVeigh hatred in, 219, 227; membership changes after Oklahoma City, 226–27; monster status of, 230–31; organizations distancing selves from, 107–8; as outsiders, 116, 155–56, 206; paramilitary tradition, 28–30; photo ops provided by, 221; in popular culture imagery, 183; positive publicity for, 89; in post-Oklahoma City popular culture, 196–97; public relations campaigns, 105; public service activities, 49, 106; public understanding militias (*cont.*)

shaped by media, 6–7, 71, 119, 225–26; racism allegations against, 59, 104, 117, 135–37, 224; Rambo imagery, 179–80; recruitment strategies, 49–51; rights of, 90; Ruby Ridge as rallying point, 35–37, 40, 42–44, 49, 140; secretive nature of, 58, 123, 223; size of movement, 30–31, 50, 51, 68–69, 126*t*, 219–20, 222–23; social-control institutions as most frequently cited source, 85; in social-problems marketplace, 56–57, 70–73; state-sanctioned militias, 179–80; structures of, 69–70; technological connections of, 144–46; television portrayals of, 197–202; terrorism involvement of, 224; terrorist portrayal of, 117–22, 194–95; testimony of, 156, 157–58; threat portrayal of, 116, 118; training events, 176; on trial, 162–66; undefined prior to Oklahoma City bombing, 7; as vigilante groups, 154; as volunteers in war on terrorism, 215, 216; Waco as rallying point, 37, 42–44, 47–48, 49, 140

Mintz, John, 159

Minutemen, 28

M.O.M. *See* Militia of Montana

Montana Freemen case, 208

Montana lifestyle, 208, *209*

Montgomery Adviser, 94

moral panics: access of deviant voices, 80–81; celebrated cases evolving into, 18–20; domestic terrorism as, 67; Great Militia Scare, 220–22; symbolic endpoints for, 173

Morgenthau, Tom, 163

Mormon Militia Battalion, 126–27

Morrell, Charles, 177

movies. *See* films

Mulder, Fox (fictional character), 183, 190, 201–2

Muller, Hans-Peter, 148–49

Murrah Federal Building, 3, 150–51, 170

Nadler, Jerrold, 161

NAFTA (North American Free Trade Agreement), 32

Napolitano, Janet, 76

National Machine Gun Association, 143

National Rifle Association: against chemical markers, 160; criticism of BATF, 108; distancing self from militias, 108, 134; lobbying of, 133; public relations, 105

National Vanguard Magazine, 28

"Nature and Threat of Violent Anti-Government Groups in America" (congressional hearing), 160–62

Neiwert, David, 30, 77

neo-Nazis, 135

networking, and militia groups, 51, 144

New World Order: articles on, 28; Bush statement, 187, 188; conservative descriptions of, 34; in Conspiracy frame, 116, 132–33; conspiracy thinking about, 188; extremist literature on, 26; Gritz on, 176; Lampley's fears of, 166; media's role in establishing, 132–33; militia fears of, 76, 101, 105, 158; in television drama, 200

New World Order, The (Robertson), 188

New York Times, 56, 60–61, 220

news: blurring of fact and fiction, 181–82; distortion of, 99; relationship with popular culture, 180–84, 198–200; routinizing unexpected nature of, 64–65; selection process by media, 14

NewsBank, 55–57, 83, 102

newspapers (*see also* media): at congressional hearings, 157; militia coverage from 1990–1998, 55–57

Newsweek, 75

Nichols, Terry, 57, 72, 163, 168, 174, 219

No Threat frame, 115*t*, 117, 138–39

Nolan, Drew, 74

North American Volunteer Militia, 128–29

NYPD Blue (television show), 182, 197–98

Ohio Unorganized Militia, 98*t*

Ohman, Jack, 64

Oklahoma City bombing: comparison to September 11 attacks, 212, 213; congressional hearing reference to, 153, 155; conspiracy theory, 104, 116–17, 158, 159, 184–87; editorial cartoons, *65*, *123*, *184*; growth of militias prior to, 61–63; images of, 150–51, 183, 213; influence on *Arlington Road*, 205; and insider claims-makers, 233–34; Lampley connection to, 163; McVeigh trial, 166–74; media coverage of, x, 56–57; as media event, 63–68; public awareness of militias following, 51; reactions to, 3–4, 141; scapegoats for,

4–5, 66–68, 193–94, 213; social-control apparatus changes following, 212, 213
Oklahoma Constitutional Militia, 162–66
Olson, Norm: as celebrity figure, 98*t*, 100–101, 102; conspiracy theory of, 184–85; disbanding militia, 220; on McVeigh, 219; reporters' preference for, 231; testimony in congressional hearing, 156, 158–59, 160; theories of, 245 n. 27; on war on terrorism, 216
Olympic Park bombing, 88, 89
Operation Super Glue, 165
Operation Vampire Killer (pamphlet), 26, 98*t*, 133
Order, The, 23, 29, 30
Oswald, Lee Harvey, 117, 189, 219
output data, 45
Outsider frame, 115*t*, 116, 128–31, 155–56

Pan Am Flight 103 (Lockerbie), 119, 162
paradox of social control, 68
paramilitary tradition, 28–30, 122
paranoid-style cultural suspicion, 187
Parenti, Michael, 111–12
Parsons, John, 98*t*, 164
Patriot, The (film), 203, 206–9
Patriot Movement, 104, 243 n. 8
Patriot Report (militia newsletter), 27
patriotism, 147
Pellington, Mark, 204–6
Pentagon attack, ix (*see also* September 11 terrorist attacks)
Perry, William, 108
Persian Gulf War, veterans in militia groups, 31
Peters, Pete, 40
Phineas Priesthood, 243 n. 8
Pierce, William, 191
Pine, Art, 108
Pinsker, Sanford, 187
pipe bombs, 217
Pitcavage, Mark, 28, 93, 129
Pittsburgh Post-Gazette, 158
Planned Parenthood, 59
Pledge of Allegiance, 136, 145
poison gases, 194
Police Against the New World Order, 26
policy analysts, as militia experts, 91
policy stories, 83–84, 96
political cartoons. *See* editorial cartoons
political chat shows, 86

political hearings. *See* congressional hearings
Political Research Associates, 59, 92–93, 125
politicians, manipulation of media coverage, 86–88
politics, of Ruby Ridge and Waco cases, 62
popular culture: and conspiracy theory, 187–91; images of terrorism, 191–96; militias after Oklahoma City, 196–97; Rambo character's symbolic power, 177, 178–80; relationship with news, 180–84, 198–200
Populist Party, 175
Porter, Charles, 183
Posse Comitatus, 23, 29–30, 114, 225
Pratt, Larry, 40
preparedness: expositions, 27–28, 176, 177; mindset, 129–30; spending after September 11 attacks, 215, 216
Preparedness Catalog, 27
Present Truth Ministry, 27
Pressley, Sue Ann, 5
Printz, Jay, 129
prisons, expanding populations of, 12
Project Worst Nightmare, 180
propaganda, 224
public awareness: frames influence on, 112, 113; influences on, 52; of militias, 51, 68–69, 164–65; of Oklahoma City bombing, 64; preconceived understandings of social issues, 232–33; shaped by media, 10–15; shared understanding of social problems, 16–17; understanding of militias, 71, 202
public organizations, as claims-makers, 78–81
public relations, by militias, 105
punishment: historical public celebrations of, 203; and social solidarity, 10–13
Purdy, Patrick, 18
Puritan life, 9–10

Quick, Abdullah, 192

racism: allegations against militias, 59, 104, 117, 135–37, 224; of Aryan Nations, 37; couched in religious rhetoric, 137–38; of Gritz, 136, 176–77; of law-enforcement officials, 89
Racist frame, 115*t*, 117, 135–37

Rambo, John (fictional character), 177–80, 206
Randall, Jeff, 98*t*
Reagan, Ronald, 18, 31, 119, 193
Reardon, Mike, 129
Reavis, Dick, 40–41
recruitment strategies, militias, 49–51
Religious frame, 115*t*, 117, 137–38
Reno, Janet: attempts to remove from office, 62; criticism of, 101; Linda Thompson on, 122; reactions to Oklahoma City bombing, 170; on Viper Militia case, 76; and Waco events, 47
reporters: academics ignored by, 95; celebrity figures preferred as sources, 102; and Conspiracy frame, 131; influential sources used by, 78–81; as lazy people, 92; and policy stories, 96; reaction to celebrated cases, 109; Web used for source material, 93
research associates, as militia experts, 91
ritual ceremonies (*see also* congressional hearings; trials): about, 148–50; designation ceremonies, 150–52; maintenance ceremonies, 174
Robbins, Tim, 204
Roberts, Julia, 189
Robertson, Pat, 34, 188
Rockefeller, David, 132, 133
Roddy, Dennis, 158–59
Roy, Joseph, 76, 220
Ruby Ridge standoff: about, 37–40; as celebrated case, 61–62; Clinton on, 87; criticism of FBI, 167; fading of memories, 227; film portrayals of, 205; Gritz as negotiator, 39, 175–76, 179; investigations into, 44–48; as McVeigh motivation, 170; militia growth following, 59–60; as militia rallying point, 35–37, 40, 42–44, 49, 140; political fallout, 62; in television drama, 198, 200
rules of engagement, 39, 43
Rules of Engagement (film), 194, 196
Rules of Sociological Method, The (Durkheim), 9
rumors, speed with technology, 64
Russakoff, Dale, 141
Rydel, Dave, 98*t*

Saint Petersburg militia, 217
Sasson, Theodore, 112
Schattenberg, Gus, 11–12

Scheingold, Stuart, 53–54
Schneider, Keith, 60–61
Schrum, Richard, 162, 165
Schultz, John, 74
Schumer, Charles, 157, 161
Schwarzenegger, Arnold, 191
Scully, Dana (fictional character), 183, 190, 201
Second Amendment, 43, 165
secret militias, 70
Segal, Steven, 206–9
Seige, The (film), 194, 196
Senate hearings. *See* congressional hearings
sensationalism in media, 14–15
September 11 terrorist attacks, ix, 182, 211–16
serial murder, public understanding of, 6
Sessions, William, 122
sexual predator laws, 62
Shaheen, Jack, 192
Sheriff Posse Comitatus. *See* Posse Comitatus
sheriffs, sympathetic to militia, 89–90, 129
Sherwood, Sam, 98*t*
Sierra Club, 59
Silverstein, Ken, 94
Simon Wiesenthal Center, 161
Simpson, O. J., 16, 62, 167–68, 188
60 Minutes, 87, 152
skinheads, 24, 135
Smith, Benjamin, 16
Smith, Brent, 161
Smith, Susan, 16, 17
social construction theory, 52
social control and media, 232–35
social-control institutions: and celebrated events, 17–18; as claims-makers, 81, 84–91; limited capacities of, 51–55; media as, 14, 150–51; media monitoring of, 71; in policy and incident stories, 84*t*; representation in militia stories, 83*t*; representation of frames by, 118*t*, 128; role affirmation for, 147; scrutiny of militias as credibility enhancement, 221; statistics provided by, 124–25; as voice of authority, 80–81
social hierarchies, 13–14
social problems: celebrated cases affecting construction of, 74–78; as commodities, 52; competition among, 53–55, 229–30; exaggerated attention in news media,

Trochmann, Randy, 98t
True Lies (film), 191–93, 194, 196
Turner Diaries, The (Pierce), 191, 217

underground militias, 70
United Nations: and biosphere reserves, 33–34; and changing world order, 34; in Conspiracy frame, 116, 131–32; Gritz on, 177; militia fears of, 103, 105; in New World Order, 26; in Populist Party platform, 175; as threat to sovereignty, 34; troop sightings, 121
United States, in New World Order, 26
United States Militia Association, 98t
United States Theater Command, 98t, 145
United States vs. Randy Weaver, 38
Universal Church of God, 165
Unorganized Militia of the United States, 121
U.S. Marshalls Service, 38–39

Vest, Jason, 121
Vietnam War: American POWs, 179; veterans in militia groups, 31, 107, 175
violence: gun violence, 18, 133; media emphasis on, 12–13
Viper Militia, 72, 74–78, 87, 88, 146, 220–21
viruses, 194

Waco: The Big Lie (videotape), 47, 98t, 100, 121
Waco: The Rules of Engagement (videotape), 47
Waco incident: about, 40–44; as celebrated case, 61–62; Clinton on, 87; criticism of FBI, 167; fading of memories, 227; investigations into, 44–48; Linda Thompson's perspective, 121–22; as McVeigh motivation, 170, 180; militia growth following, 58–60; as militia rallying point, 37, 42–44, 47–48, 49, 140; political fallout, 62; pyrotechnic tear-gas rounds, 44, 46; questions about, 44; in television drama, 198, 200
Wagner, Diane, 75
Walker, Sam, 60
Wallace, William, 191
Wanted: Dead or Alive (film), 194, 196
Warren Commission investigation, 188–89
Washington Post, 108, 121, 125, 144, 159

Washington State Militia, 72, 77, 89, 146, 220–21
watchdog groups: on dangers of militias, 61; fund-raising tactics of, 94; on growth of militias, 63; as militia experts, 91–93; on militia growth, 59; size estimates of militia movement, 126t, 220, 222–23
Watts, Thomas G., 126
weapons seizures, 156, 162, 217
weather control systems, 158
Weathermen, 23
Weaver, Randy: as celebrity figure, 100; and Gritz, 175–76, 177; as martyr, 30; prosecution of, 42–43; Ruby Ridge standoff, 37–40; Trochmann friendship, 136
Weaver, Sam, 38–39
Weaver, Vicky, 39, 43, 205
Web. *See* World Wide Web
weekend warriors, 69
West Virginia Mountaineer Militia, 72, 89, 96, 146, 220–21
West Wing, The (television show), 182
White Patriot Party, 30
white supremacists: Aryan Nations, 37; militia linkages, 59
Wicks, Wayne, 169
Wiegand, Linda, 177
Wilkinson, Beth, 171–72
Wolf, David, 199, 200
Woodward, Louise, 16
World Bank, 101
World Church of the Creator, 23
world order, changing, 34–35
World Trade Center: 1993 attack, 4, 5, 66, 119, 193, 213; 2001 attack, ix, 211 (*see also* September 11 terrorist attacks)
World Wide Web (*see also* Internet): coverage of celebrated cases, 64; expert sources found on, 93; linkage of militias, 144; militia materials posted on, 26; militia recruitment, 49; as statistics source, 124

X-Files (film), 183
X-Files (television show), 200–202, 208

Y2K fears, 217
Yousef, Ramzi, 213

ZOG (Zionist-Occupied Government), 37